Kiplinger's™ CA-Simply Money™

For Microsoft Windows

SPOKE WITH KIETH PLEINES @ CA
8-23-92. SEND DISK BACK 8-26-93.
HE SAID APPROX. 2-WKS FROM 8-23,
I SHOULD HAVE NEW DISK.

User Guide

Version 1.0

COMPUTER® ASSOCIATES
Software superior by design.

How to Use This Guide

Welcome to Kiplinger's CA-Simply Money. There are two routes through this guide: All first-time users should take the route that introduces financial planning and gives steps for getting started in the program. Advanced users—those familiar with personal finance as well as with computers—can get started fast by skipping to the Practice Session after installing.

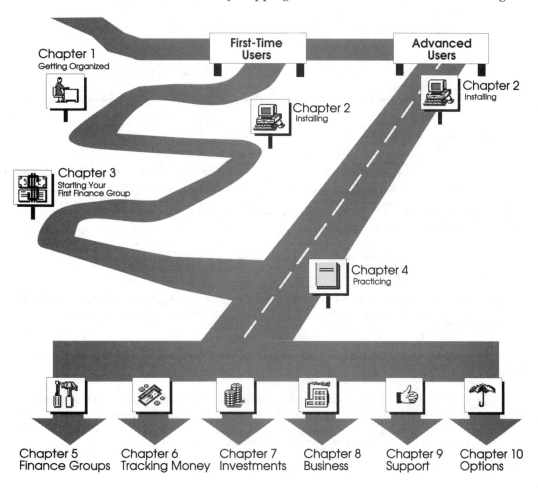

First-Time Users

If you are new to CA-Simply Money, read all chapters. The step-by-step instructions give you a solid grounding in money management and ensure that you use the program correctly:

Learn:	By reading:
The basics of money management.	Chapter 1, "Getting Organized"
How to install CA-Simply Money.	Chapter 2, "Installing"
How to set up your own finances.	Chapter 3, "Starting Your First Finance Group"
About advanced program features using complete sample data.	Chapter 4, "Practicing"
About a specific feature of the program.	Chapters 5-10 (see the Table of Contents or the Index)

Advanced Users

Experienced users may want to start quickly on their own:

If you want to:	Do This:
Install CA-Simply Money.	Follow instructions in Chapter 2.
Try features using several months of sample data.	See Chapter 4, "Practicing."
Learn how to use a specific feature of the program.	Go to Chapters 3 and 5-10. Refer to the Table of Contents or Index.

Quick Reference

At the back of this guide is a *Quick Reference* that summarizes the menus, procedures for basic tasks, and the tools and actions you use most in CA-Simply Money. Use it when you just need a quick summary or reminder of how to perform an action.

Contents

Chapter 1: Getting Organized

Chapter 2: Installing

Chapter 3: Starting Your First Finance Group

Chapter 4: Practicing

Chapter 5: Setting up Your Finances

Chapter 6: Tracking Your Money

Chapter 7: Managing Your Investments

Chapter 8: Business Applications

Chapter 9: Support Tools

Chapter 10: Other Options

Appendix

Glossary

Index

Quick Reference

Chapter 1
Getting Organized

Chapter 1
Getting Organized

Kiplinger's CA-Simply Money is an easy-to-use yet powerful tool for recording and monitoring your personal and business finances. You'll soon find that Kiplinger's CA-Simply Money (or just CA-Simply Money) is much more than check-writing software. It's a complete system that will help you manage your money more effectively. But more importantly, CA-Simply Money can actually help you reach your personal financial goals. This chapter shows you how to get there.

What Are Your Goals?

You bought this package for a reason: Perhaps you want to be better organized for taxes this year. Maybe it's finally time to figure out where all the money that comes in is going. Or perhaps you'd like to start saving for a special goal, and you need some help getting started.

CA-Simply Money provides all the tools you'll need. The key, however, is to zero in on your objectives so you'll be able to use these tools most effectively. Money is, after all, simply a means to an end. What do you want your "end" or goal to be? Enough money to put the kids through college? A comfortable retirement? Getting out from under revolving credit card debt? Putting aside enough capital to start your own business?

Setting specific goals is important. If you just say "I want to get out of debt," you may fall back in again. If you decide to get out of debt *and* discipline your spending patterns to avoid falling back into debt, you have a plan for future success. And if you decide to get out of debt and then build a college or retirement fund, you're on your way to real security.

Do You Really Need to Balance Your Checkbook?

Before you can make progress toward your goals, you need to know *exactly* how much you make and spend. In this exercise "fudging" does not help: accuracy is important. So for you "fudgers," the answer is yes, you do need to balance your checkbook. CA-Simply Money helps get you started on the right track.

Income

It's fairly easy to track income—your paycheck, money you make outside of your regular job, interest earned on investments (and in bank accounts), dividends from securities, and so on. Start by looking at last year's tax return. To begin tracking this year's income, save your paychecks and receipts or statements of other income.

Just about all income is taxable. Net income is what remains after you've subtracted federal, state, social security and other tax expenses. You may also have paycheck deductions for a 401(k) plan or disability insurance. Be sure to subtract all deductions to get your true net income. With CA-Simply Money, you can track all types of income with great care and accuracy. A special paycheck feature automatically keeps track of standard tax and all other deductions every time you deposit your paycheck into an account. You always know exactly how much you are making.

Expenses

Expenses can be more difficult to track. You must account for all spending: checks you write, out-of-pocket cash you spend, credit card usage, and so on. The best way to get a handle on expenses is to gather your check register and credit card statements. You might even want to start keeping a log of your cash expenditures, too. CA-Simply Money provides special accounts for tracking check, credit card, *and* cash spending to make it easy. If you've been using another program, such as Quicken® or Microsoft® Money, you can quickly load all of your financial data into CA-Simply Money (see *Exporting and Importing Data* on page 9-53).

Being accurate makes you more honest about your spending habits. You might say, "I spend about $3 a day on lunch," but you're really spending about $4.50. Realism is the first step toward reaching your financial goals.

Cash Flow

Money passing in and out of your control is cash flow. Your net cash flow is your net income minus your total expenses. If this number is less than zero, you have negative cash flow: You are spending more than you are earning. If you want to get ahead—and stay out of trouble—you must cut expenses now. If you have positive cash flow, you have money left over to apply toward your goals.

From now on, you can use CA-Simply Money to track all of your income and all spending from checking accounts, credit cards, and cash. CA-Simply Money alerts you when an account is about to be overdrawn. It also provides reports and graphs to give you an overall view of your cash flow. When you experience the satisfaction of having this kind of control over your money, you may even enjoy balancing your checkbook!

Where Is All the Money Going?

In addition to knowing how much you are spending, you need to know *where* you are spending the money. How much goes to food? How much to housing? How much to clothing? By categorizing your expenses, you can see where to cut spending in order to increase your cash flow.

Expense Categories

Categories are general groups, such as automobile expenses, home improvement, and insurance. Some people keep folders or envelopes for category expenses. If they spend $5 at the corner grocery, that receipt goes in the "Groceries" folder. If they spend $250 at the supermarket, that receipt goes in the groceries folder, too. Their "Utilities" folder might include receipts for gas, electricity, water, and telephone bills.

CA-Simply Money provides basic categories to use for all your transactions. It keeps your category "folders" up-to-date automatically as you spend the money.

Tax-related Categories

Categories are especially useful when tax time comes around. Business expenses—travel, equipment, and so on—may be tax-deductible. "Charities" should be one of your tax-related categories, as should "Mortgage Interest," and "Child Care." Tracking tax-related categories year-round saves you time and money when you prepare taxes or hire a tax consultant.

CA-Simply Money automatically tracks all tax-related categories. Before meeting with your tax consultant, just print out a Tax Summary report. Or you can export your data to any of the leading tax preparation programs. Finding out where the money is going is as easy as viewing a graph or printing a report.

How Much Are You Worth?

Suppose you made $25,000 four years ago. Today you make $40,000. You are better off today than you were four years ago, right? Not necessarily. Your *worth* depends on more than just what comes in and goes out of your checking account.

Assets

Anything you own that has value is an asset. Assets add to your worth. Assets might be cash, stocks, bonds, savings certificates, your home, collectibles (such as jewelry, antiques or art), and so on. Assets can be exchanged for money (although collectibles are not as liquid or reliable). Someone with very little income who has a portfolio of blue-chip stocks may be worth more than appears from the outside.

Liabilities

Anything that you owe someone else is a liability. Liabilities subtract from your worth. Liabilities are mortgages, credit card balances, loans, etc. Someone may have a high income, but have massive debts and be worth much less than it appears. If your liabilities increase along with your income, you are not necessarily making more than you used to.

Net Worth

Your net worth is your assets minus your liabilities. To get ahead, you want your net worth to be increasing each year. If it isn't, you just aren't getting ahead. If it is, you will be able to achieve your goal sooner.

CA-Simply Money makes it easy to track assets and liabilities. Investment and loan accounts are automatically associated with asset and liability categories. You can track the performance of your savings, your investment funds, your IRA, and even the resale value of that old coin collection. You can stay on top of your car loan and credit cards. CA-Simply Money also tracks your home as both an asset (its value and improvements) and a liability (the outstanding balance of any mortgages). With all information in place, getting a report on your net worth is easy.

How Can You Achieve Your Goals?

Once all your expenses are assigned to categories, you are on the way to developing a budget. The next step is deciding where to continue spending and where to cut.

Budget

Your budget is your plan for dealing with living expenses. It allows certain amounts to be spent for each category. If you want to improve your cash flow, use your budget as a kind of "diet" for cutting spending in certain categories. Looking at your expenses, you can see two main kinds: fixed and variable.

Fixed Expenses

Fixed expenses are the inevitable bills you pay every month, quarter, or year. These are rent or mortgage payments, utilities, insurance, and so on. Although fixed expenses are easier to track, they are usually more difficult to cut. There are a few things you can do: Refinance your home to lower your mortgage payment. Reduce your insurance rates by setting higher deductibles or shopping around. Change your lifestyle to avoid a loan payment or membership fee. Kiplinger's Financial Advisor, which comes with CA-Simply Money, will make some of these recommendations for you.

Variable Expenses

Variable expenses are rarely exactly the same. These are grocery bills, entertainment expenses, gas for the car, and so on. Variable expenses are more difficult to track, but easier to cut. For example, suppose you are surprised to discover (by tracking receipts and credit card statements) that dining out is costing you about $800 a month. That's $9600 a year. If eating out is important to you, you might try cutting just the bottle of wine to save over $100 a month. If you're willing to cook at home more often, you can save hundreds more.

There are many ways to cut variable expenses. Reduce grocery bills by planning economical meals and using coupons for shopping. Plan free entertainment events: a picnic, a walk on the beach, a hike in the country. Go to a Sunday matinee instead of opening night at the theatre. Car pool. Use your imagination to expand this list.

Priorities

It's your decision when it comes to cutting expenses. Match your spending to your priorities. If dining out is important to you, maybe you should find other areas to cut. Don't have unrealistic expectations about what you can change. A budget is no good if you can't stick to it. And it does no good to feel guilty or pass blame among family members. Base your budget on reality, fix what you can, and focus on the positive outcome.

CA-Simply Money provides complete tools for making difficult budget decisions easier. Once you have recorded several months of financial data, you can get an automatic budget. Various reports help you study your spending habits. With the reports as your reality check, you can adjust both fixed and variable expenses in the budget until you come up with an outcome that pleases you. A budget report makes it convenient to compare your actual spending against your budget.

Plan

Your goals and budget give you the tools to draw up a financial plan. Positive cash flow gives you extra money above living expenses. Your plan for directing that money might be to:

1. **Get rid of all debt with non-deductible interest.**
   This includes credit card balances, car loans, etc. Money that goes to pay interest each month could be going toward achieving your goal.

2. **Set up emergency, liquid savings equal to at least three months of living expenses.**
   This account prevents you from going into debt when the car breaks down. Use a bank account or money market fund. Whenever you draw on the fund, replenish it.

3. **Invest money to make more money.**
   Once you have your emergency fund salted away, start investing the extra cash to achieve your goal. CA-Simply Money will give you advice and tips on possible investments that fit your needs. You may also want advice from a financial professional.

Establish Good Habits

Set aside regular time to let CA-Simply Money work for you: daily, once a week, or once a month. Good habits are as hard to break as bad ones. Like exercising and eating right, saving money becomes a reward in itself. You are not likely to go back to "fudging" or falling carelessly into debt once you have the satisfaction of seeing your money grow. CA-Simply Money increases that satisfaction by making it easy to track and control income, expenses, and investments. Especially if you use the check printing feature, CA-Simply Money can become the Grand Central Station for all your money transactions.

Where to Go Next

If you want to:	Do This:
Install CA-Simply Money.	Follow instructions in Chapter 2.
Get started tracking your money right away.	Gather your latest account statements, checkbook register, and paycheck stub (or other receipt of income). Go to Chapter 3 in this guide for easy steps.
Try features using several months of sample data.	See Chapter 4 for a Practice session.
Learn how to use a specific feature of the program.	Go to Chapters 5-10. Refer to the Table of Contents or Index.

Chapter 2
Installing

Chapter 2
Installing

What You Need

There are a few minimum requirements to run Kiplinger's CA-Simply Money successfully.

Software

- Microsoft Windows 3.1 or higher
- DOS 3.1 or higher

Note: See your Windows documentation for details and procedures for using Windows. Many CA-Simply Money actions are the same as Windows actions.

Hardware

- IBM PC or compatible with 80286, 80386, or 80486 processor
- 2 megabyte (MB) of memory (4 MB or higher recommended)
- 5 MB of available hard disk space
- VGA / Super VGA graphics card
- Mouse

Installing Kiplinger's CA-Simply Money

Use the easy Setup program to install the software. Do not copy files directly from the installation disk. The files must be converted into usable files during the Setup process.

To install CA-Simply Money:

1. If you are at a DOS prompt, type **win** to start Windows. For example: c:\ **win**

2. Insert the CA-Simply Money disk in any active disk drive.

3. Open the Program Manager window, if it is not open.

4. From the File menu, choose Run. The Run box appears.

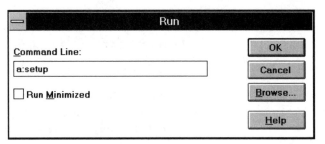

5. In the Command Line text box, type

   a:setup

   or

   b:setup

   specifying the drive where the CA-Simply Money disk is inserted. Then press Enter. The installation begins.

6. Follow the instructions on screen.

Uninstalling

If you ever need to remove CA-Simply Money from your computer:

1. Delete all CA-Simply Money files that are in the \S-MONEY directory. Delete the directory also.

2. Remove CASMALRT.EXE and its path from the LOAD= statement in your WIN.INI file.

Purchasing Checks

Computer Associates offers custom printed checks designed to work specifically with CA-Simply Money and your printer. Using printed checks saves you time and ensures accuracy. You need only enter transactions once—CA-Simply Money updates your checking account register and prints the check in one easy step. See *Writing Checks* on page 6-15 of this guide for instructions on writing checks from the computer.

To order checks, either use the Ordering Supplies command from the System menu of CA-Simply Money, or see the catalog enclosed in your CA-Simply Money package.

Installing

Where to Go Next

If you want to:	Do This:
Get started tracking your money right away.	Gather your latest account statements, checkbook register, paycheck stub (or other receipt of income), and go to Chapter 3 for easy steps.
Try features using several months of sample data.	See Chapter 4 for a Practice session.
Learn how to use a specific feature of the program.	Go to Chapters 5-10. Refer to the Table of Contents or Index.

Chapter 3
Starting Your First Finance Group

Chapter 3
Starting Your First Finance Group

CA-Simply Money can help you achieve your financial goals.
This chapter shows you how to get started, how to set up your
own finances, and concludes with a plan for tracking your
complete financial picture. To get started, let's look at how
CA-Simply Money is designed to help you organize your
finances.

What Is a Finance Group?

CA-Simply Money manages your money in what is called a
finance group. A finance group is a collection of *income sources,
accounts*, and *payees*. It is where you track all money coming in
and going out of your possession.

My Finance Group

Income	Accounts	Payees
Paycheck	Personal Checking	Albert's Foods
Dividends	Credit Union	Uptown Salon
Rentals	Stendall Brokers	County Bell
	401(k)	Barton's Drugs
	Ace Credit Card	Home Shop
	Home Mortgage	Central Electric

Income sources are where your money comes from such as your
paycheck or savings account interest. Accounts are set up for
your checking, savings, credit cards, loans and other accounts.
Payees are bills that you pay other than credit cards or loans; for
example, utilities, groceries, cable TV, and so on.

Although most people will need only one finance group, you
can set up many finance groups with CA-Simply Money. You
might have a finance group for your family accounts, another

for an older relative's accounts, and a third for your small business. CA-Simply Money allows you to create up to ten finance groups to keep the "books" separate.

Original Group
My Finances

A personal finance group contains information for tracking household income and expenses. You can include business with personal, if you wish.

Income	Accounts	Payees
Paycheck	Personal Checking	Albert's Foods
Dividends	Credit Union	Uptown Salon
Rentals	Stendall Brokers	County Bell
	401(k)	Barton's Drugs
	Ace Credit Card	Home Shop
	Home Mortgage	Central Electric

Second Group
Grandma's Finances

Using discrete finance groups makes budgeting and tax preparation easier.

Income	Accounts	Payees
Social Security	First Bank Checking	County Bell
	First Bank Savings	Barton's Drugs
		Dr. Smith
		Central Electric

Third Group
Jim's Lawn Service

Business finance groups have special categories for tracking tax liabilities and deductions, as well as the "bottom line."

Income	Accounts	Payees
Fees	Big Bank Checking	ABC Suppliers
Other Income	National Bank Loan	D. Jones (Employee)
	Payroll	R. Blain (Employee)
	Payables	F. Gomez (Employee)
	Receivables	

This chapter leads you through creating your first (and possibly only) finance group. You set up your basic accounts, income sources, and payees in this group. When you complete the chapter, your finance group will look something like the one shown on the next page, except the names and pictures on your buttons will be different.

Income sources are the funds you earn.

Accounts include bank accounts, credit cards, investments, loans, and other vehicles through which you move money.

Payees are the people and companies to whom you pay money.

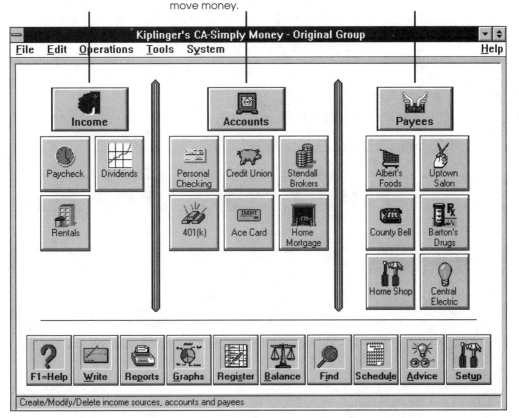

The Home window shows your finance group. You choose the name and picture on each income, account, and payee button.

In this chapter, you learn how to:

- Start CA-Simply Money.
- Create a new finance group.
- Set up and manage your checking account.
- Add and manage a savings account.
- Track your paycheck.
- Manage your credit cards.
- Take the next step in managing your finances.

When you complete this chapter, you will have set up your basic accounts and started using CA-Simply Money to manage your finances. Once you have mastered your first finance group, you may wish to add others. The other chapters in this *User Guide* provide more detailed explanations of the basic and advanced functions of CA-Simply Money.

Starting Kiplinger's CA-Simply Money

1. If you are not in Windows, type **win** at the DOS prompt. Open the Program Manager, if it is not open.

2. Open the CA-Simply Money group window.

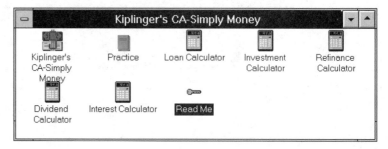

3. Double-click the Kiplinger's CA-Simply Money icon.

Tip: If you see a Read Me icon in the CA-Simply Money program group, double-click on it to see the latest CA-Simply Money information.

Welcome to Your First Session

The first time you use CA-Simply Money on your PC, a special Welcome helps you get started quickly. Read the Welcome screens. Click the buttons at the bottom of the screens to make choices.

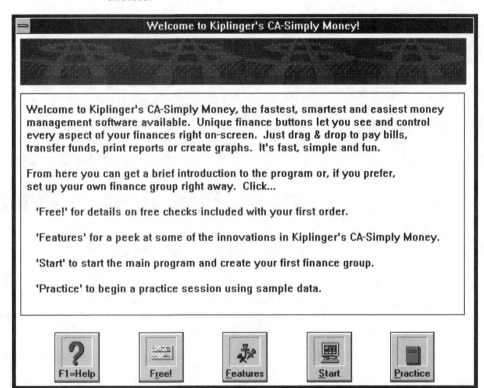

Welcome to Kiplinger's CA-Simply Money!

Welcome to Kiplinger's CA-Simply Money, the fastest, smartest and easiest money management software available. Unique finance buttons let you see and control every aspect of your finances right on-screen. Just drag & drop to pay bills, transfer funds, print reports or create graphs. It's fast, simple and fun.

From here you can get a brief introduction to the program or, if you prefer, set up your own finance group right away. Click...

'Free!' for details on free checks included with your first order.

'Features' for a peek at some of the innovations in Kiplinger's CA-Simply Money.

'Start' to start the main program and create your first finance group.

'Practice' to begin a practice session using sample data.

F1=Help   Free!   Features   Start   Practice

Note: If you do not see this screen, you see an existing finance group. You need to create a new finance group. Pull down the CA-Simply Money File menu and choose New. Enter a finance group name in the dialog box that appears. You can enter descriptive information in the Comment area. Click OK. Skip to Step 2 on page 3-8.

Starting Your First
Finance Group

Creating Your First Finance Group

Creating a finance group is the first step in using Kiplinger's CA-Simply Money. A finance group organizes your financial information. Think of it as a set of ledger books where you record all income and outflow activity.

As you start your first finance group, have your most recent statements for your checking, savings, and credit card accounts and any receipts of income available. To create your first finance group:

1. At the Welcome screen, choose Start to start your finance group. Click OK on the next screen.

2. Choose a type of finance group to create: Personal, Business, or Both. Your choice affects the kinds of expense categories that are automatically set up.

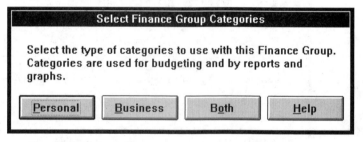

Select Finance Group Categories

Select the type of categories to use with this Finance Group. Categories are used for budgeting and by reports and graphs.

[**Personal**] [**Business**] [**Both**] [**Help**]

- To enter your family accounts, choose Personal.

- To record only business information, choose Business.

- To include consulting or business information with your family accounts, choose Both.

3. If you were in the Welcome, a message tells you that the Welcome is complete. Click OK.

4. CA-Simply Money asks if you want to create an account to get started. Click Yes.

Setting up Your First Checking Account

Most people use a checking account for paying bills, so we'll start your finance group with one. A CA-Simply Money checking account can really help you keep track of inflow and outflow and stay on top of your account balance.

When you choose to create an account, this box appears:

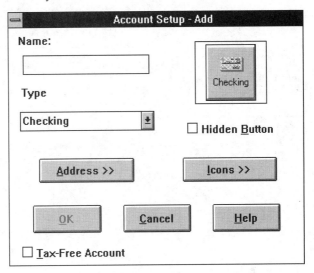

Tip: Newcomer Hints pop up each time you try a new feature. Hide them by clicking elsewhere on the screen.

1. Enter a name for your checking account. Use the bank name or other descriptive name. (We'll use "Personal Checking.")

2. Click on OK. A box asks for your starting account balance.

3. From your last checking account bank statement, enter the ending balance or an approximate amount to update later. You can enter a decimal point, but no commas.

   Starting with the ending balance from your last statement makes it easy to balance your checkbook later. Don't worry if this is not your *current* checking balance.

4. Click OK to create the button.

You now see the Home window with your new finance group containing the checking account button. Your Home window may look somewhat different, depending on the resolution of your computer screen.

Menu bar. Use menus as you do in any Windows program.

Finance buttons. You will set up new buttons representing your income sources, accounts, and people you pay under these three general buttons.

Financial Advisor. Click on the Advisor window to close it. Click the Advice button to see detailed advice from Kiplinger.

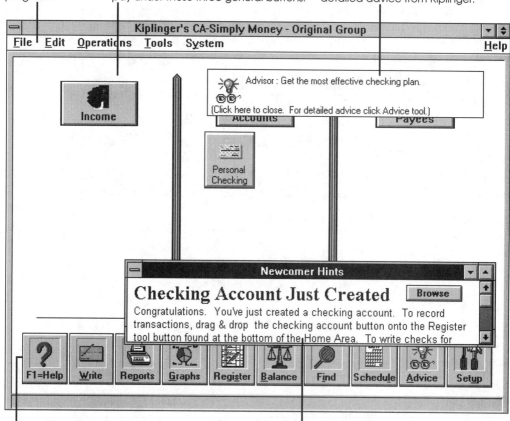

Tool rack. These buttons provide a variety of support functions.

Newcomer Hints. Newcomer Hints pop up each time you try a new feature. To hide a hint after reading it, click anywhere on the screen outside the hint. To turn Hints off altogether, pull down the System menu, select Settings, and General. Then click to clear the Newcomer Hints checkbox in the dialog box that appears.

Managing Your Checkbook

The CA-Simply Money checking account is going to act as your checkbook. To get your checkbook up-to-date, you need to record all checking transactions made since the last statement. *Transactions* include checks you have written, withdrawals, transfers, and deposits. It may take up to an hour to get completely up-to-date, depending on how many checks you have written. Have the following items near at hand:

- Your last checking account statement.

- Your checkbook register and ATM and bank receipts that you may not have recorded in your register.

Note: Before recording a paycheck deposit in your checking account, read *Tracking Your Paycheck* on page 3-22 of this chapter.

Viewing the Register

The CA-Simply Money checking account has a register where you can list all transactions, just as your regular checkbook does. To view the register:

1. Place your mouse pointer on the checking account button and press and hold the mouse button.

2. Drag the checking account button down to the Register button in the tool rack. Then release the mouse button.

Drag the account button to the Register button, or vice versa.

Tip: This procedure is called drag and drop. You can drag and drop buttons to complete many tasks quickly.

Dragging and dropping   A symbol appears when drag and
changes the button shape.   drop cannot take place.

When you "drop" the checking account button, the checkbook
register appears. The only entry so far is your starting balance.

Date	Via	C	Pay To / Deposit From	Payment	Deposit	Balance
03/31/93		☒	Starting Balance		505.34	505.34
04/01/93		☐				

Tip: Another way to see an account register is to double-click
on the button for that account.

Changing the Starting Balance

The Starting Balance should match the ending balance shown on
your checking statement. Update the date and amount if
necessary.

Changing the Date   1.   To change the date, click on the first number in the Date
column. Type the statement date over today's date.

**Changing the
Amount**   2.   To change the amount, double-click on the amount in the
Deposit column and enter the correct amount.

3.   Click on the Record button to make the change(s).

Recording a Check Payment

Look at your checking account statement and checkbook register to see which checks have not cleared (checks you have written that are *not* shown on the statement). Begin entering these checks in the register.

Entering the Check Date

1. In the first blank row, click on the first number in the Date column. Type the date of the check over today's date.

"Cleared" checks are marked   Balance updates automatically

Date	Via	C	Pay To / Deposit From	Payment	Deposit	Balance
03/31/93		⊠	Starting Balance		505.34	505.34
04/01/93	1234 ▭	☐	County Bell ❶ ❷ Utilities\Telephone ❸	50.00		455.34

Type over the date to change it.

Type the check number. Click the icon to select means of payment.

1. Payee. Type to get a Browser.
2. Memo space.
3. Category. Type to get a Browser.

Click the arrow to split a payment between categories.

Tip: Click anywhere on the register to make an entry, or use Tab to go forward and Shift+Tab to go backward through the register fields. If you click outside the current transaction area, CA-Simply Money assumes you are ready to go on to the next transaction and displays a message.

Entering the Check Number

2. Tab to the Via column and type the check number.

The icon below the check number indicates payment by check. You can click on this icon to display a list of payment methods. Double-click on a method to select it.

Adding a New Payee

3. Tab until you get to the Pay To/Deposit From column. Type the name of the person or company to whom you wrote the check.

As soon as you begin typing, the Payee Browser box appears. Since you have no payees yet, the Browser is empty. Once you have a list of payees, the Browser tries to match your typing to a listed name.

CA-Simply Money Browsers save you typing time.

For a new finance group

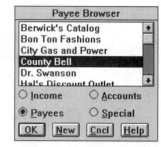

With payee buttons added

4. After typing the entire name of the payee, click on the New button in the Browser box.

   The Payee Setup box appears, showing the name you typed and the button you are about to create.

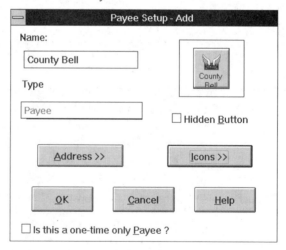

Adding Payee Information

■ If you wish, click on the Address button and type in the address, telephone number, contact person and/or account number for the payee. Click OK.

Changing the Payee Button Icon

■ If you wish, click on the Icons button to see a window of icons. Choose one of these for your payee button by clicking on it. Then click OK.

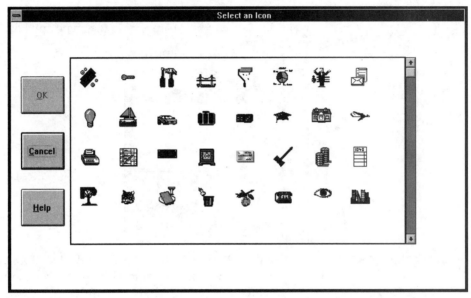

Click on the down arrow at the right of the screen to see more icons.

Tip: If you will not write many checks to this payee, you can "hide" the payee button so it won't take up space on the Home window. Click the Hidden Button checkbox on the Payee Setup box. Hidden payees still show up in the Payee Browser.

5. Click OK on the Payee Setup box to return to the register.

6. Enter the check amount in the Payment column.

Assigning a Category

Categories group similar transactions for budgets, reports, and graphs. Try to assign categories to every transaction you make. For more on categories, see *Where Is All the Money Going* on page 1-5.

7. Tab until you get to the category field, the third line in the Pay To/Deposit From column. Type the first letter of the category you want (for example, type *u* for Utilities). If you don't know which category to use, type any key.

The Category Browser appears:

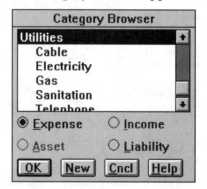

- Continue typing, or scroll through the list, until you see the category or subcategory you want. (For example, if you are paying your phone bill, the category is Utilities, and the subcategory is Telephone.)

- If necessary, click on your choice to highlight it.

- Click OK or press Enter to accept the category.

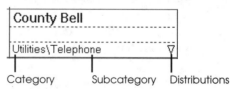

Tip: If you need to assign the amount to more than one category (also called making a distribution), click on the Distributions arrowhead in the category space (or press Ctrl+DnArrow). When multiple categories have already been assigned, the arrowhead is black.

Recording the Payment

8. Click Record. The checkbook balance is updated, and you move on to the next transaction line.

Tip: Typing Alt+R is the same as clicking on Record.

To speed things up, the next time you enter a payment to the same payee, CA-Simply Money automatically remembers and enters the category and amount you last used with that payee.

9. Continue entering uncleared check payments. Click Record to complete each payment.

Tip: Right now you are using CA-Simply Money just to track your finances. By using CA-Simply Money to print checks, too, you save time since you enter transactions only once—in the computer—rather than on a check and then in the computer.

To print checks with CA-Simply Money, order your checks now. See the catalog that came with this package or pull down the System menu and select Order Supplies.

Withdrawing Cash from an ATM

Recording cash withdrawals is similar to recording payments by check. Here is what you do differently:

■   In the Via column, click on the icon. In the menu that appears, double-click on ATM.

■   When you enter a payee, in the Payee Browser box click on the Special button. From the Special list, select Withdrawal and click OK.

Click Record or type Alt+R to complete the withdrawal.

Tip: If you want to take more detailed control of your money, you can set up a cash account button to track your "out-of-pocket" spending money. You can transfer funds into your cash account by dragging the Savings or Checking account button to the Cash account button. Tracking cash allows you to categorize your spending accurately, as it occurs. Learn more about tracking cash accounts in *Cash and Savings Accounts* on page 6-31 of this guide.

Editing Transactions

You can go back and change any transaction in the register. Just double-click on the space you want to change and type new information. In a payee or category space, type any key to get the Browser. When you click Record, the balance updates.

Returning to the Home Window

After entering transactions in your checkbook register, return to the Home window:

■ Click the Home button.

Don't worry if you are not completely up-to-date. CA-Simply Money saves information each time you "Record," so you can leave the program, then come back later and start where you left off.

Your Home window now contains the checking account button and all payee buttons you added while recording payments. It looks something like the window shown on the next page, with more or fewer payees. The names of your payees, of course, are different than those shown, reflecting your own personal finances.

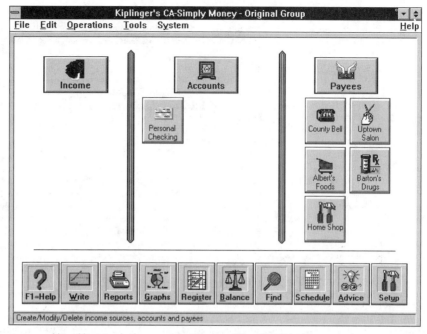

Your Home window now looks something like this. You may have more or fewer payees, as a result of updating your checking account register.

Managing Your Savings Account

As you update your checkbook, you may need to record transfers. To do this, you should set up buttons for the other accounts you transfer to and from. If you have a savings account, now is a good time to set it up. Find your last savings statement and have it ready.

Setting up a Savings Account

1. Drag and drop the Accounts button on the Setup button.

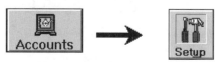

This box appears:

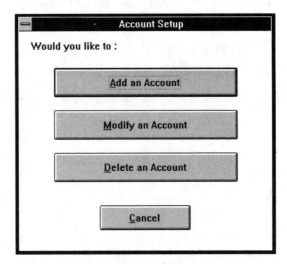

2.   Click the Add an Account button.

Tip: The Account Setup box also lets you change information about an account (choose Modify an Account). For example, you can add an account number or change the button icon.

3.   The Account Setup box that appears is the same one you used to set up your checking account. Fill in account information just as you did for the checking account, except this time:

   ■   Click on the arrow next to the Type box to display a list of account types. Choose Savings.

   ■   When you click OK to get the Account Balances box, enter the ending balance shown on your savings statement.

4.   Click OK to create the button and return Home.

Getting Your Savings Account Up-to-Date

The savings account register is identical to the checking account register, and you can update it in the same way. But you may find it easier to work from the buttons on the Home window. Here's how:

Withdrawing from a Savings Account

1. To record a withdrawal, click once on the savings account button. Then click Withdrawals. Fill in the box that appears and click Record to go to the next withdrawal.

Payee: Type here to get the Payee Browser. The Payee Browser also lets you choose Special payees (such as Withdrawal) and Accounts (to transfer funds).

Category: Type here to get the Category Browser. Click the arrow if you need to distribute the amount to more than one category.

Buttons: All buttons relate to the savings account. For example, clicking Register takes you directly to the savings account register.

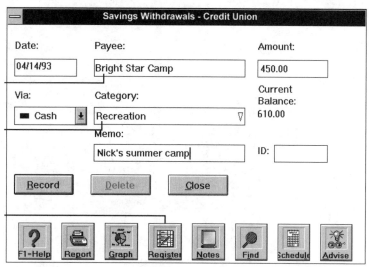

When you record more than one withdrawal, a scrollbar appears to let you scroll through your work.

2. Click Close to return to the Home window.

Transferring from a Savings Account

To record a transfer from your savings to your checking account, drag the savings account button to the checking account button in the Home window. In the box that appears, fill in the amount and select the Transfer Via option. Click Transfer to record the transfer and return to the Home window.

The savings account register and any other relevant account registers are automatically updated, complete with the right "payees" and categories.

Your Home window now has a checking and a savings account button, plus all payees that you have added.

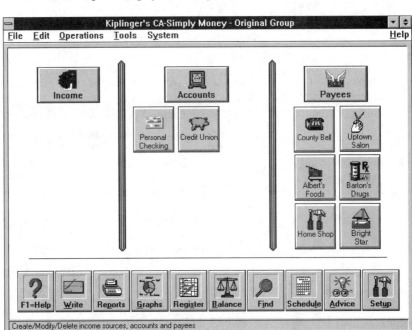

Your finance group may contain many payee buttons, if you have updated both your checking and savings account.

Tracking Your Paycheck

Before you deposit a paycheck to your checking or savings account, you should add a paycheck button to your Home window under "Income."

Setting up a Paycheck

Adding an income source is essentially the same procedure as adding an account:

1. Drag the Income button down to the Setup button.

2. Click Add Income Source. The Income Source Setup box appears. This box is similar to the Account Setup box.

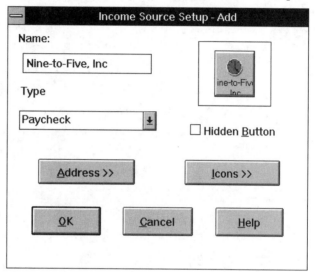

3. Enter a name for the button. We'll call the button "Nine-to-Five," but you should give it your company name.

4. If "Paycheck" is not displayed as the income source type, click the arrow next to the Type box to select it from a list.

5. Change the icon, if you wish, then click OK.

Note: CA-Simply Money treats each income source specially. If you have income other than a paycheck to record, select the appropriate income source type from the Type list. For more information, see *Adding Income Sources* on page 5-9 and *Recording Income* on page 6-4.

Setting up a 401(k) Asset Account

If you have 401(k) deductions taken from your paycheck, CA-Simply Money makes it easy for you to track this asset in a separate account. Start by setting up an asset account:

1. Drag the Accounts button to Setup on the tool rack. Then click Add an Account.

2. In the Account Setup box:

   ■ Enter a name such as "401K."

   ■ Click on the arrow next to the Type box to display a list of account types. Choose Asset Account.

   ■ Click "Tax-Free Account."

   ■ When you click OK to get the Account Balances box, you can enter the ending balance shown on your last 401(k) account statement, if you wish.

3. Click OK to create the button and return Home.

Your 401(k) asset account is updated automatically each time you deposit your paycheck.

Depositing a Paycheck

To deposit your paycheck:

1. Drag the paycheck button across to your checking or savings account button. The Record Income box appears.

2. Enter the deductions as they appear on your paycheck stub (the numbers shown in this box are examples):

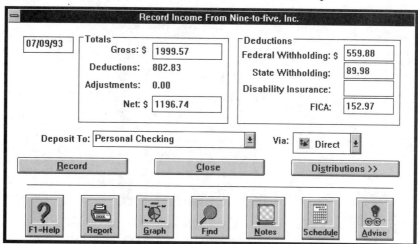

CA-Simply Money automatically assigns tax categories to the standard deductions.

3. If you have a 401(k) or other deductions, click Distributions to display all paycheck distributions in a register.

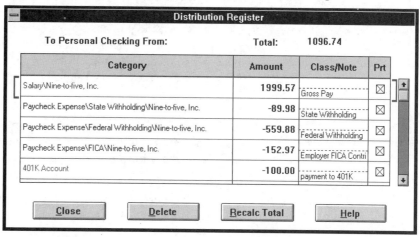

Enter extra deductions in this register. The 401(k) deduction appears in blue to indicate an asset account.

When the category browser appears, click to select Asset in the lower left, then select your 401(k) account. Click OK.

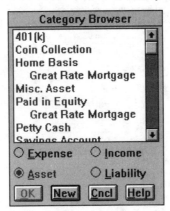

Enter negative amounts for your 401(k) and other deductions. When you finish, click Close on the Distribution register.

4. Click Record to deposit the funds, or Close to cancel the transaction, and return to the Home window.

The deposit is automatically recorded in your checking or savings account register. From now on, when you deposit your paycheck, the Record Income box appears showing the deduction amounts and categories as you last entered them. Just press Enter to record the deposit, or, if your income or deductions change, make changes as needed

Tip: The 401(k) deduction you entered went into your 401(k) asset account automatically. You can see it by double-clicking on your 401(k) account button to open the register.

To learn more about using your paycheck button, see *Recording Paycheck Income* on page 6-4.

Your Home window now contains an income source and a 401(k) asset account in addition to your checking account, savings account, and payees.

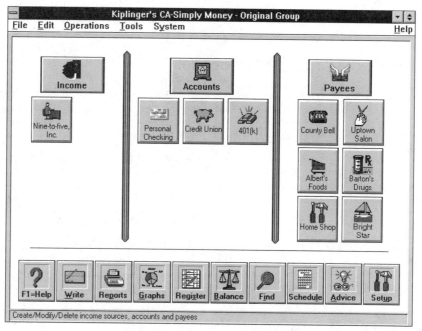

Notice the status line at the bottom of the Home window. This gives hints on using the button or area below your cursor.

Tip: You can move the two divider bars to make more room for accounts or payee buttons. Just click on a bar and drag. The buttons are automatically rearranged.

Managing Your Credit Cards

If you carry a balance on your credit cards, you should set up accounts for them and track them as you do your other accounts. Have your last credit card statements handy.

Setting up a Credit Card Account

1. Drag the Accounts button to Setup on the tool rack. Then click Add an Account.

2. In the Account Setup box:

   ■ Enter the name of the card issuer (the name you write a check to when paying your bill).

   ■ Choose Credit Card as the account Type.

   ■ When you click OK to get the Account Balance box, enter the balance from your last credit card statement and your credit limit (usually found on the statement).

3. Click OK to create the button and return Home.

Using Your Credit Card

Like the savings account, the credit card account has a standard register, but is easier to use from the Home window:

Recording a Credit Card Charge

1. To record a credit card charge, click once on the credit card button. Choose Use Card. Fill in the box that appears and click Record to go to the next charge.

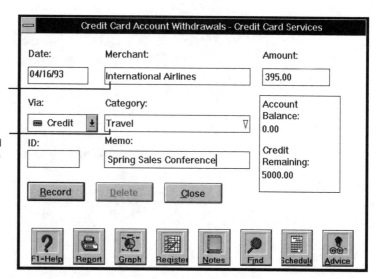

Merchant: Type here to get the Payee Browser.

Category: Type here to get the Category Browser. Click the arrow if you need to distribute the amount to more than one category.

Buttons: All buttons relate to the credit card. For example, clicking Register takes you to the credit card account register.

When you record a charge, the Balance updates and a scroll bar appears.

2. Click Close to return to the Home window.

Paying a Credit Card Bill

When you are ready to pay your credit card bill have your most recent statement with you. Click once on the credit card button and choose Pay Bill. When you pay your credit card bill, CA-Simply Money balances your account at the same time. Enter the ending balance from your statement and any finance charges. Check off all the charges that show up on your latest statement. Then, click Home to write a check or record payment of the bill. When the amount is recorded, you return to the Home window. Turn to *Balancing Credit Card Accounts* on page 6-47 for detailed instructions.

Your Home window now contains a credit card account and the payees you have added as a result of updating the account.

When there are too many buttons to display, a scroll bar appears. In this example, you would use the scroll bar to view more payees.

Taking the Next Steps

Now that your basic accounts and paycheck (or other income source) are set up, you can keep them up-to-date and begin to get control of your finances. Enter all checking, savings, and credit card transactions at least once a week.

Here are the steps we suggest taking next:

1. Practice using CA-Simply Money with sample data.

2. Add the rest of your accounts.

3. Stay on top of all account transactions.

4. Check your progress toward your financial goals regularly.

Practicing to Learn More

Dragging and dropping buttons is particularly efficient when all of your financial information is in place. If you want to practice using a complete, sample finance group:

1. Exit out of the CA-Simply Money program: From the File menu, choose Exit.

2. Back up your finance group. Select a drive and/or directory, then click OK.

3. When you return to the Program Manager, double-click the Practice icon in the CA-Simply Money group. (Go to Chapter 4, "Practicing," for more information about using the Practice group.)

Using the Practice finance group, try some of the advanced CA-Simply Money features to get a feel for how they work. Decide what you need in your own finance group, then continue to set up accounts.

Adding the Rest of Your Accounts

So far you have set up checking, savings, and credit card account buttons, an income source button (your paycheck), and several payee buttons. This is only the beginning. You may have loans, mortgages, and investments as well. The more complete your finance group is, the better CA-Simply Money can help you track your money.

Accounts you can set up are listed in the following table. Set up any account by dragging the Accounts button to Setup (or vice versa), then selecting the appropriate account Type. Some accounts—credit card, mortgage, investment, credit line, liability, and payroll—need explanation. See Chapter 5 for instructions on setting up each kind of account, Chapter 6 for directions on using the accounts, and Chapter 7 for investment information.

Account type	Description	Page
Checking	For writing checks.	5-13, 6-15
Savings	For tracking interest-bearing accounts such as savings accounts and CDs.	5-13, 6-31
Credit Card	For paying and tracking credit card balances.	5-16, 6-29
Cash	For tracking the cash you spend.	5-13, 6-31
Mortgage	For making mortgage payments. Tracks principal, tax-deductible interest, equity, and home improvements.	5-14, 6-36
Investment	For buying and selling securities. Records and tracks taxable and non-taxable interest, short- and long-term capital gains and losses, dividends, margin interest, and miscellaneous expenses.	Chapter 7
Credit Line	For paying bank lines of credit such as home equity loans. Tracks the balance, amount of credit remaining, and amortization information. Useful for tracking your car or boat loans.	5-16, 6-33
Liability	For paying loans, such as personal loans, that are not covered elsewhere, or for tracking accounts payable.	5-16, 6-40
Asset	For tracking assets such as coin or art collections, or for tracking accounts receivable.	5-16, 6-40
Payroll	For paying wages. Itemizes taxes and deductions as liabilities and expenses.	8-19

With all accounts and income sources in place, your Home window begins to fill up, like this:

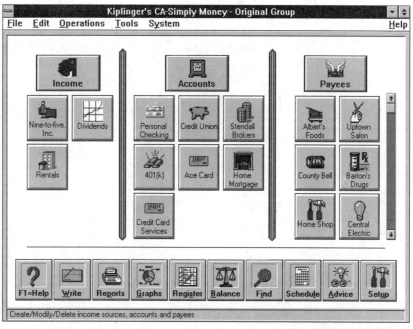

Buttons that you use most frequently will "migrate" toward the top left position, by default. To turn off automatic button layout, pull down the System menu, choose Settings, and General. Clear the Auto Button Layout checkbox in the dialog box that appears. You can then arrange buttons yourself by pressing Shift while you drag a button to a new position.

Keeping All Accounts Up-to-Date

Once you have account buttons set up for all of your checking, savings, credit card, and other accounts, you'll begin to enjoy the power of CA-Simply Money. Here are some things you can do to stay on top of your finances:

Balance Accounts

If you stay up-to-date, reconciling your CA-Simply Money accounts is easy. Just drag the account button to the Balance button on the tool rack. Enter ending statement balance, service charge, and interest earned. Click OK. Then, go down the list of cleared transactions on your statement and click to mark the same transactions as cleared in CA-Simply Money. (Page 6-43, *Reconciling Accounts*, has complete instructions.) You'll be surprised at how easy and satisfying it is!

Num	Date	C	Pay To / Deposit From	Amount	Memo
545	06/28/93	☑	Great Rate Mortgage	-502.63	
	06/29/93	☑	Nine-to-five, Inc.	1196.74	
546	06/30/93	☑	Satellite Cable	-25.63	45678
547	06/30/93	☐	Regal Daycare	-350.00	
548	06/30/93	☐	City Gas and Power	-87.46	

Checks in the "C" column mark cleared transactions.

Write Checks by Computer

Writing checks from CA-Simply Money (using special checks in your computer printer) makes staying on top of checking transactions a lot easier. Any checks you write are automatically added to your checking account register. Order your free checks right away to take advantage of this valuable feature. Practice writing checks using the Practice data (see Chapter 4, "Practicing"), if you wish.

Schedule Transactions

Another way to simplify the task of staying up-to-date is to use the Schedule button. You can have the Scheduler remind you when important transactions are due. For example, you could schedule a loan payment at the beginning of every month. See page 9-40, *The Scheduler*, for complete instructions on using the Schedule button.

Checking Your Progress Toward Financial Goals

With all accounts up-to-date, you can get an entire financial picture to see how close you are to achieving your goals. Here are some ways to check up on your financial progress:

Use Graphs

Graphs help you see general trends. Click on the Graph button to get a list of graphs.

- Use Expense Trend graphs to check your spending trends.
- Use Portfolio Value graphs to get a quick picture of how your investments are doing.

See *Graphs* on page 9-29 for complete information.

Use Reports

Reports gather useful information. Click on Reports to get a list of reports.

- Cash Flow and Net Worth compare your spending to your earnings and your liabilities to your assets.
- Category Summary shows exactly where you are spending money.
- Budget reports let you check your actual spending against your budget.
- The Tax Summary saves time when you prepare your taxes.

See *Reports* on page 9-14 for complete information.

Get Advice

Kiplinger's CA-Simply Money provides professional advice based on your personal financial data. Be sure to click the Advice button when an Advisor message appears. See *Kiplinger's Financial Advisor* on page 9-43 for complete instructions on using the Advisor. The Financial Advisor can help you save and even make more money!

Create a Budget

Budgets help you set financial goals and monitor your progress toward achieving those goals. To set up a budget, pull down the Edit menu and select Budget. See *Budgeting* on page 6-60 for details.

Getting Help

CA-Simply Money provides comprehensive online Help. Help answers questions about terms, procedures, and commands. To get Help, click on the Help button or choose Help from the menu bar.

Help buttons in registers and dialog boxes display information for the part of the program you are in. You can always choose Contents from the Help window to get to other Help subjects.

If you have never used Windows Help before, you may want to return to the Program Manager and choose How to Use Help from the Help menu on the Program Manager menu bar.

Quitting CA-Simply Money

To exit from CA-Simply Money:

1. From the File menu, choose Exit. The CA-Simply Money Backup Finance Group Before Exit dialog box appears. It gives you the opportunity to back up the current finance group before exiting.

   Note: We strongly recommend that you back up your data to a diskette every time you exit.

2. To perform the backup, select a drive and/or directory, then click OK.

   To exit without backing up, click on Exit.

The Windows Program Manager or an underlying application appears.

Where to Go Next

If you want to:	Do This:
Try additional features using several months of sample data.	See Chapter 4 in this guide to learn how to use the Practice session.
Learn how to use a specific feature of the program.	Go to chapters 5-10 in this guide. Refer to the Table of Contents or Index.

Starting Your First
Finance Group

Chapter 4
Practicing

Practicing

Chapter 4
Practicing

This chapter shows you how to use the CA-Simply Money Practice session. The Practice session gives you a chance to try many features using several months of sample data that is already in place. Once in the Practice finance group, feel free to select menu options or drag buttons just to see what happens. Don't worry about destroying the sample data. Nothing you do is saved after you exit Practice.

Viewing the Sample Finance Group

You can access the sample data in two ways:

- If you have started the main program for the first time, you can click Practice at the first Welcome screen.

Practice

- From the Program Manager, you can double-click the Practice icon in the CA-Simply Money group. If you are already running CA-Simply Money, select Exit from the File menu, then double-click the Practice icon.

The Practice finance group is shown on the next page. The position of the buttons depends on your screen resolution. Scroll bars appear if buttons are off the screen. You may need to scroll to see and use some of the buttons.

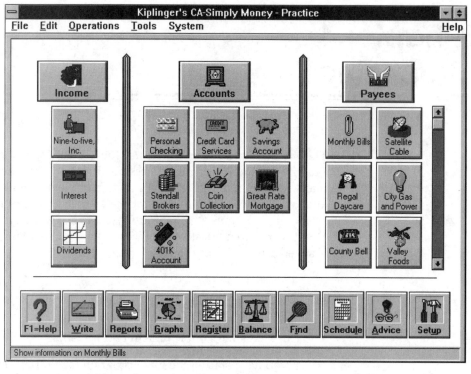

If you have already started your own finance group (as described in Chapter 3) you know the basics of using the buttons. Finance buttons are those under Income, Accounts, and Payees. Tool rack buttons are at the bottom of the window. You can:

- Drag and drop one finance button on another to perform a transfer, deposit, or other action.

- Drag and drop finance buttons to tool rack buttons to perform actions.

- Click once on a button to get information or begin a procedure.

- Double-click on account buttons to see a register.

- Press Alt plus the underlined letter to perform menu operations.

This Practice finance group gives you the opportunity to try any and all button maneuvers.

Experimenting on Your Own

Practice by experimenting. Here are some ideas:

- Generate a quick transaction report. Drag the Personal Checking button to the Reports button on the tool rack.

- Generate a quick graph. Drag the Savings account button down to the Graphs button.

- Get information about a payee. Click once on the County Bell payee button.

- Pay the mortgage. Click once on the Great Rate Mortgage button. Click Pay Mortgage. Click OK to accept the amortized payment, then record the payment from the Personal Checking account. Choose whether to record and prepare a check for printing or just record payment. See *Mortgages* on page 6-36 for details.

- Try writing a check. Drag the Personal Checking button to Joe's Gas Station payee button. Record the check (click Register to see the updated check register), then click Home. Use this method to print checks from the computer, otherwise, just record handwritten checks in the register.

- Try using the Monthly Bills payee *group* button. Click on it once, or drag it onto the Personal Checking button. Group buttons save time when you write checks for regular bills and let you produce reports or graphs on several buttons at once. To group buttons, see *Grouping Buttons* on page 6-56.

- Deposit a paycheck by dragging Nine-to-Five to Personal Checking. Click the Distributions button and note the 401(k) deduction. Close the Distribution register and record the deposit. Double-click on the 401K asset account to see the updated register.

- Look at a budget. From the Edit menu, choose Budget. You see all fixed monthly budget categories first. Click Variable to see a budget for the whole year.

- View a budget report. Click once on Reports, click the Miscellaneous Reports button, then select a Budget report from the report list.

Practicing

- Record capital gains or losses by clicking on the Stendall Brokers button.

- If a modem is connected to your PC, try updating stock prices. From the System menu choose Settings and Modem. Click OK to use the CA-Simply Money 900 securities quote line (the cost is $1.00 per minute, subject to change), or enter your own CompuServe information. From the Operations menu, choose Modem Stock Update and watch as security prices are downloaded. See *Updating Stock Prices by Modem* on page 7-31 for details.

- Check each security from the Edit menu by choosing Investments, then Securities. Use the scroll bar to move back through each security.

Quitting the Practice

The Practice session is provided for you to try features using sample data. Do not enter your own financial data during the Practice session, because it will not be saved. To leave the Practice session:

1. From the File menu choose Exit.

2. Click OK on the box that appears. You return to the Program Manager.

Where to Go Next

If you want to:	Do This:
Create your first finance group and start tracking your own money.	Gather your latest account statements, checkbook register, and paycheck stub (or other receipt of income). Go back to Chapter 3.
Learn how to use a specific feature of the program.	Go to Chapters 5-10. Refer to the Table of Contents or Index.

Chapter 5
Setting Up Your Finances

Setting Up Your
Finances

Chapter 5
Setting Up Your Finances

With CA-Simply Money you organize your finances into "finance groups." You can have a finance group for your personal finances, another for your business, and still another for a relative who lives with you. You can create up to ten finance groups, each one separate from the others.

This chapter explains how to create and open finance groups, and how to add and maintain the finance buttons that represent your finances.

Creating and Opening Finance Groups

A finance group is a collection of financial income and outflows. Each finance group has buttons representing:

- **Income Sources**, which are the sources of your money.

- **Accounts**, which hold your money and let you record fund transfers. Examples are checking, credit card, and savings accounts.

- **Payees**, which are the persons or companies that receive your bill payments.

The different types of finance groups, personal, business, and both, contain categories that help you organize and track your money. Typical categories in a personal finance group are Dental, Groceries, and Clothing. For a business group some categories are Advertising, Leasing, and Commissions. Personal and business groups also have some categories in common, such as Insurance, Utilities, and Auto. For a list of the expense categories associated with each type of finance group, see the Appendix.

Categories let you group similar transactions for budgets, reports, and graphs. For example, you might want to budget a certain amount of money for groceries. At tax time you probably want a report of tax-related earnings and expenses. Or, you may generate a graph showing the trend of medical payments over the past year.

You do not have to set up categories now, while setting up your finance group. You assign categories later, when recording income, updating accounts, and writing checks. For example, when writing a check to the phone company, you can allocate the amount to the category Utilities.

Besides using the categories that come with CA-Simply Money, you can add your own. See Chapter 6 for details about categories.

Creating a New Finance Group

To create a new finance group:

1. From the File menu, choose New. The New Finance Group box appears.

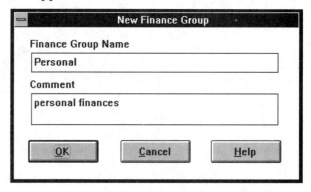

2. Type a name that characterizes the group.

3. If you wish, type a comment. Comments help you distinguish one finance group from another.

4. Choose OK. The Select Finance Group Categories box appears.

5. Choose the type of finance group you want to create:

    ▪ **Personal** sets up a finance group with categories for personal finances.

    ▪ **Business** uses categories that apply to business operations.

    ▪ **Both** sets up a finance group with a combination of the Personal and Business categories.

6. Choose OK.

The new finance group becomes the current group on the screen. You can begin adding buttons to the group, as explained in *Adding and Maintaining Finance Buttons* later in this chapter.

Opening an Existing Finance Group

When you start CA-Simply Money, the finance group that was last used appears.

To switch to another finance group:

1. From the File menu, choose Open. The Open Finance Group box appears. It lists all existing groups, and highlights the current group.

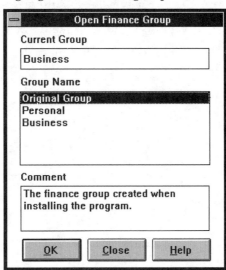

2. Choose a finance group. The comments for that group appear in the Comment box.

3. Double-click on the finance group name
   -or-
   Choose OK to open the finance group.

The Income Sources, Accounts, and Payees for that finance group appear on the screen.

Note: You can also open an existing finance group when you start CA-Simply Money. For more information, see *Customizing Some Operations at Startu*p in the Appendix.

Modifying a Finance Group

You can change the name of a finance group and edit the comments about it.

1. From the File menu, choose Change Name. The Select Finance Group box appears.

2. From the Group Name box, choose the group you want to rename.

3. Choose Edit Name. The Modify Finance Group box appears.

4. Type a new name or edit the comments.

5. Choose OK to return to the Select Finance Group box.

6. Choose Home to return to the main window.

Deleting a Finance Group

When you delete a finance group, all transactions for that group are also deleted. Make sure you have backup copies of any important finance groups before you delete them. For more information, see *Backup* in Chapter 10.

1. From the File menu, choose Delete. The Select Finance Group box appears.

2. From the Group Name box, choose the finance group you want to delete.

3. Choose Delete.

Note: You cannot delete the finance group that is currently open. If you want to delete the current group, you must first open a different finance group.

Adding and Maintaining Finance Buttons

Your finances are represented by three columns of buttons in the main window: Income, Accounts, and Payees. A typical payee might be your doctor. The button for your doctor appears in the Payee section, identified by an icon and a name.

You do not have to add all buttons at once. In fact, you can start entering transactions after you have added only one account. You can add other accounts, plus income sources and payees, as you pay bills, record income, and update accounts.

This section explains how to add, modify, and delete Income Sources, Accounts, and Payees. It also discusses Specials, which are for transactions such as balance adjustments, voided checks, and account withdrawals.

Setup Methods

You can add, modify, or delete buttons with either the Setup button or the Tools menu. Most of the procedures in this chapter describe button setup using the Setup button.

Setting up Your Finances

Using the Setup Button

To use the Setup button, follow one of these procedures:

1. Click the Setup button. The Setup box appears.

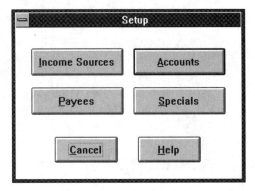

2. Choose Income Sources, Accounts, Payees, or Specials. A setup box for your choice appears.

Or:

1. Click and drag the Setup button onto the Income, Accounts, or Payees button. A Setup box appears.

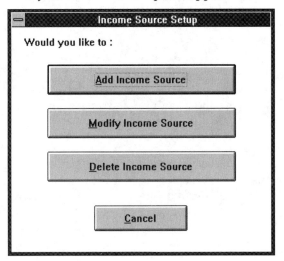

2. Choose Add, Modify, or Delete.

Using the Tools Menu

To set up buttons with the Tools menu:

1. From the Tools menu, choose Setup. The Setup box appears.

2. Choose Income Sources, Accounts, Payees, or Specials. A Setup box for your choice appears.

3. Choose Add, Modify or Delete.

Adding Income Sources

Income source buttons represent where your money comes from. Typical income sources are paycheck, interest, and dividends.

To add a new income source:

1. Drag and drop the Income button onto the Setup button. The Income Source Setup box appears.

2. From the Income Source Setup box, choose Add Income Source. The Income Source Setup-Add box appears.

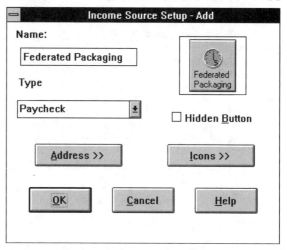

3. In the Type box, click on the down arrow to see a list of income source types. Choose a type. The type you choose appears in the Type box.

   Note: Some types create categories and subcategories. For example, if you choose the type Paycheck,

CA-Simply Money creates a Salary category with the income source as the subcategory. It also creates a Paycheck Expenses category with subcategories Federal Withholding, FICA, State Disability, State Withholding, and Misc.

4. In the Name box, type the name you would like to appear on the Income Source button. You can use the same name as the Type if you wish.

    Example: If you receive paychecks from only one source, you can call your income source "Paycheck." But if you have several jobs, you need to label each income source with the company name.

Adding Additional Information If you wish, add an address, telephone number, contact name, and/or account number.

5. Click the Address button. The Additional Information box appears.

6. Type an address, telephone number, contact person, and/or account number.

    Tip: You can copy the name on the income source button to the first line of the address by pressing Ctrl+P.

7. Choose OK to return to the Setup-Add box.

Changing the Icon If you want your button to have an icon different from the one shown in the Setup-Add box, follow steps 8 and 9:

8. Click the Icons button. A gallery of over 200 icons appears. Use the scroll bar to display the many different icons.

9. Double-click on the icon of your choice.
    -or-
    Single-click on the icon and on OK.

Hiding the Button If you do not expect to use a button very often, you can "hide" it from view in the main window. You may want to do this for consulting income that you do not receive regularly.

All the transactions for a hidden button remain intact. You can unhide a button at any time. Even when hidden, a button name still appears in the browser box so you can use it.

10. In the Setup box, click on the Hidden Button check box.

Returning to the Main Window 11. Choose OK to create the income source and return to the main window.

Adding Accounts

Accounts hold your money and let you record fund transfers. Examples of accounts are checking, savings, and credit card.

Adding an account is similar to adding an income source. However, you must enter additional information. For example, checking accounts require starting balances, and mortgages require down payment information.

This section explains the various types of accounts you can have, then shows how to set them up.

Note: The procedure for setting up investment accounts is in Chapter 7, "Managing Your Investments."

Note: To make an account tax-free, make all the categories associated with it tax-free. See *Using the Category Editor* in Chapter 6.

Setting up Your Finances

Types of Accounts   The account types and their uses are listed below:

Checking. For check-writing accounts.

Savings. For interest-bearing deposit accounts.

Credit Card. For major credit card use. You can set up a credit card account for each credit card you use.

With a credit card account you can reconcile your charge statement, and keep track of outstanding charges and remaining credit. You can print a check for your credit card payment through the account, and have the check appear in the checking account register. For more information about credit card accounts, see *Setting Up a Credit Line or Credit Card Account* later in this chapter, and *Tracking Credit Cards* in Chapter 6.

In some cases you may want to set up your credit card company as a payee rather than an account:

- if you pay your card in full every month

- if you use BillPay USAsm to pay your credit card bill (see Chapter 9)

- if you do not care to track account balance, available credit, and interest

Cash. For tracking on-hand currency.

Mortgage. For making mortgage payments, broken down into principal and tax-deductible interest. Helps you keep track of home improvements and equity.

A mortgage account keeps track of principal and interest by using the amortization table you can calculate when you set up the account. A mortgage account calculates your net worth by balancing the value of your home, including home improvements, against your mortgage debt. You can print a check for your mortgage payment through the account, and have the check appear in the checking account register. Your mortgage payments are distributed properly to liability, asset, and interest categories. See *Setting Up a Mortgage Account*, later in this section, and *Making a Mortgage Payment* in Chapter 6.

If you pay your mortgage via BillPay USA, set up your mortgage as a payee rather than an amount.

Investment Account. For buying and selling securities. Use an investment account to record and track taxable and nontaxable interest, short- and long-term capital gain and losses, dividends, margin interest, and miscellaneous expenses.

Credit Line. For bank lines of credit (such as home equity loans) and loans for which interest is paid (such as car and boat loans). Keeps track of balances and amounts of credit still available (credit remaining).

Liability Account. For loans or amounts owed that are not covered in other accounts (such as personal loans).

Asset Account. For keeping track of assets such as a 401(k) account, coin and art collections, or loans you have made to others. Also for tracking accounts receivables.

Payroll. For paying wages. Automatically itemizes taxes and deductions for liability and expense categories.

Setting Up a Checking, Savings, or Cash Account

The procedure for setting up checking, savings, and cash accounts is the same.

1. In the Account Setup-Add box, type an account name.

2. From the Account Type list, choose Checking, Savings, or Cash.

3. Choose OK. The Account Balances box appears.

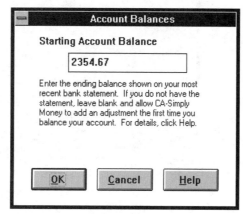

4. Type the starting account balance. If you want the balance to have a date other than today's date, press Alt+D and enter the date.

5. Choose OK.

Setting Up a Mortgage Account

To set up a mortgage account:

1. In the Account Setup-Add box, type the name of the company that holds your mortgage. This name prints on checks and appears in the mortgage account register.

2. From the Account Type list, choose Mortgage.

3. Add any additional information such as address or account number, choose an icon, or hide the button.

Tip: If you are going to print checks and use windowed envelopes, add the payee name to the address. A quick way to do this is to press Ctrl+P.

4. Click OK. The Account Balances box appears.

```
┌─────────────────────────────────────────────┐
│ ▬            Account Balances                │
├─────────────────────────────────────────────┤
│                                             │
│     Current Loan Balance                    │
│       ┌─────────────────────────┐           │
│       │ 100000.00               │           │
│       └─────────────────────────┘           │
│     Current Market Value                    │
│       ┌─────────────────────────┐           │
│       │ 150000.00               │           │
│       └─────────────────────────┘           │
│     Down Payment + Improvements             │
│       ┌─────────────────────────┐           │
│       │ 40000.00                │           │
│       └─────────────────────────┘           │
│                                             │
│   ┌──────┐ ┌──────────┐ ┌────────┐ ┌──────┐ │
│   │  OK  │ │ Amortize...│ │ Cancel │ │ Help │ │
│   └──────┘ └──────────┘ └────────┘ └──────┘ │
└─────────────────────────────────────────────┘
```

5. In the Current Loan Balance box, type the outstanding loan amount. If you want the balance to have a date other than today's date, press Alt+D and enter the date.

6. In the Current Market Value box, type the current value of your home.

7. In the Down Payment + Improvements box, type the sum of your down payment plus the cost of any home improvements (as distinct from repairs or maintenance) you have made.

8. If your mortgage has a fixed rate, follow the next procedure, *Amortizing Loans*. Otherwise, click OK to return to the main window.

Amortizing Loans When you amortize a mortgage or other interest-bearing loan (credit line account type), you create an amortization schedule that lists how much of a fixed loan payment is principal and how much is interest. The amortization table causes CA-Simply Money to distribute the correct amounts of principal and interest automatically when you pay off the mortgage or loan.

1. At the end of creating or modifying an account, the Account balances box appears. Choose Amortize.

    The Amortize button also appears on the box for paying mortgages and credit lines.

2. Choose Principal, Payment, or Interest Rate. CA-Simply Money will calculate this value for you.

3. Type the appropriate amounts in the other two boxes.

4. In the Number of Years box, type the length of the loan.

5. In the Payments Made box, choose the payment frequency.

6. If the mortgage is new, leave "1" in the Payment Number box. If it is not new, type the next payment number.

7. If payments are made at the end of the period, click the Payments Made at End of Period box.

8. Click Solve. CA-Simply Money fills in the missing value.

9. To view an amortization table for this loan, choose Schedule. The Payment Schedule appears.
    -or-
    Choose OK to complete the amortization set up.

Note: You may also use the Amortization Setup box to remove amortization information. Simply choose UnAmortize.

Setting Up a Credit Line or Credit Card Account

To set up a credit line or credit card account:

1. In the Account Setup-Add box, type the name to appear on payment checks (usually the bank name).

2. From the Account Type list, choose Credit Line or Credit Card.

3. Add any additional information such as address or account number, choose an icon, or hide the button.

    Tip: If you are going to print checks and use windowed envelopes, add the payee name to the address. A quick way to do this is to press Ctrl+P.

4. Click OK. The Account Balances box appears.

5. For a credit line, type the Starting Account Balance and the Total Credit Line. For a Credit Card, enter the Credit Limit.

    If you want these amounts to have a date other than today's date, press Alt+D and enter the date.

6. For a credit line with a fixed rate, follow the previous procedure, *Amortizing Loans*. Otherwise, click OK to return to the main window.

Setting Up an Asset or Liability Account

To set up an asset or liability account:

1. In the Account Setup-Add box, name your account.

2. From the Account Type list, choose Asset Acct. or Liability Acct.

3. Click on OK. The Account Balances box appears.

4. Type the current asset value or the current loan balance. If you want the asset value or the loan balance to have a date other than today's date, press Alt+D and enter the date.

5. Choose OK to return to the main window.

Adding Payees

Payees are the persons or companies that receive your payments. To add a new payee:

1. Drag and drop the Payees button onto the Setup button. The Payee Setup box appears.

2. From the Payee Setup box, choose Add Payee. The Payee Setup-Add box appears.

3. In the Name box, type a name for the payee. The name appears on the payee button and on checks.

4. Add any additional information such as address or account number, choose an icon, or hide the button.

Tip: If you are going to print checks and use windowed envelopes, add the payee name to the address. A quick way to do this is to press Ctrl+P.

5. Choose OK to return to the main window.

Adding Specials

Some transactions are not transfers of funds from one button to another. Examples are balance adjustments, voided checks, and account withdrawals. For these types of transactions you can use "specials." You can also use specials for transactions that require a transfer of funds but do not warrant setting up a payee button.

Specials have a browser box just as income sources, accounts, and payees do. The browser enables you to choose specials when you record transactions in an account register.

Example: To record an ATM withdrawal from your checking account, use the special "Withdrawal."

This section describes the types of specials already set up in CA-Simply Money, and explains how to add your own.

Setting up Your Finances

Types of Specials   The CA-Simply Money Specials are:

Balance Adjustment. CA-Simply Money adds this automatically during account reconciliation if you choose to make an adjustment to an unbalanced account.

A Balance Adjustment is distributed to the Misc. Equity category, which is used to add money to an account without recording it as income.

Deposit. Use Deposit when the payee is the account itself.

Interest Earned. Interest earned and added to an account automatically by the account institution.

Interest Paid. Interest expenses deducted from an account automatically by the account institution.

Refund. Funds that are restored by a bank or other institution.

Service Charge. Overdraft, ATM, and other charges.

Starting Balance. The first entry in the register for an account is the starting balance. You enter the starting balance when you add an account.

A Starting Balance is distributed to the Misc. Equity category, which is used to add money to an account without recording it as income.

Transfer. For transfers between accounts.

Void. Use Void for checks that have been destroyed.

Withdrawal. For money you take out of an account for your own use, as opposed to a payment to yourself as payee.

Setting up a Special   You add specials in the same way you add other buttons.

1. Choose the Setup button. From the Setup box, choose Specials. The Special Button Setup box appears.

2. Choose Add Special. The Special Button Setup-Add box appears.

3. Type a name for the Special, and click OK.

Modifying a Button

You can change most information for any button at any time. The only attributes you cannot change are the Account Type and Starting Balance for an account. (If you want to change the Starting Balance of an account, enter the change as a Balance Adjustment, which is a Special transaction; see *Handling Out of Balance Accounts* in Chapter 6.)

If you want to merge several payee buttons into one button and combine their transaction history, see *Merging a Payee Group into One Button* in Chapter 6.

If you want to make an account tax-free, make the categories associated with it tax-free. See *Tax Considerations for Categories* in Chapter 6.

To modify a button:

1. Drag and drop the button you want to modify onto the Setup button. The Single Button Setup box appears.

2. Choose Modify. The Setup-Modify box appears. It contains the information you entered when you set up the button.

3. Edit any information you want to change: Name, Address, Telephone Number, Contact, and/or Account Number. You can also change the Icon, or hide the button.

If you are going to print checks and use windowed envelopes, you may need to add the payee name to the address. A quick way to do this is to press Ctrl+P.

4. For some types of accounts, the Account Balances dialog box appears. You cannot change the starting account balance, but you can modify other amounts such as Credit Limit for a credit card account or Current Market Value and Down Payment and Improvements for a mortgage account. Change an amount if you wish. This generates an adjustment transaction.

   If you want the adjustment to have a date other than today's date, press Alt+D and enter the date. Click on OK to get back to the main window.

5. Choose OK to return to the main window.

Deleting a Button

If an account is inactive but contains information you want to keep, you can delete the button. Before deleting it, you should make a backup (see *Backup* in Chapter 10). You can also "hide" a button instead of deleting it. To delete a button:

1. In the Setup box, choose the button type: Income Source, Account, Payee, or Special. Then choose Delete. The Setup-Delete box appears.

2. Click the Next or Previous button until the item you want to delete appears in the Name box, and choose OK.

   A Delete box appears. The Delete boxes for Income Sources, Accounts and Payees contain a warning that deleting the button will make it impossible to reference transactions associated with the button.

   ■ You can choose to keep the categories and transactions associated with an income source. Any transactions you keep will have either "Withdrawal" or "Deposit" in place of the deleted source name. References to any deleted categories are moved to the "Miscellaneous" category.

- You can choose to keep the transactions associated with a payee. Any transactions you keep will have either "Withdrawal" or "Deposit" in place of the deleted payee name.

- Categories associated with an account are deleted.

- You can delete specials you created but not the default ones that come with CA-Simply Money. The deleting options are the same as for a payee.

3. Click on OK, then click on OK again to confirm deleting the button.

Chapter 6
Tracking Your Money

Tracking Your
Money

Chapter 6
Tracking Your Money

After you have set up at least one account, you can start recording income and paying bills. CA-Simply Money can translate this information into reports and graphs to help you understand where your money comes from and where it goes.

Categorizing Your Finances

To track your finances properly, you need to allocate the funds you receive and spend to categories that reflect your lifestyle or business needs. Typical categories are child care, dental, and groceries. By recording transactions in various categories, you can get reports that show how much you earned from one area, and how much you spent in another. These reports can help you define a budget and prepare for tax time.

CA-Simply Money provides default categories that are appropriate for personal and business finances. The categories (and subcategories) are assigned when you create a finance group, based on the type of finance group you choose to create: Personal, Business, or Both. You can also create your own categories (see *Using the Category Editor* later in this chapter).

CA-Simply Money divides most of your financial information into four areas: income, expense, asset, and liability. Each area has categories. For example, some typical income categories are Commissions, Interest, and Dividend. Typical expense categories are Clothing, Medical, and Groceries. The asset and liability areas also have categories.

Each time you set up an income source or account, CA-Simply Money creates one or more categories or subcategories, based on the type of income or account you set up. For example, when you create a paycheck income source,

CA-Simply Money creates a Salary category and a subcategory with the name of the income source. Also created is an Expenses category with the subcategories Federal Withholding, FICA, State Disability, State Withholding, and Misc.

You assign funds to categories when you record income and make payments. You can allocate an amount to one category, or split it among several categories (called making a distribution). You see how to assign categories in *Writing Checks* later in this chapter. If you do not choose a category, CA-Simply Money automatically assigns the funds to the default Miscellaneous category.

Note: The Misc. Equity category is a special category for balance adjustments and starting balances. It is not an income, expense, asset, or liability category, and is used to add money to an account without recording it as income.

Recording Income

Recording income in CA-Simply Money is as simple as typing a number—and sometimes simpler. After you set up your income sources, as described in *Adding Income Sources* in Chapter 5, and entered information about your first deposits from those income sources, a single click of the income source button brings up a dialog box with the current date and all the information from the last deposit. If your income is steady from month to month, another click of the mouse records the current payment.

Recording Paycheck Income

When you deposit income, CA-Simply Money automatically records amounts in the expense categories for Federal and State withholding, disability insurance, and FICA. This saves you effort at tax time.

1. Click once on your paycheck button.
   -or-
   From the Operations menu, choose Record Income, then select your paycheck name from the Income Source list:

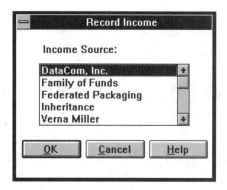

The Record Income box for your paycheck appears. If you have not recorded a paycheck before, the Record Income box is empty. If you have, the information from the last transaction appears.

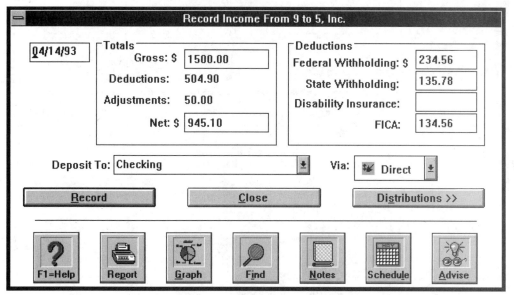

2. If necessary, enter amounts for Gross pay and Deductions, or change amounts that are already there.

3. Click the down arrow at the right of Deposit To and select the account into which you want to deposit the income.

4. Click the down arrow at the right of Via and select the payment method (for example, check or direct deposit).

Contributing to a 401(k)

5. If you contribute to a 401(k), click on the Distributions button. (Your 401(k) must already be set up as an asset account; see *Setting Up an Asset or Liability Account* in Chapter 5.) The Distribution register appears.

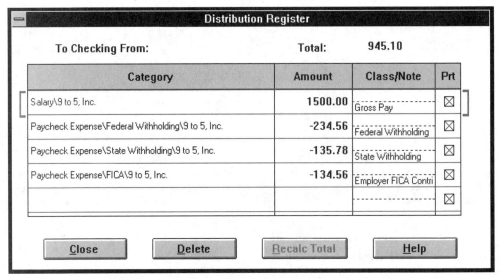

Distribution Register			
To Checking From:	**Total:**	**945.10**	
Category	Amount	Class/Note	Prt
Salary\9 to 5, Inc.	1500.00	Gross Pay	☒
Paycheck Expense\Federal Withholding\9 to 5, Inc.	-234.56	Federal Withholding	☒
Paycheck Expense\State Withholding\9 to 5, Inc.	-135.78	State Withholding	☒
Paycheck Expense\FICA\9 to 5, Inc.	-134.56	Employer FICA Contri	☒
			☒

Close | Delete | Recalc Total | Help

6. On the first blank line, start typing the name of the 401(k) account. A browser box appears.

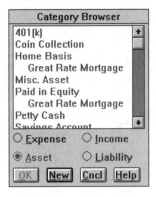

Category Browser
401(k)
Coin Collection
Home Basis
Great Rate Mortgage
Misc. Asset
Paid in Equity
Great Rate Mortgage
Petty Cash
Savings Account

○ Expense ○ Income
◉ Asset ○ Liability

OK | New | Cncl | Help

7. Select Asset at the bottom of the browser. Then click on your 401(k) account from the list, and press OK.

8. In the Amount column of the Distribution register, type the contribution amount as a negative number.

401(k)	-50.00		☒

Entering Other Paycheck Deductions

9. To add other deductions such as medical insurance, repeat steps 6 through 8, except click on Expense in the browser.

Recording the Paycheck

10. Press Close. The Record Income box reappears.

11. Click Record to record your paycheck income and deductions. The Net amount on the Record Income box, your gross income less all deductions and adjustments, is added to the destination account automatically. The 401(k) amount is added to your 401(k) asset account.

Recording Other Income

You might have income from other sources, for example, consulting income, inheritance, royalties, or social security. The dialog boxes for these sources differ slightly from that for a paycheck, but recording the income is similar.

1. Click on the button for your income source.
    -or-
    Choose Record Income from the Operations menu and select the name of your income source from the Income Source list.

    The Record Income box for this income source appears.

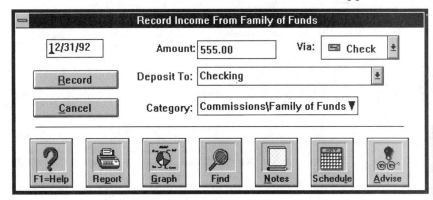

2. Type the amount, choose the deposit method (Via), and select the destination account.

3. Begin typing the category name in the Category box, and choose your category from the Category Browser.

4. Click Record to record this income.

Using an Account Register

One of the most common ways to view and update your financial data is through an account Register. Each account has its own Register, which shows all transaction information for that account. Registers vary slightly for the different types of accounts, but they work in the same manner.

Tasks you might use a register for include:

■ Viewing transactions.

■ Deleting transactions.

■ Changing transactions.

■ Distributing transactions to categories and subcategories.

■ Recording deposits and withdrawals.

■ Recording transactions that have a check number (for example, a check drawn against a checking account).

■ Recording, changing, or deleting transactions while reconciling an account.

Opening an Account Register

Use any of the following methods to open an account register.

Double Clicking. Double-click on an account button.

Dragging & Dropping. Click and drag an account button and drop it on the Register button.

Tools Menu. From the Tools menu, choose View Register. The View Register box appears.

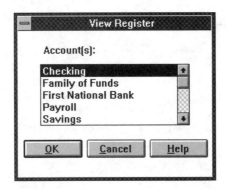

Choose an account by double-clicking on the account name.

-or-

Click on the account name and choose OK.

Register Button. Click on the Register button. The View Register box appears. Choose an account.

Register Columns

The standard columns for account registers are:

Date. Contains the transaction date.

Via. Contains either a check number or a P, which indicates a check is ready to print. Also contains an icon indicating the transaction method (check, ATM, wire, and so on).

C. Indicates whether the transaction has cleared.

Pay To/Deposit From. When a register is in standard register format (see *Setting Register Sort and Display Options* later in this chapter), this column has three lines. The first line is for a name, the second is for an optional memo, and the third is for a category. In Credit Card accounts this column is labeled Merchant/Paid From.

Payment. Contains the purchase amount. In Credit Card accounts this column is labeled Charge.

Deposit. Contains the deposit amount. In Credit Card account, this column is labeled Payment.

Balance. Contains the balance CA-Simply Money calculates.

Recording a Deposit in a Register

This procedure is for recording a deposit from most income sources. Do not use it for recording paycheck income, however. Use the procedure described in *Recording Paycheck Income* earlier in this chapter.

1. Open the register of the account to which you want to make a deposit.

2. Type the name of the income source from which your deposit will come.

3. Type the amount in the Deposit column.

4. Choose Record.

Using an Account Register to Pay Bills

If you do not use CA-Simply Money to print checks, record your handwritten checks in the account Register.

You can record payments in most registers. The exceptions are the registers of Payroll and Mortgage accounts. Do not use the register to record payroll checks. Record mortgage payments in the register only if you use BillPay USA to pay your mortgage. For more information, see *Making a Mortgage Payment* later in this chapter and *Writing Payroll Checks* in Chapter 8.

Tip: If you use the check printing feature, it may be more convenient to write checks through the Checkbook rather than in the Register. See page 6-15 for instructions on writing checks.

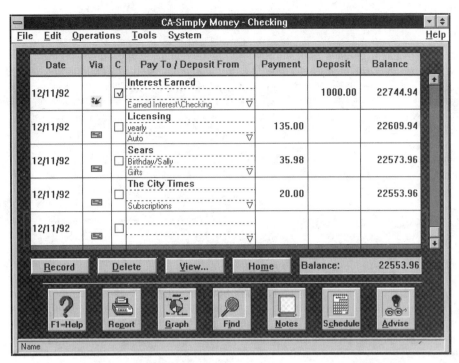

When you first open the Register window, CA-Simply Money provides you with an empty transaction line to begin a new transaction. After recording a transaction by pressing the Record button, a new blank line appears just below it. If you predate or postdate a transaction, the transaction automatically moves to its proper chronological location in the register.

While you move through the Register, the message line at the bottom of the screen indicates the information required in each field. (The Drag & Drop Info On setting needs to be turned on; see *Changing System Settings* in Chapter 10.) To move the cursor from field to field, use the Tab key or Enter key.

Tracking Your Money

To record a payment:

1. Double-click on the checking account button to open the register.

2. Click on the first line in the Pay To column of the empty transaction area. Each transaction line in the Pay To/Deposit From column is divided into three parts: Name (Payee), Memo, and Distribution (category).

Name

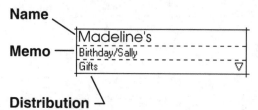

Memo

Distribution

3. Start typing the name of the payee on the Name line. The Payee Browser box appears.

   If you want to add a new payee, click New. (See *Adding Payees* in Chapter 5.) The Payee Setup-Add box appears. Fill in the payee information.

   If a new payee will not receive checks often, you can record the check without adding the payee to your payee list. In the Payee Setup-Add box, select "Is this a one-time only Payee?" If you need to use a one-time payee again, simply type its name. Although the name is not in the browser list, CA-Simply Money will accept it as an existing payee. You can also make a button for it by adding a payee with the name of the one-time payee. CA-Simply Money will associate all the previous transactions with that button.

   If the payee already exists, select it from the list in the browser and click OK. If you entered an address when you set up the payee, the address appears on the check. If needed, change the address. Changing the address here also updates the payee button.

4. In the Payment column, type the transaction amount.

Tip: You can use the Windows Calculator while you are in the Register by choosing Calculator from the System menu.

5. In the Memo line, type an optional memo.

Tip: You can use the Note button to attach a note to the transaction. See *The Notes Feature* in Chapter 9.

6. Assign one or more categories to your payment by typing on the distribution line. For details about distributing payments, see *Distributing a Payment to a Category* on page 6-18 or *Distributing a Payment to More Than One Category* on page 6-19 in this chapter.

Tip: You can open the Distribution Register by pressing Ctrl+DnArrow.

7. In the Date column, type the transaction date if it is different from today's date.

8. In the Via column, type the check number for your handwritten check, or type P if you want to print the check.

Tip: If you want to clear the Distribution Register and reenter categories, place the cursor on the distribution line of the account register and press Ctrl+D.

9. When you have entered all transaction information, choose Record. CA-Simply Money updates your balance, and a new transaction line appears.

10. Continue entering transactions, or choose Home to return to the main window.

Note: If you do not assign a category, CA-Simply Money uses the Miscellaneous Expense category. If you should ever move an amount assigned to Misc. Expns. from the Payment column to the Deposit column, the category changes to Miscellaneous Income. Both categories do not appear in the register, but show as miscellaneous expense or income on reports.

Tracking Your Money

Editing a Register Transaction

You can change a transaction at any time: during or after completion, or during account reconciliation. Any changes you make to an amount automatically change the account balance.

If the transaction line is yellow, you must edit the transaction in the account where you made the transaction (usually checking).

1. Open an account register.

2. In the register, use the scroll bar to locate the transaction you want to edit. Change the transaction.

Note: If you should ever move an amount assigned to the Misc. Expns. category from the Payment column to the Deposit column, the category changes to Miscellaneous Income. The category does not appear in the register, but shows as miscellaneous income on reports.

Tip: CA-Simply Money prompts you to confirm every change. You can turn this confirmation message off with the Confirm Cancel setting. See *Changing System Settings* in Chapter 10.

Deleting a Register Transaction

You can delete a transaction any time.

1. Click on the transaction line, then click Delete. A confirming message appears.

2. Choose Yes. The transaction line disappears, and CA-Simply Money updates your balance.

Setting Register Sort and Display Options

You can specify how transactions in a register are sorted, and collapse or expand the space for each transaction.

1. In the Register, choose View. The Register View Options box appears.

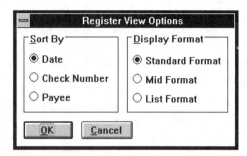

2. Choose one of the Sort By options.

   Date. To list transactions by date.

   Check Number. To list transactions by check number.

   Payee. To list transactions alphabetically by payee.

3. Choose one of the Display Format options.

   Standard Format. To display three lines per transaction, for the payee name, the memo, and the distribution.

   Mid Format. To display two lines per transaction, dividing the second line between the memo and distribution.

   List Format. To display one line per transaction, showing just the payee name and payment information, excluding the memo and distribution.

4. Choose OK to return to the Register.

Writing Checks

You can pay bills two ways: by "writing" checks in the Checkbook, or by recording payments in the account Register. If you are going to print custom checks when you pay your bills, use the Checkbook for making your payments. If you do not print checks, record your payments in the Register. See *Using an Account Register to Pay Bills* on page 6-10 in this chapter for instructions on how to use the register.

The Checkbook is a CA-Simply Money window that looks like a check. You can write checks as you receive bills, or you can write checks for all your bills at the same time. Whichever you choose, you can print the checks at any time. Writing and printing checks are separate activities.

Tip: If you pay several bills at the same time every month, you may want to automate the check writing procedure by grouping those payees. See *Grouping Buttons* later in this chapter.

Whenever you write a check, CA-Simply Money remembers the amount. The next time you write a check to that payee, the information from your last payment automatically appears on the check. Printing checks from the Checkbook saves time and reduces errors when you make recurring payments.

Tip: CA-Simply Money can remind you to pay recurring bills. See *The Scheduler* in Chapter 9.

Note: CA-Simply Money can import information from BillPay USA[sm], which is an online bill-payment service available through Prodigy. The imported payments are incorporated into your records just as payments made any other way, and your balances are adjusted accordingly. (See *Importing BillPay USA Records* in Chapter 9.)

You need a Prodigy membership to use BillPay USA; see the Prodigy brochure in your CA-Simply Money package.

Opening the Checkbook

You can open the checkbook by clicking with the mouse, dragging and dropping a button, or selecting from the Operations menu.

Using the Mouse. Either click once on the button of the checking account you want to use, or click on the Write button.

If you have more than one checking account, the Write Checks box appears, containing a list of all your checking accounts. From the Select Account box, choose a checking account.

Using Drag & Drop. Drag the checking account button to the payee button, or the payee button to the checking account button. Or drag the Write button to the checking-account button.

Using the Operations Menu. From the Operations menu, choose Transfer Funds or Pay Expenses. From the Use Account box, select the name of the checking account you want.

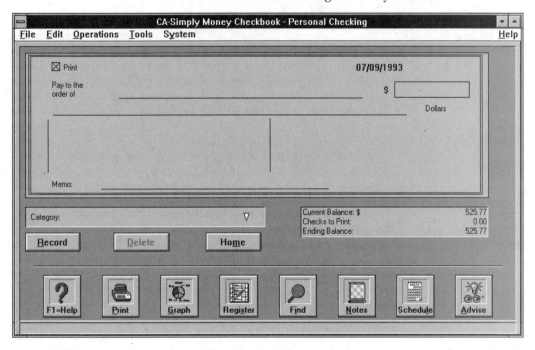

Writing a Check

You can write a check to a payee you have already set up, or you can create the payee while writing the check.

Use the Tab key or the Enter key to move the cursor to the various fields on the check.

Tip: If you wish, you can change the function of the Enter key to make it record the check rather than move from field to field. See *Customizing Some Operations at Startup* in the Appendix.

1. Change the date if necessary.

2. In the Pay to the order of line, type the name of a payee. If the payee is new (not in the Payee Browser list), choose New and set up the payee button. (See *Adding Payees* in Chapter 5.)

Tip: To add the payee name to the address, click on the first line of the address and press Ctrl+P. (Press Return to move to the second line). The name appears on the printed check and is added to the address information for the payee.

3. In the $ box, type the amount of the check. CA-Simply Money writes the amount in words on the next line.

4. If you wish, type a memo on the Memo line. The memo appears on the printed check (it may be truncated) and in the Register.

Tip: You can use the Note button to record a note with the transaction. See *The Notes Feature* in Chapter 9.

Distributing a Payment to a Category

Use the following steps 5 and 6 if the whole check amount is for one category. If you want to distribute the amount to more than one category, skip to step 7.

5. Click in the Category box, and begin typing a category. The Category Browser box appears.

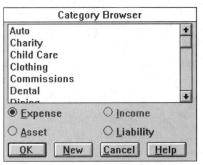

As you type, CA-Simply Money searches the browser list, and highlights the matching category name.

6. Choose OK.

Note: If you do not assign an amount to a category, CA-Simply Money puts it into the Miscellaneous category. The Misc. Expns. category does not appear in the register, but shows as a Miscellaneous Expense on reports.

Distributing a Payment to More Than One Category

In CA-Simply Money the term "distribution" means splitting a transaction to more than one category. For example, if you are paying a pharmacy bill that includes food and a prescription, you might distribute the amount to the Groceries and Medical categories.

7. Click on the arrowhead in the Category box of the Checkbook. The Distribution Register opens.

Tip: You can also open the Distribution Register by placing the cursor on the category line and pressing Ctrl+DnArrow.

8. In the Category column of the Distribution Register, start typing the first category. The category browser appears. Select the category and click OK.

If you want to use a new category, you can add it at this time by typing the category name and choosing New.

Note: If the category you choose is a subcategory, the top level category appears in the Distribution Register along with the subcategory, separated by a backslash (\).

The entire payment amount appears in the Amount column:

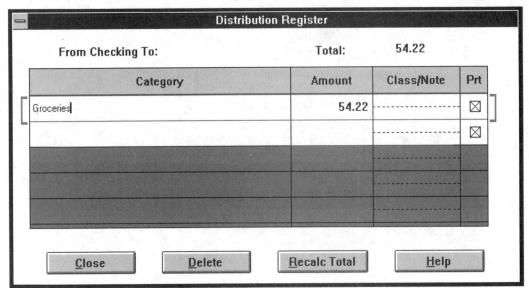

Note: An X in the Prt column indicates that the category prints on voucher-style checks.

9. In the Amount column, type the amount to distribute to that category. The remainder of the payment amount appears on the next category line.

| | Total: | 54.22 | | |
Category		Amount	Class/Note	Prt
Groceries		34.22	----------------	⊠
		20.00	----------------	⊠

Tip: You can use the Windows Calculator while you are in the Distribution Register by choosing Calculator from the System menu.

10. In the next Category line, type another category. If you plan to add more categories, change the Amount to the amount you want to distribute to that category. The remainder of the payment amount appears on the next line.

11. Repeat step 10 for all categories you want to add.

   If you want to delete a category line, click anywhere on the line, then click on Delete and on Recalc Total.

   If you end up with an excess amount, you can eliminate it by pressing the Recalc Total button. The new total is transferred to the check.

   Note: If you do not press Recalc Total, any undistributed amount goes into the Miscellaneous category. The Misc. Expns. category does not appear in the register, but shows as a Miscellaneous Expense on reports.

   Note: You can also make distributions before typing an amount on the check. The distribution values are automatically totaled and the total is used on the check.

12. Click Close to return to the Checkbook.

Tip: If you want to clear the Distribution Register and reenter categories, place the cursor on the category line of the Checkbook and press Ctrl+D.

Finishing the Check

13. If you want to print the check, make sure the Print box in the upper left corner contains an X.

14. In the Checkbook click on Record. A new check appears.

15. Continue writing checks, or click on Home to return to the main window.

Tracking Your Money

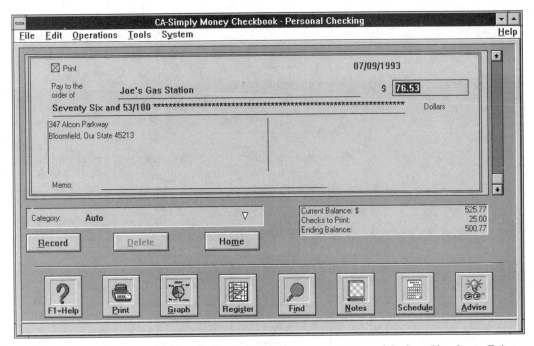

As you write checks, the amounts are added to Checks to Print in the lower right of the Checkbook, and subtracted from the Ending Balance. The Current Balance stays the same until you print checks.

Printing Checks

You can print checks from a dot-matrix, ink jet, or laser printer. Order check stock using the supplies catalog, online order form, or toll-free number (see *Ordering Supplies* in the Appendix).

Follow this general procedure for printing checks:

1. Edit any unprinted checks, if necessary.

2. Delay printing specific checks, if necessary.

3. Set the check printing options.

4. Set check layout and alignment.

5. Send the checks to the printer.

Editing an Unprinted Check

Checks remain in the Checkbook until they are printed, so you can change them if you wish

1. Open the Checkbook by clicking once on an account button. Use the scroll bar to locate the check you want to edit.

2. Click on any part of the check you want to change and edit the transaction information.

3. Choose Record. The new transaction information replaces the old on the check and in the account Register, and the next check in the Checkbook appears.

4. When you have finished editing checks, choose Home.

Delay Printing Specific Checks

If your checks total more than the funds in your checking account, the Ending Balance is a negative amount (shown in red on color monitors). You can selectively delay the printing of some checks until you add more money to your account.

1. In the Checkbook, use the scroll bar to find a check you do not want to print yet.

2. Click to remove the X from the Print box at the top left corner of the check, then click on Record.

3. Repeat steps 1 and 2 for every check you want to delay printing.

The Ending Balance changes as you choose the checks not to print. When the Ending Balance is a positive amount, you can click on the Print button to print the checks that still have an X. You can print the other checks after you deposit more money.

The Register for your checking account shows a negative balance reflecting the amount you still owe.

Setting Check Printing Options

You can select three printing options and four date formats.

Tracking Your Money

1. From the System/Settings menu, choose Check Printing. The Check Printing Settings box appears.

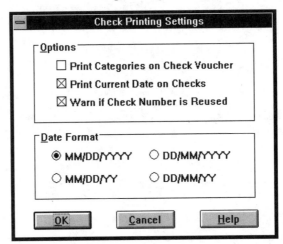

2. From the Options box, choose one or more of these options:

   Print Categories on Check Voucher, for use with the voucher-style checks

   Print Current Date on Checks, to date all checks with today's date

   Warn if Check Number is Reused, to guard against entering an incorrect starting number

3. From the Date Format box, choose a format.

4. Choose OK to return to the main window.

Setting Check Layout

Because you can order several different check styles, you may need to specify what kind of checks you have. If you have pin-feed, standard checks, the default, you can skip this procedure.

1. If you are not already in the Checkbook window, click on the checking account button.

2. Click on the Print button. The Print Checks box appears.

3. In the Print Checks box, click on Check Layout. The Check Layout box appears.

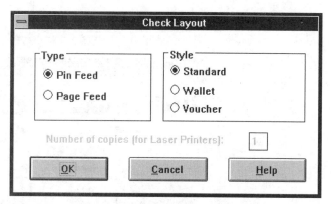

4. In the Type area, select either Pin Feed or Page Feed. Laser printers use page feed stock.

5. In the Style area, select Standard, Wallet, or Voucher. Wallet-style checks are not available for laser printers.

6. If you are using a laser printer, you can request multiple copies of the check for a multi-part check form.

7. Click on OK to return to the Print Checks box.

Setting Check Alignment

To verify that the alignment of checks is correct, you may want to print a sample check.

You may also want to verify that your printer setup is correct. For laser printers, be sure paper size is 8.5 by 11 inches and a paper cassette is chosen.

After you set the check alignment, CA-Simply Money remembers it from session to session so you only need to do it once unless you change check style or get a new printer.

Printing a Sample Check

1. In the Print Checks box, click on Print Sample.

2. Feed enough check stock into the printer to gain traction. If you are using a pin-feed printer, note where the check lines up with the printer guides. The first check in each print run should start in the same position.

3. Click on Print Sample Check.

Tracking Your Money

4. Examine the printed check, then align your checks using the following procedure for pin-feed or page-feed printers.

Aligning Checks On a Pin-Feed Printer

The Continuous Feed Checks-Alignment box appears for most pin-feed printers.

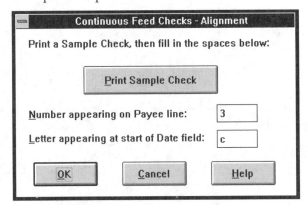

1. The sample check for pin-feed printers has two columns of numbers and one row of letters. Position an actual check under the sample check and see where the numbers and letters line up. One of the numbers should line up on the Payee line and one of the letters should line up with the left edge of the Date line.

2. In the Continuous Feed Checks-Alignment box, type the number appearing on the Payee line and the Letter appearing at the start of the Date field.

Aligning Checks On a Page-Feed Printer

The Page Feed Checks-Alignment box appears.

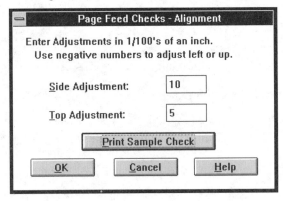

1. If the information on the sample check was too far left, right, up, or down, you can enter adjustments in 1/100ths of an inch. For example, if the information is 1/2 inch too far to the right, enter -50 in the Side Adjustment field.

2. Print another sample check to verify the new alignment. (You may want to use regular paper to save check stock. Put the paper on top of a check to verify the alignment.)

Sending Checks to the Printer

To print checks:

1. Make sure the printer is ready and check stock is loaded.

2. If you are not already in the Checkbook window, click on the checking account button.

3. Click on the Print button. The Print Checks box appears.

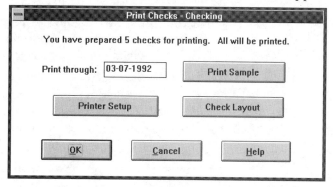

4. If you want to print only those checks written before a certain date, enter a date in the Print through box. The default is today's date.

   If you have recorded more checks than your account balance can support, print only those within your balance. See *Delay Printing Specific Checks* earlier in this chapter.

   Important: *Before continuing, you may need to change the check printing layout and/or the printing alignment.*

5. Choose OK. The Check Number box appears.

6. Look at your check stock. Type the number of the next check in the Next check # area. Choose OK. The Confirm Printing box appears.

Printing Partial Pages of Checks

7. If you are using standard page-feed checks, the Standard Checks - Page Feed dialog box appears. It enables you to print on a partial page of checks. Standard laser checks come three on a page. After printing checks the last time, you may have a partial page of only one or two checks.

   If the first page you are going to feed into the printer has three checks, you do not need to use this dialog, so click on OK to close it. Skip ahead to step 11.

8. In the Number of Checks area, select the number of checks on the first page you will feed into the printer: 2 Checks or 1 Check.

9. In the Orientation area, select Normal Feed or Sideways Feed. The most common choice is Sideways Feed, which is appropriate for the HP Laserjet II, III, IIp, and the Apple Personal LaserWriter. Normal Feed is usually appropriate for bubble jet printers such as the HP DeskJet.

   If your printer uses Sideways Feed, experiment with inserting the checks face up or down and with the left or right edge leading. A good first try is face up, right edge.

10. In the Alignment area, select Centered or Along Left Edge. Centered applies to popular printers such as the HP Laserjet II and III. Use Along Left Edge for the HP Laserjet IIp and the Apple Personal LaserWriter.

Confirming Printing

11. If all your checks printed correctly, choose OK. Then choose Home to return to the main window.

    If your checks did not print correctly:

    ■ In the Confirm Printing box, type the number of the first check that misfed.

    ■ Choose OK to return to the Print Checks box.

    ■ Repeat steps 5 and 6.

    When all checks have printed successfully, the Register is updated with the check numbers.

    Note: You should record any spoiled checks in the register by using the Special "Void."

12. Choose Home to return to the main window.

Reprinting Checks

If your printer jams, you may need to reprint checks after you have left the Print Checks box. Open the Register. Find the check(s) that need reprinting, and type P over the check number in the Via column. The check is selected for printing and will be included in the next check printing run.

Tracking Credit Cards

You can track your credit card payments in two ways: fast payments and detailed payments.

Fast Payments

Use the fast payments method when you have set up your credit card as a payee rather than an account. You would do this if any one of the following situations applies to you:

- you pay your credit card bill in full every month

- you use BillPay USA to pay your credit card bill

- you do not care to track account balance, available credit, and interest

Simply pay the credit card bill from your checking (or other) account. You will not have a record of the merchants you purchased from, but you can record purchase categories when you pay bills. You cannot reconcile your credit card statement.

Detailed Payments

Use the detailed payments method if your credit card is an account. This method lets you track and categorize credit card charges, and reconcile your account from statements.

The reconciliation procedure for credit card accounts performs two functions. First, it lets you confirm the charges on your statement. Second, it lets you pay your credit card bill, partially or in full, from your checking, savings, or other bank account. You can reconcile the account when you make a payment, or reconcile the account at another time.

Tracking Your Money

Recording Credit Card Usage

To record detailed credit card usage:

1. Select your credit card account button. The Account Activity box appears.

2. From the Account Activity box, choose Use Card. The Credit Card Account Withdrawals box appears.

3. If the transaction date is different from the current date, type the date in the Date box.

4. If the transaction is a purchase, in the Merchant box, type the place of purchase. The Payee Browser box appears.

5. In the Amount box, type the amount of the purchase.

6. If the transaction is a withdrawal from an ATM, or a check written against the credit card account, click the down arrow in the Via box. Select the appropriate transaction.

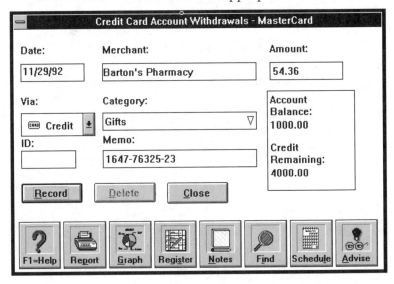

7. You can optionally add a Memo or an ID number.

   Note: The memo could include the ATM slip number or credit card transaction number. The ID could be a check number if you write checks against your credit card.

8. In the Category box, select a category. See *Distributing a Payment to a Category* or *Distributing a Payment to More Than One Category* earlier in this chapter.

9. Choose Record to accept the transaction. The amount of the transaction is added to the Account Balance amount and subtracted from the Credit Remaining amount.

10. Choose Close to return to the main window.

Recording Detailed Payments   To use the detailed payment method, make your payment while reconciling the account. See *Balancing Credit Card Accounts* later in this chapter.

Cash and Savings Accounts

If you want to keep track of how you spend your cash, you can create a Cash account to accept transfers from other accounts. You can record individual cash transactions, or record a monthly or weekly lump sum that you use for spending money.

For example, you stopped at an ATM on your way to go shopping and withdrew $50. While shopping, you used $15 for lunch. To record this transaction, drag your Checking account button to the Cash button and make a $50 transfer via ATM. Then use your Cash account to distribute the $15 to a category like Food or Dining. As you spend the rest of the $50, distribute the payments singly, or distribute them all at the same time.

If you withdraw spending money from your Savings account, you do not need to transfer from your Savings to your Cash account. Just use the Savings account button to record the withdrawal and distribute the expenditures.

Clicking once on a Cash or Savings account button brings up a dialog box with buttons labeled Deposits and Withdrawals. You can also record deposits and withdrawals in the account register as a Special transaction. Clicking on the buttons is faster, however, because you can bypass the register.

Tracking Your Money

Recording Withdrawals

To record cash or savings account withdrawals:

1. Select your cash or savings account button. The Account Activity box appears.

2. From the Account Activity box, choose Withdrawals. The Cash Out or Savings Withdrawal box appears.

3. In the Payee box, add a new payee or select an existing one. To use a Special, choose Specials.

4. In the Amount box, type the amount of cash you spent. You can optionally type a memo or an ID, or change the date.

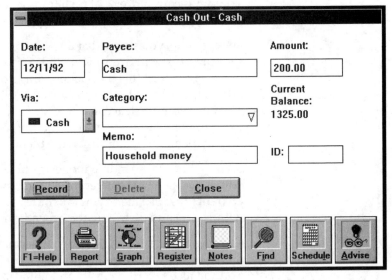

5. Use the Category box to record how you spent the money. See *Distributing a Payment to a Category* or *Distributing a Payment to More Than One Category* earlier in this chapter.

6. Choose Record to accept the transaction. The amount of the transaction is subtracted from Current Balance, and a new Cash-Out or Savings Withdrawal window appears.

7. When you are finished recording withdrawals, choose Close to return to the main window.

Recording Deposits

To record cash or savings account deposits:

1. Select your cash or savings account button. The Account Activity box appears.

2. From the Account Activity box, choose Deposits. The Cash In or Savings Deposits box appears.

3. In the From area, type the source of the funds. The Income Source browser box appears. If the funds came from an account, choose Accounts to see the Account Browser box. If you want to use a Special, choose Specials to see the Special browser box.

4. Choose an account or income source and click on OK to return to the Cash In or Savings Deposit window.

5. Complete the transaction by following steps 4 through 7 of the previous procedure, *Recording Withdrawals*.

Credit Line and Loan Accounts

Use credit line accounts to keep track of lines of credit such as home equity loans.

Example: Your son is in college and needs money for expenses. Your bank extends a credit line of $5000 to you. You open a joint bank account with your son and draw on the credit line.

Using Your Credit Line

To use your credit line:

1. Select your credit line account button. The Account Activity box appears.

2. From the Account Activity box, choose Use Credit. The Use Credit box appears.

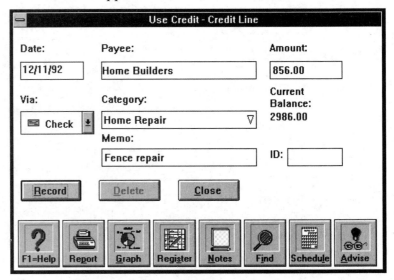

3. In the Payee box, begin typing a payee. The Payee Browser box appears. If the payee is an account, click on Accounts to change the Browser list. Choose an account or payee and choose OK to return to the Use Credit box.

4. Type the Amount, and optionally type a memo, an ID, or change the date.

    Note: The ID could be used for the trace number on an account transfer.

5. If you are tracking your distributions, select one or more categories in the Category box. See *Distributing a Payment to a Category* or *Distributing a Payment to More Than One Category* earlier in this chapter.

6. Choose Record to accept the transaction. The amount of the transaction is added to the Current Balance, and a new Use Credit window appears.

7. Choose Close to return to the main window.

Paying Off Your Credit Line

You can record payments to credit lines by using the Register, the Checkbook, or the Pay Off Credit box (which appears when you click on the credit line account button). The Pay Off Credit box is easiest to use because CA-Simply Money automatically enters principal and interest distributions; you do not have to enter them yourself in the Distribution Register.

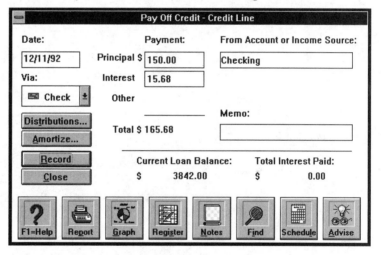

The Pay Off Credit box displays the Current Loan Balance and Total Interest Paid (which includes interest paid since recording payments in CA-Simply Money).

To pay off your credit line:

1. Select your credit line account button.

2. From the Account Activity box, choose Pay Off Credit. The Pay Off Credit box appears with information from your last payment. The Amortized Payment box also appears if you amortized this credit line. If you did not amortize, you can do so now. See *Amortizing Loans* in Chapter 5.

3. If necessary, type the Principal and Interest, and choose the Account or Income Source the funds are coming from by using the Browser boxes. You can optionally type a memo, or change the date.

4. If you are tracking your distributions, click on the Distributions button to open the Distribution Register. See *Distributing a Payment to a Category* or *Distributing a Payment to More Than One Category* earlier in this chapter. The total distributions are displayed in Other in the Pay Off Credit Line box.

   The transaction amount is subtracted from Current Loan Balance and displayed in Total. Total interest is shown, and appears the next time you pay off your credit line.

5. Choose Record to accept the transaction. The Print Record box appears.

6. In the Print Record box, choose Prepare Check for Printing or Just Record Transaction. Choose OK.

Mortgages

The best way to keep track of mortgage payments is to create a mortgage account and record payments in the account. When you create a mortgage account, CA-Simply Money creates the following categories:

- Mortgage Principal (a liability, top level category)

- Mortgage Interest (an expense, Interest Expenses subcategory), flagged for tax reporting

CA-Simply Money properly balances the liability of the mortgage against the asset of your equity (realized and unrealized) to reflect a positive net worth when the mortgage is considered.

Two of the CA-Simply Money calculators may be useful with mortgage accounts: the Loan Calculator and the Refinance Calculator. For information, see *The Financial Calculators* in Chapter 9.

Note: If you print checks with CA-Simply Money, use the name of your loan institution on the mortgage account button. For example, if you pay your mortgage to Federal Bank, the name on the mortgage account button should be "Federal Bank."

Making a Mortgage Payment

To make a mortgage payment:

1. Click on your mortgage account button. The Account Activity box appears.

2. From the Account Activity box, choose Pay Mortgage. The Mortgage Payment box appears. If you made a previous mortgage payment, the information from the last payment is displayed.

   If you amortized your mortgage, the Amortized Payment box appears on top of the Mortgage Payment box.

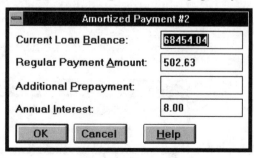

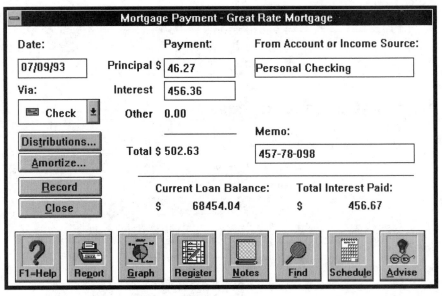

3. If the Amortized Payment box is on your screen, verify the information. If it is correct, click OK. The information goes into the Mortgage Payment box. If it is not correct, click Cancel.

4. If necessary, in the Mortgage Payment box, type the principal and interest amounts, and choose the Account or Income Source the funds are coming from. You can optionally type a memo or change the date.

    The amount of the transaction is subtracted from Current Loan Balance and displayed in Total. The Total Interest Paid to date is displayed.

5. Choose Record to accept the transaction. The Print/Record Check box appears.

6. Choose either Prepare Check for Printing (if you print checks with CA-Simply Money) or Just Record Transaction (if you write your own checks). A check number box appears with the next sequential check number. Change the check number if necessary.

7. Choose OK to complete the payment and return to the main window.

Editing Mortgage Payments

When you make a mortgage payment, you do not pay a payee, but you transfer money between accounts, usually from checking to the liability and expense categories of your mortgage account. Mortgage payments split between liability and expense appear in yellow in the mortgage register, indicating you cannot edit them there. You must edit the transaction in the source account, usually your checking account.

Recording Other Mortgage Costs

Some mortgages have insurance or other costs that you can record when you make your payment.

1. In the Mortgage Payment box, click on Distributions.

2. In the Distribution register, enter one or more categories with negative amounts.

3. Click on Record to return to the Mortgage Payment box. The other costs are displayed in Other.

Recording Home Improvements

To receive the appropriate tax deductions on your home, you must keep accurate records of additions to your home basis equity. When you use CA-Simply Money to record improvements to your home, the value of the improvements is automatically added to your equity.

1. Select your mortgage account button. The Account Activity box appears.

2. From the Account Activity box, choose Record Improvement. The Record Home Improvements box appears.

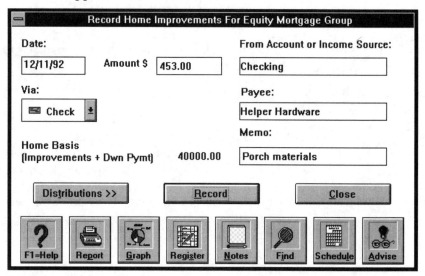

3. In the Amount box, type the cost of the improvement.

4. Select the account or income source you used to pay for the improvement.

5. In the Payee box, select the vendor from whom you purchased the improvement.

6. You can optionally type a memo or change the date.

7. Click on the Distributions button to categorize the amount. See *Distributing a Payment to a Category* or *Distributing a Payment to More Than One Category* earlier in this chapter.

8. Choose Record. The Print/Record Check box appears.

9. Make a selection, then click on OK.

10. Choose Close to return the main window.

Asset and Liability Accounts

An asset account is for tracking assets such as coin or art collections. In a business finance group, an asset account is for tracking accounts receivable. A liability account is for personal loans that are not mortgages or credit lines. In a business finance group, a liability account is for tracking accounts payable.

Note: An asset account is also used to track the value of a 401(k) account. Do not use the following procedure to record deposits to a 401(k), however. Instead, use the procedure described in *Recording Income* earlier in this chapter.

To record asset or liability account transactions:

1. Click on the Asset or Liability account button. The Account Activity box appears.

2. From the Account Activity box, choose Record Decreases or Record Increases. The appropriate box appears.

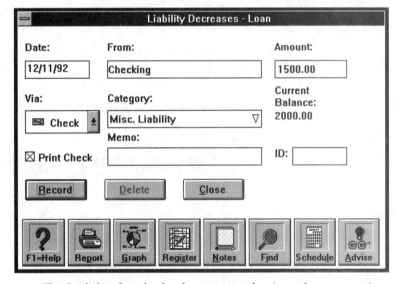

The Liability box looks the same as the Asset box except it has a From text box instead of a Payee text box. The Asset Increases and Liability Decreases windows have the Print Check box.

3. Begin typing an account name in the Payee or From box. The Account Browser box appears. Choose an account, and click on OK.

4. Type the Amount. You can optionally type a memo or an ID, or change the date.

5. If you are tracking your distributions, select one or more categories in the Category box. See *Distributing a Payment to a Category* or *Distributing a Payment to More Than One Category* earlier in this chapter.

6. Choose Record. The Current Balance is adjusted to reflect the transaction.

7. Select Home to return to the main window.

Transferring Funds

You can transfer funds between any accounts except Mortgage, Credit Line, and Payroll. For example, you might transfer from savings to checking to add enough funds to pay your bills.

1. Drag the button for the account the money will come from to the account to receive the funds. The Account-to-Account Transfer box appears.

Note: If you drag a button to a mortgage, credit line, or payroll account (or vice versa), CA-Simply Money assumes you want to make a payment or write a payroll check.

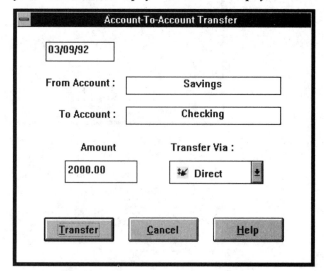

2. If needed, change the date.

3. Type the Amount to be transferred.

4. In the Transfer Via box, choose a method of transfer, such as Direct or ATM.

5. Click on Transfer.

Editing Transfers Between Accounts

Use the register of the source account to edit or delete a transfer between accounts, if the amount is distributed to more than one category. Only the part of the transaction distributed to a destination account appears in that account's register, so the transfer needs to be edited in the source register, where the whole transfer is recorded.

Transferring by Check

If you use CA-Simply Money's check printing feature and you want to transfer funds from checking to another account by writing a check, type the name of the account to receive the funds in the Category box of the check.

Reconciling Accounts

You can reconcile (balance) most accounts, except for mortgage and payroll accounts. The accounts most commonly reconciled are checking, credit card, savings, and credit line.

When you click on the Balance button or select Balance Accounts from the Tools menu, CA-Simply Money displays:

- The Balance Account dialog box, where you enter your statement balance and any service charge or interest earned. CA-Simply Money deducts any service charge from the Balance, adds interest, and adds these amounts to your account Register as individual transactions.

Tracking Your Money

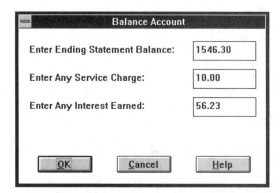

- The Balance window, which contains account transactions.

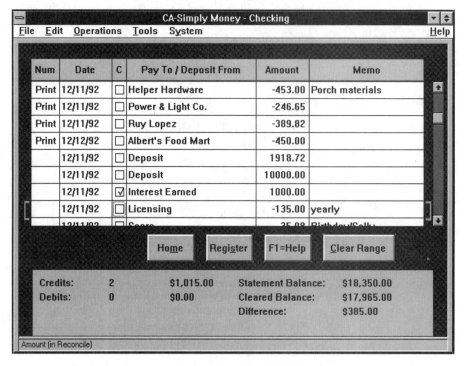

Interpreting the Balance Window

The Balance window contains five numbers at the bottom:

Credits. The number and total amount of deposits and interest earned that you have checked as cleared in the register list in the Balance window.

Debits. The number and total amount of payments that you have checked as cleared in the register list in the Balance window.

Statement Balance. The balance on the statement.

Cleared Balance. The balance of your account excluding the credits and debits that have not yet cleared.

Difference. The Statement Balance less the Cleared Balance.

Balancing a Bank Account

To balance a bank account:

1. Drag the button of the account you want to balance to the Balance button. The Balance Account box appears.

2. From your current statement, type the ending balance and any service charge (for example, the bank's monthly service charge, or a stop-payment charge for a checking account, or a late-payment charge for a credit card account). For a Liability Account, type the current liability.

3. Enter the interest shown on your account statement. For a Liability Account, type any interest paid.

4. Choose OK. The Balance window appears. It shows the transactions that have not yet cleared. A minus sign (-) in front of a transaction amount indicates a debit. Credits have no sign.

5. In the column labeled C (Cleared), click on the boxes of transactions that have cleared on current statement.

    If a range of checks have cleared, you can enter them all at once. Click on the Clear Range button. The Clear Range box appears.

Tracking Your Money

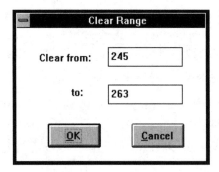

In the Clear from and to boxes, type the lowest and highest check numbers in the range, and choose OK.

As you clear items, the amount of the transaction is deducted from the Cleared Balance. The Difference between the Statement Balance and the Cleared Balance is also updated. Debits and Credits are totaled on the bottom left of the window.

6. If any items on your statement are not recorded or need to be modified, choose the Register button so you can add or change them.

   From the Register, choose List if you want to return to the Balance window to clear any newly recorded transactions.

7. From the Register or from the Balance window, choose Home. If the account balances, the Reconcile box appears. Click on OK to complete the account reconciliation.

Handling Out of Balance Accounts

If an account does not balance (the Difference amount is not $0.00) the Balance Adjustments box appears.

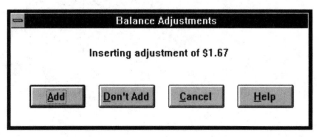

Add. Adds the positive or negative difference to your register as a transaction called "Balance Adjustment." The Balance Adjustment amount is distributed to the Misc. Equity category. This is a special category for balance adjustments and starting balances. It is not an income, expense, asset, or liability category, and is used to add money to an account without recording it as income.

Don't Add. Leaves the register unbalanced.

Cancel. Returns to the Balance window, allowing you to check off items and access the register.

If the Difference is small, a few cents to a few dollars, you may want to ignore it and let CA-Simply Money add it to the account. In this case, click on Add.

If the Difference is large, you may want to figure out why. Perhaps you forgot to enter a transaction, or entered the wrong amount. In this case, click on Cancel or Don't Add.

Balancing Credit Card Accounts

When you reconcile a credit card account, you can balance the account and pay the bill at the same time.

Balancing the Account

1. Drag the credit card account button to the Balance button
    -or-
    Click on the account button, choose Pay Bill, then OK.

    The Balance window appears.

2. Follow the previous steps for reconciling an account in *Balancing a Bank Account*. The differences are:

    - The Service Charge might be a late payment charge.

    - "Enter Any Interest Paid" takes the place of "Enter Any Interest Earned."

3. If needed, make corrections in the Register. When the Difference is equal to zero, choose Home. The Pay Off Credit Card Balance box appears. The current account balance appears in the Amount box.

Tracking Your Money

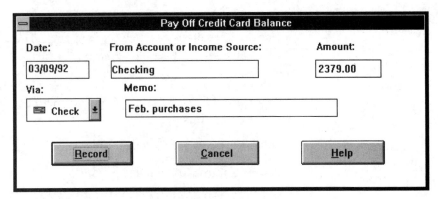

4. If you do not want to make a payment, select Cancel to return to the main window.

Paying the Bill

5. If needed, change the date (today's date).

6. In the From Account or Income Source box, type the name of the income source or account the payment comes from.

7. If necessary, type the payment Amount. CA-Simply Money automatically fills in the total amount owed, but you can enter a different amount.

8. In the Via box, select a method of payment (such as Check).

9. Type an optional Memo.

10. Choose Record, then choose whether to print a check or just record the transaction.

Using the Category Editor

By allocating your income and expenses to categories, you can generate reports, graphs, and budgets that show your financial status. CA-Simply Money comes with default categories, and makes more when you add accounts. You can also add your own categories and edit or delete existing ones. You can add descriptions to categories, and mark categories as tax-related.

Adding a New Category

This procedure shows how to add a new category by using the Edit menu.

Note: You can also create new categories on the fly, as you record your transactions. Just add the new categories in the browser boxes.

1. From the Edit menu, choose Categories. The Category Editor box appears.

2. In the Category Editor box, click on Expense, Income, Asset, or Liability. A list of categories for that financial area appears.

3. In the Create box, click on Top Level. The Create Top Level Category box appears.

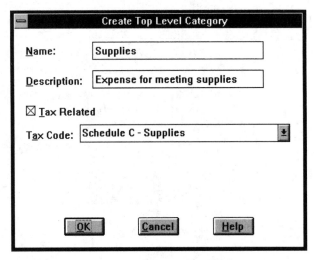

4. In the Name box, type the name of the new category.

5. Type an optional description. It prints on voucher-style checks. See *Printing Checks* earlier in this chapter.

6. If you want this category to appear in the Tax Summary report, click the Tax Related box and choose a Tax Code from the list box. Tax Codes apply only to Income and Expense categories. Categories with Tax Codes appear in exported TXF files and in the Tax Schedule Report.

7. Click on OK. CA-Simply Money places the new category in its alphabetical position in the list.

Tax Considerations for Categories

Be sure to set up separate categories for items that are tax-related. For example, some donations are tax-deductible and others are not. For tax-deductible donations, create a category (or use the Charity category that CA-Simply Money provides) and make sure the Tax-related box is checked. For donations that are not tax-deductible, create a separate category (such as Donations - Not Deductible) with the Tax-related box blank. Record donations against the proper category. The Tax Summary report will list the transactions assigned to Charity but not the transactions assigned to Donations - Not Deductible. (See *Reports* in Chapter 9.)

To make an account tax-free, make all the categories associated with it tax-free. When you set up the account, CA-Simply Money sets up categories and/or subcategories with the account name. Find each expense and income category with the account name, and make sure the Tax-related box is checked.

Creating a Subcategory

You can divide categories into subcategories. Subcategories allow you to group related categories together for reporting or graphing purposes.

Example: The standard Personal finance group has an expense category called Auto. You may want to break it down further into gas and maintenance subcategories.

To create a subcategory:

1. In the Category Editor box, select the top level category for which you want to create a subcategory.

2. In the Create box, click on Subcategory. The Create Subcategory box appears.

3. Type the subcategory name and description.

4. Click on the Tax Related box if the subcategory will be used in assembling your tax information.

5. Choose OK to add the subcategory and return to the Category Editor box. CA-Simply Money adds the subcategory under the top level category you had selected.

Modifying a Category

You can change the name, description, or tax status of a category at any time.

1. In the Category Editor box, click on the category name you want to modify.

2. Choose Modify. The Modify Category box appears.

3. Type the changes you want to make to the Name, Description, or Tax Related boxes.

Tracking Your Money

4. Click OK to make the change and return to the Category Editor box.

Moving a Category

You can move a top level category to become a subcategory of another top level category. You can also promote a subcategory to a top level category, or move it to another category.

Caution: You can move categories *across* category types. For example, a liability category could become an expense. Make sure you understand the accounting ramifications before you move categories across types, however.

1. In the Category Editor box, click on the category name you want to move.

2. Choose Move. The Move Category box appears.

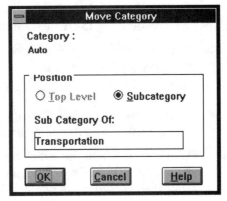

3. In the Position box, choose Top Level if you are changing a subcategory to a top level category. Choose Subcategory if you are changing a top level category to a subcategory or a subcategory from one top level category to another.

Note: The Top Level box will be disabled if the category you have highlighted is already a top level category.

4. In the Sub Category Of box, type a top level category. Use the Category Browser box to find a top level category.

5. Choose OK to return to the Category Editor box, then Home to return to the main window.

Merging Categories

If you rarely use a category, merge it into another. For instance, if you use the Dining category only once or twice a year, you might want to merge it into the Entertainment category.

You can merge any category or subcategory into any other category or subcategory. When you merge categories, CA-Simply Money replaces distributions to the first category with distributions to the second. The first category or subcategory vanishes from your category browser.

Caution: You can merge categories *across* category types. For example, a liability category could become an expense. Make sure you understand the accounting ramifications before you merge categories across types, however.

To merge categories:

1. In the Category Editor box, click on the category name you want to merge.

2. Choose Merge. The Merge Category box appears.

3. In the Position box, select the category or subcategory which will replace the category chosen in step 1.

4. Choose OK to return to the Category Editor box, then Home to return to the main window.

   The merged category or subcategory name vanishes from the category browser.

Deleting Categories

When you delete a Top Level category, the transactions assigned to that category go into the Miscellaneous category. When you delete a subcategory, the transactions associated with it are assigned to the next highest level of category or subcategory. If you delete a category with subcategories, the subcategories are also deleted.

Certain categories such as Mortgage Principal are "linked" to accounts, so you cannot delete them. The delete button is disabled for categories that cannot be deleted.

Tracking Your Money

You never lose a transaction by deleting a category. Transactions are permanently stored. You can only remove transactions through the Register.

After you delete a category, you can no longer access it. So, before deleting categories, you may want to:

- Run a Category Summary Report. This report displays transactions by category. If the category you want to delete has amounts associated with it, you may want to merge it with another category instead of deleting it. This prevents incomplete reports in the future.

- Look at the whole "tree" before deleting a category, because subcategories are deleted along with the category above them. Select Categories from the Edit menu, and look at the category to be deleted. Any subcategories are listed immediately below the category and indented slightly to the right. Make sure you are not deleting anything you may need in the future.

To delete a category:

1. In the Category Editor box, click on the category name you want to delete.

2. Choose Delete, then OK to confirm that you want to delete the category.

Classifications

Classifications are used to group related categories. Some common uses for classifications are:

- **Clients/Jobs:** If you want to track accounts receivable by client or job, create a classification for each client or job.

- **Charity:** If you want to know how much you give specific charities each year, create a classification for each charity.

You can produce reports that identify amounts distributed to the classifications within a category. For information about Classification Reports, see *Miscellaneous Reports* in Chapter 9.

Using Classifications in Distributions

You assign classification as you record transactions. First you enter one or more categories (see *Distributing a Payment to More Than One Category* earlier in this chapter).

1. In the Distribution Register, click on the first line in the Class/Note column. Begin typing your classification. The Classification Browser box appears.

2. Enter a classification, using the same procedure as for entering a category.

Using the Rental Income Classification

If you want to track rent payments by tenant, create a classification for each tenant. Distribute the income to the rental income category and the tenant classification. If you want to track rental income by property, create a classification for each piece of property.

Example: You have a Rent income source. Create a Rental Income category with a Rent subcategory. Create classifications for each tenant (such as Jim Smith and Jane Jones). When Jim sends in his rent check, record it with a distribution to the Rental Income category and the Jim Smith classification.

Adding a New Classification

You can create Classifications as you assign categories during transactions (see *Distributing a Payment to More Than One Category* earlier in this chapter), or by using the Edit menu.

To add a new classification using the menu:

1. From the Edit menu, choose Classifications. The Classification Editor box appears.

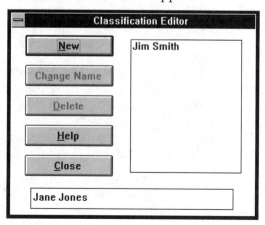

Tracking Your Money

2. In the text entry box, type the name of the classification you want to add.

3. Choose New. The new name appears in the list box.

4. Choose Close to return to the main window. Now you can apply the classification to your categories.

Changing a Classification Name

To change a classification name:

1. From the list of classifications in the Classification Editor box, choose the classification name you want to change.

2. In the text entry box, type the new classification name.

3. Choose Change Name. The highlighted name changes to the one you have typed.

4. Choose Close to return to the main window.

Deleting a Classification

To delete a classification:

1. From the list of classifications in the Classification Editor box, choose the classification name you want to delete.

2. Choose Delete, then Yes to confirm deleting the classification.

3. Choose Close to return to the main window.

Grouping Buttons

The Group feature of CA-Simply Money is a powerful way to view your finances and automate tasks. You can group any number of income sources, accounts, or payees.

For example, you may want to view your total grocery bill for the month, but you shop at three different stores and have a separate payee button for each. You can group the three grocery store buttons and drag the group button to the Reports button to create a monthly category summary report. The report displays data only for the grouped buttons.

With just a single click on a grouped button you can display summary information about all buttons in a group. You can also record transactions to groups of payees. For example, to pay bills that are due at the same time each month, drag the group to your checking account button. CA-Simply Money presents a check for each of the grouped payees, one after another.

You can make two types of groups: permanent and temporary. Temporary groups are ones you create on the fly. They are easy to make and easy to undo. You can create temporary groups as often as necessary, and keep them as long as you need them.

Permanent groups are represented by a button. Make permanent groups when you use a certain combination of buttons on a regular basis.

Although groups are most useful for payees, you can use groups for income sources and accounts in order to generate reports and graphs. You can use one button in more than one group. The only limitation is you cannot combine different types of buttons; groups must be either payees, accounts, or income sources, not a mixture. You can create a maximum of 32 groups, temporary or permanent.

Note: Group actions do not apply to the Write Checks, Register, Balance, and Advice functions.

Creating a Temporary Group

To create a temporary group:

- Hold down the Shift key and click on the buttons you want to add to the group. A frame appears around each button.

Tip: To deselect a button, Shift+Click again. To deselect all buttons (undo the temporary group) click anywhere on the background.

When you drag any of the grouped buttons, the icon changes to a paper clip. The result of dragging and dropping affects all buttons in the group.

Tracking Your Money

Creating a Permanent Group

To create a permanent group:

1. Create a temporary group by holding down the Shift key and clicking on the buttons you want to merge. Then drag the button for any member of the group to the Setup button.
    -or-
    From the Operations menu, choose Make Group. The Make Groups box appears. Choose the type of group you want to make.

    The Group-Add box appears. The buttons of any temporary group are already highlighted in the Group Members list box, which shows every income source, account, and payee.

2. Click on the name of buttons you want to include (if they are not highlighted) or exclude (if they are highlighted) from the group.

3. In the Group Name box, type a name for the group button.

4. Click OK. The added group becomes a permanent button.

Tip: If you create a permanent group, you may find you do not need the individual buttons displayed. Use the Hidden Button feature to "hide" them (see *Hiding the Button* in Chapter 5).

Using Find with a Group

Suppose you create a group of the three grocery stores you frequent. If you drag the Find button and drop it on one of the grouped buttons, CA-Simply Money finds all transactions for the grouped buttons.

Modifying a Group

To modify a group:

1. Drag the button for the group to the Setup button. Click on Modify this Button.
   -or-
   From the Operations menu, choose Modify Group. Choose the type of group you want to modify, then highlight the group you want to modify and click OK.

   The Modify Group box appears.

2. Click on any names you want to include or exclude.

3. In the Group Name box, type a new name for the group, if desired. You can also choose to hide the button.

4. Click OK.

Merging a Payee Group into One Button

Importing files from Quicken often produces several buttons for one payee. You can merge a group of payee buttons into one button. The new button replaces all the payee buttons in the group, both onscreen and in your records.

For instance, if you combine buttons for "Moe's supermarket," "Moes Supermarket," and "Moz Supermarket" into one button named "Moe's," CA-Simply Money merges all transactions associated with any of the spellings into the new Moe's button. Future transactions affect only the new Moe's payee.

To merge a group of payees:

1. Create a temporary group by holding down the Shift key and clicking on the buttons you want to merge.

2. Drag one of the buttons in the temporary group to the Payee button. The Merge Payees box appears.

Tracking Your Money

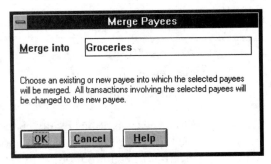

3. Type a name for the new button. You can choose an existing name from the Payee browser or use a new name.

4. Click OK to replace the whole temporary group with the new button.

Budgeting

Budgeting is a critical component of any financial plan. You set financial goals for yourself or your business, and you use a budget to attain your goals. Budgets, and your success at sticking to them, define your financial progress in clear terms: Were you over budget or under budget? With which categories do you have trouble? Does your income meet your expectations? Where can you trim your budget to advance your rate of savings? With CA-Simply Money, you can create a budget, use reports to assess the rate at which you are over or under spending, and adjust either your budget or your spending, or both.

The CA-Simply Money budget feature allows you to create a fixed budget by listing expenses for just one month and projecting them for twelve-months. Or, you can create a variable budget by listing expenses for each month or season separately. Expenses can be entered for subcategories (like Electricity and Gas) and then be listed by top-level categories (like Utilities). Your budget can also include expected income. The AutoBudget feature can extrapolate from your past income and expenses to an entire year's budget, even including seasonal variations in some expenses.

The CA-Simply Money budget tool works like an electronic spreadsheet. Once you have entered values into your budget, CA-Simply Money calculates monthly and annual totals for the various categories. Whenever you change a value, CA-Simply Money recalculates the totals. If a monthly expense changes, the new expense can be projected for the rest of the year at the new level, leaving the old amounts unaffected.

You can evaluate a budget by generating special reports and graphs. The reports display the difference between the actual and budgeted amounts. (Budget reports are Miscellaneous Reports; see *Miscellaneous Report*s in Chapter 9.)

Making a Monthly Budget

This procedure explains how to add expenses to a monthly budget. To add income, see *Adding Income to a Budget* later in this chapter.

1. From the Edit menu, choose Budget. The Monthly Budget box appears, showing a column for a fixed budget.

    The left column, Expense, lists categories. The right column, Amount, contains empty cells. At the bottom of the budget sheet, the Totals row gives the monthly expense total. The Total Income row has a single cell that shows total monthly income.

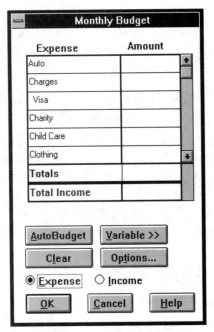

2. In the Amount column, type expense amounts for the expenses you have incurred or know you will incur in the current month, and those you expect to incur, if you want to include upcoming costs in your estimate. You can change any value later.

3. Click OK when you have finished. This saves the budget and returns you to the main window.

Making a Yearly Budget

A yearly budget can be either fixed or variable. A fixed budget is a monthly budget projected for twelve months. A variable budget has different expenses for each month. Procedures for making both types of budgets are explained below.

These procedures explain how to add expenses to a budget. To add income, see *Adding Income to a Budget* later in this chapter.

Fixed Budget   To make a fixed budget:

1.   From the Edit menu, choose Budget. The Monthly Budget box appears, showing a column for a fixed budget.

2.   Type the appropriate expense amount for each category.

3.   If you wish, click on Options to limit the budget to only main categories, or to sort the budget by amount rather than category. For more information, see *Budget Display Options* later in this chapter.

Variable Budget   To make a variable budget:

1.   From the Edit menu, choose Budget. The Monthly Budget box appears.

2.   In the Monthly Budget box, click on Variable. The box expands to include columns for several months and a Totals column.

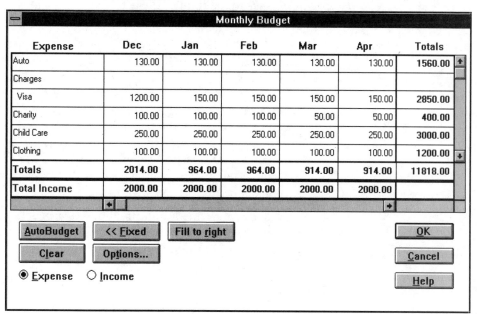

Note: The number of columns displayed depends on the resolution of your monitor.

The Totals column shows expense and income totals for twelve months, beginning with the current month. Variable budgets, unlike Fixed budgets, reflect monthly or seasonal changes in your expenses and income, so the months you can see may not have the same subtotals as the others. You can see the other months by using the horizontal scroll bar.

3. Type the appropriate expense amount for each category in each month.

   If an expense is the same amount each month for some or all of the year:

   ■ Type the amount in the first month it occurs.

   ■ Click on Fill To Right. The amount is copied to all columns to the right.

Tip: You can use the Fill To Right command from any cell in the row. All rows to the right of the cell where you choose Fill To Right will contain the amount of that cell.

Example: Your cable TV bill is the same every month. You have created a subcategory under Entertainment called Cable. In the first cell in the Cable row, you type the monthly amount. You then click on Fill To Right and the amount is entered for the rest of the year. After three months, however, your cable bill goes up. In the cell for that month, you type in the new amount, and click on Fill To Right. The following months show the new amount, and the preceding months show the old amount.

4. If you wish, click on Options to limit the budget to only main categories, or to sort the budget by amount rather than category. For more information, see *Budget Display Options* later in this chapter.

5. To return to the single-month budget, click on Fixed.

Adding Income to a Budget

To add income to a budget:

1. In the Monthly Budget box, click on the Income button.

    If you have made changes to the Expense budget, the Save Budget box appears. Choose OK to save the Expense budget.

    The income categories appear in green in the Income column.

2. Type values for your income. CA-Simply Money totals your entries in the Totals row.

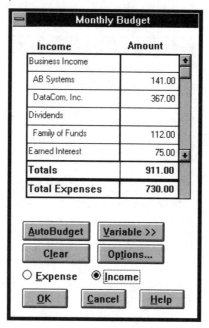

Tip: If income is the same amount each month for some or all of the year, click the Variable button. Type the amount in one column, then click Fill to Right. The amount is copied to all columns to the right.

3. When you have finished entering income amounts, choose Expense, then OK to save your income entries.

The Expense budget appears. The total income appears in the Income row.

Using AutoBudget to Create a Budget

If you have at least one month's worth of transactions, you can have CA-Simply Money automatically create either a fixed or variable budget based on your current financial patterns.

1. From the Monthly Budget box, click on AutoBudget. The Automatic Budgeting box appears.

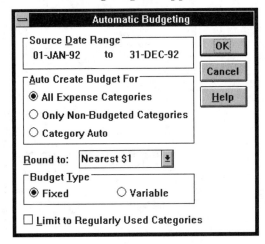

2. In the Source Date Range area, type the beginning and ending dates of transactions you want CA-Simply Money to use in calculating the budget.

Note: If you later generate budget graphs or reports, use the same date range to generate them that you used for the Automatic Budgeting. You may get unexpected results if the date ranges do not match.

3. In the Auto Create Budget For area, specify the options for creating your budget:

- If you want a budget created for all of your expense categories, choose All Expense Categories.

- If you have already created a budget for some of your categories and want CA-Simply Money to finish the job, choose Only Non-Budgeted Categories. CA-Simply Money will calculate budget amounts for those budget categories that don't yet have a value.

- If you want a budget calculated for a single category, choose Category. (The category displayed is the one in the Monthly Budget box that the cursor is on.) In this example, a budget is calculated for the Auto category.

4. In the Budget Type box, choose Fixed or Variable.

5. Click on OK.

Budget Display Options

You can display your budget information in three ways.

- All categories, sorted by category name

- Top-level categories, sorted by value (expense amount)

- Top-level categories, sorted by name

Sorting by value has the advantage of showing just the categories with expenses, and not categories you have not used. You probably want to see all categories and subcategories when you enter your expenses, but not when you view your expenses.

Displaying All Categories

To display all categories:

1. Choose Options on the Monthly Budget box. The Budget Options box appears.

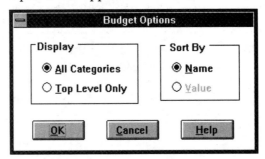

2. In the Display area, choose All Categories to display categories and subcategories so you can enter detailed expenses. When you choose All Categories, the Sort By box is limited to sorting by category name.

3. Choose OK to return to the Budget box.

Displaying Only Active Categories

To display only active categories:

1. Choose the Options button. The Budget Options box appears.

2. In the Display box, choose Top Level Only.

3. In the Sort By box, choose Value.

   Sorting by value places the expense categories you have already used at the top of the category list, beginning with the highest amount. The categories you have not used are at the end of the list.

4. Choose OK to return to the Budget box.

Displaying Only Top-Level Categories

When you display only top level categories in a budget, values for subcategories are included in the total for each top level. The top levels are sorted by name.

1. Choose the Options button. The Budget Options box appears.

2. In the Display box, choose Top Level Only.

3. In the Sort By box, choose Name.

4. Choose OK to return to the Budget box.

Chapter 7
Managing Your Investments

Chapter 7
Managing Your Investments

CA-Simply Money can help you track your investments. Mutual funds, stocks, bonds and other investments can be integrated with your other finances. With CA-Simply Money you can record the buying and selling of securities, increases in mutual funds, dividends, stock splits, interest and expense.

You can update the value of your investments by entering the latest prices of your securities—either manually or electronically. The easy-to-use Modem Stock Update tool gives you access to the latest prices through CompuServe or the Kiplinger's CA-Simply Money Stock Quote Service. You can also classify your various types of investments and assign them goals. This lets you evaluate the performance of your portfolios.

Considerations for Investment Accounts

An investment account, also called a portfolio, consists of investment instruments that you want to track as a group. The advantage of grouping investments is the financial reports and graphs that CA-Simply Money can generate to help you measure the performance of the group. Set up your portfolio according to the way to you want to see your investment information. Create as many portfolios as you like.

Some portfolios may contain securities, which are investment instruments with a value expressed in shares. Stocks, mutual funds, and bonds are examples of securities.

Other portfolios may contain investment instruments that maintain a constant price, such as money market funds and certificates of deposit. By setting up these types of investments in investment accounts, you can track the return on investment through the CA-Simply Money financial reports.

Other portfolios might represent your brokerage account, a family of mutual funds, or investments that have the same goal.

Here are some typical portfolios you may want to create:

Individual security. If you directly own a security, such as shares of a stock or mutual fund, you can set up a portfolio for that specific security.

Brokerage account. You can create an account that represents the account your broker uses for you. As you receive your statements, you can copy the transactions into CA-Simply Money. Set up a separate portfolio for each of your managed accounts.

IRA. Set up portfolios for you and your spouse. Since you can add more than one security to a portfolio, this is an ideal place to track your IRA investments. For example, you could enter all of your mutual fund purchases into one investment account, even if they are from different fund managers.
CA-Simply Money can provide performance reports on your IRA as a whole. Since it is desirable to be able to view your IRA performance as a group, it is best to include your CDs and other non-fluctuating investments. CA-Simply Money can also set up your portfolios as tax-free accounts. See *Tax-Free Investment Accounts* later in this chapter.

401(k). Set up a 401(k) as an asset account. Record contributions as you enter paycheck income, as explained in Chapter 6.

Money market account. f you are writing checks from a money market account, you may want to set it up as a checking Account. Money market investments can also be tracked through an Asset account.

Cash management account. CMAs are best handled with two separate accounts. Create a checking account for the checking transactions and set up an investment account for all other transactions. When you need to transfer funds to the checking account, you can drag the investment account button to the checking account button and record the transaction.

Mutual fund. You can set up a mutual fund in two ways: with detailed past transactions, or with just the current shares and price. The detailed method gives you accurate capital gains, but is more time-consuming.

To show detail, set up an investment account with your opening deposit as the account balance. Then enter your purchases and reinvested earnings. If you reinvest all earnings, the Increase Securities operation (explained later in this chapter) is the easiest way to record it, though you could also record it as a receipt of earnings and a purchase of shares.

To track just from your last statement, set up an investment account with no account balance. Then use the Increase Securities operation to enter the number of shares owned and the price per share. After initial setup, track all account activity just as for the detailed type of mutual fund investment account.

Broker margin account. A broker margin loan is similar to any other type of loan, except the securities in your account are the collateral. One way to set up a broker margin loan is as a credit line account, and make its category for interest tax-free. Interest on margin loans is generally deductible if used for investing, with some tricky exceptions.

Another way is to use a liability account for the principal amount of the loan. For example, suppose you borrow $10,000 on your security account. To record the loan in CA-Simply Money, set up a liability account with 0 as the account balance. Drag and drop from the liability account to your checking account, and deposit the $10,000. As you pay off the loan, enter the principal in the liability account as a decrease. Enter the margin interest in your investment account.

Setting Up an Investment Account

Setting up an investment account is like setting up any other account in CA-Simply Money.

1. Drag the Setup button to the Accounts button. The Account Setup box appears. Choose Add an Account.

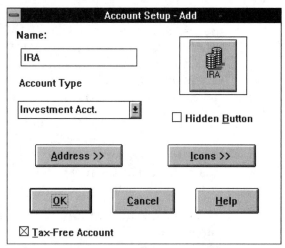

2. In the Name box, type a name for your account.

   If the account represents a brokerage account, you could use your broker's name. A collection of Mutual Funds could be called "Mutual Funds." Use any name that makes sense to you.

3. From the Account Type list, choose Investment Acct. The Account Balances box appears.

4. In the Starting Account Balance box, type the cash balance.

   - If you are adding all previous transactions for a security, you do not need a starting balance. Instead, record the initial cash in the account as a transfer from another account (see *Transferring Funds* in Chapter 6).

   - If you want to avoid adding previous transactions, just enter the current balance of the investment account as the starting balance. Performance reports for the account will not be accurate.

- If you are creating an account for mutual funds and you want to avoid adding previous transactions, do not enter a starting balance. Instead, enter the current number of shares and the share price (see *Increasing Number of Shares* later in this chapter).

    If you want the cash balance to have a date other than today's date, press Alt+D and enter the date.

5. If you are setting up a tax-free account such as a Keogh, SEP-IRA, or IRA, click on Tax-Free Account.

    ☒ **Tax-Free Account**

    CA-Simply Money excludes tax-free income from the Tax Summary report. For procedures on contributing to and withdrawing funds from tax-free accounts, see *Tax-Free Investment Accounts* later in this chapter.

6. Choose OK to return to the main window. The new investment button appears with your other accounts.

    To enter the current number of shares you hold and the share price, see *Increasing Number of Shares* later in this chapter.

Making Investment Transactions

CA-Simply Money provides two ways to make an investment transaction:

- The Operation window, which is most useful for recording new transactions

- The Investment Register, which is most useful for modifying existing transactions

Using the Operation Window

Click once on any investment account button to display the Operation For: box for that account. This box is divided into four sections, each with several buttons. For instance, you can transfer funds in or out of the investment account by clicking the In or Out button in the Transfer Funds area. The more complicated sections are explained below.

Income Types   **Interest.** You can record interest earned on your investments and specify that income as **Taxable** or **Non-taxable**. For example, you may receive income earned on a money market fund that is the cash balance of a brokerage account.

Capital Gain/Loss. CA-Simply Money automatically records the gain or loss when you sell your securities. However, with mutual funds you may receive cash distributions of capital gains. You can record those distributions using the Capital Gain button and specify the distributions as **Short Term** or **Long Term**.

Dividend. Distributions of dividends may be in the form of additional shares of stock or as cash. Use this category for cash dividends.

Miscellaneous. You can use the Miscellaneous category for any income other than interest, capital gains, or dividends.

Expense Types   **Margin Interest.** If you borrow funds from your broker, you can record the interest using this category.

Miscellaneous. You can use the Miscellaneous category for any expense other than margin interest.

Using the Investment Register

The Investment Register is similar to the other CA-Simply Money registers. You access it by dragging and dropping an investment account button onto the Register button. The Investment Register is most useful for modifying existing transactions and specifying a return of capital. You can change dates, view balances, add memos, and delete transactions.

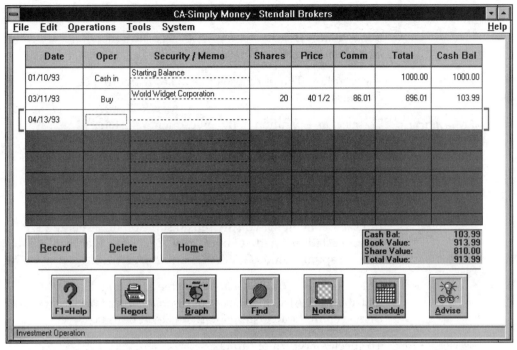

The following columns make up the Investment Register:

Date. The date of the transaction.

Oper. Type of investment transaction (or operation). These selections correspond to the buttons on the Operations box.

Security/Memo. You can enter the name of a security along with memos and distributions.

Shares. The number of shares of the transaction.

Price. The price of the shares at the time of the transaction.

Comm. The commission (if any).

Total. The total cost of the commission plus the cost of the shares (number of shares multiplied by price).

Cash Bal. The cash balance of the investment account as of the date of the transaction.

The values in the box in the lower right are:

Book Value. The purchase price of securities (net of commissions) plus the cash balance.

Share Value. The purchase price of securities (net of commissions).

Selecting an Operation

To select an operation in the investment register:

- Click on the Oper column and select an operation from the Browser box.

Specifying a Return of Capital

The Oper box of the Investment Register contains a choice called "Return of Capital." Return of capital is a non-taxable transaction in which you are repaid some or all of the funds you invested in a particular security. Securities that may return capital include GNMAs and unit trusts.

Note: Return of capital is not the same as a capital gains distribution. Also, the Return of Capital choice is only displayed in the Register, not in the Operations box.

To specify a return of capital:

1. In the Oper box of the Investment Register, select Return of Capital.

2. Complete the rest of the transaction and Record it like any other transaction.

Transferring Funds

To pay for securities purchases, you need to add funds from other accounts. When you sell securities or receive dividends, you need to remove funds from your investment account. Transferring funds to and from investment accounts is similar to transferring between other accounts in CA-Simply Money.

If transfers occur at the time of a transaction, you can perform the purchase and the transfer at the same time.

Adding Funds

To add funds to an investment account:

1. Drag the account button representing the source of funds and drop it on the investment button.
   -or-
   Click on the investment button. From the Operation window, choose Transfer Funds In. Select the account name.

   The Account-to-Account Transfer box appears.

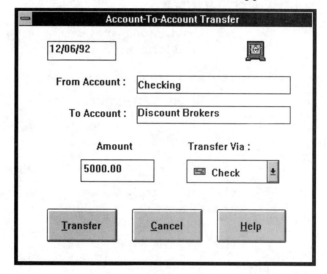

2. In the Amount box, type the amount of the transfer. In the To Account box, type the destination account. Choose a method in the Transfer Via box.

3. Click on Transfer to complete the transaction. The funds are transferred directly to the investment account.

If you want to view the transaction and current balance of the investment account, click on the Reports button in the tool rack.

Removing Funds

Transferring funds out of an investment account is essentially the same as transferring funds into it.

1. From the Operations box, choose Transfer Funds Out.

2. Type the destination account and transfer amount and click on Transfer to complete the transaction.

Recording Securities

CA-Simply Money provides dialog boxes for recording the information involved with investment transactions, including:

- Buying and selling securities.

- Recording information about each security.

- Recording the increase and decrease in shares due to reinvestment or stock splits.

- Recording income and expense.

Note: CA-Simply Money will remind you to make investment transactions if you schedule those transactions. See *The Scheduler* in Chapter 9.

Buying Securities

To record security purchases you enter the name of the security, the number of shares, share price, and commission. You can fund the purchases from the cash in the investment account or by transferring funds from another account.

1. Click on the investment button for which you want to record a transaction. The Operations box appears.

2. From the Operations box, choose Buy. The Buy Securities box appears.

The balance for the current investment account appears in the lower right of the box. If you have already transferred funds into the account, you see a positive balance.

3. If you need to transfer funds, click on Funds To/From. The Funding Account Options box appears.

   Type the name of the account that will fund the buy. The current balance of that account appears.

┌─ **Funding Account Option** ──────────────────────────────────────┐
│ ☒ **Eunds To/From:**   │Savings   │   **Balance: $ 6000.00** │
└──┘

4. In the Date box, type the date of the purchase.

5. Type the name of the security you are buying. The Security Browser box appears. If you are purchasing a security for the first time, you will have to add information about the security. Also, "inactive" securities do not appear in the browser box. See *Adding New Securities* later in this chapter.

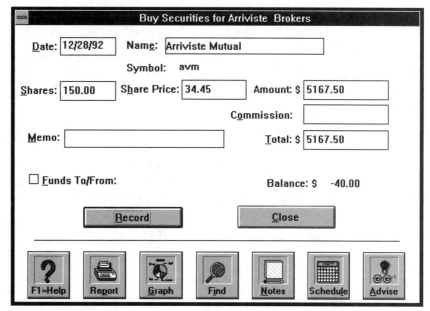

6. In the Shares box, type the number of shares.

7. In the Price box, type the current price of the security. If you have purchased the security before, the last recorded price for that security appears. You can enter the share price in decimal (3.5) or fractional (3 1/2) notation.

The total amount of the transaction is automatically calculated and displayed when you click in the box. See *Entering Share Prices* later in this chapter.

Note: You can also add historical pricing for your securities. See *Recording Security Price History* later in this chapter.

8. In the Commission box, type the amount of the commission and fees.

The total of the Amount and Commission boxes is automatically calculated and displayed when you click in the Total box.

9. You can type a memo in the optional Memo box.

10. Click on Record to complete the transaction. The Operations box appears.

The transaction amount is deducted from the balance of the investment account. You can view the balance through a report or the register.

Adding New Securities

Typically, you add a new security while completing a buy transaction, as shown here. However, you can enter a new security while completing any investment transaction.

For your convenience, the ticker symbols for the DowJones Industrial Average and the S&P 500 are set up in CA-Simply Money. You can use CA-Simply Money to compare the performance of securities you own against the performance of these averages. For more information, see *Updating Stock Prices by Modem* or *Updating the Price Manually* later in this chapter.

1. Click on the investment button for which you want to record a transaction. The Operations box appears.

2. From the Operations box, choose Buy. The Buy Securities box appears.

3. In the Name box, type the name of the new security you are buying. The Security Browser box appears.

4. Click on New to add the security to the list. The New Security box appears.

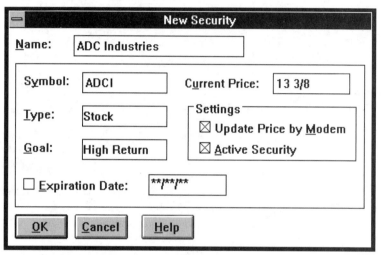

5. In the Price box, enter the current security price.

6. Click on OK to record the new security. The Operations box you were previously working with appears. Symbols and/or expiration dates for the new security now appear along with the security name. Finish your transaction.

Note: You can also add a new security from the menu bar on the main window. From the Edit menu, choose Investments, then Securities. The Edit Security box appears.

Updating the Price Manually

To update the price of a security manually, follow this procedure. To update by modem, see *Updating Stock Prices by Modem* later in this chapter.

1. From the Edit menu select Investments/Securities. The Edit Security box appears.

2. In the Symbol area, type the ticker symbol for the security.

3. Click on Update Price by Modem if you want the security price to be updated by the automatic price update feature. Only securities flagged in this way are included in the updates.

Making Securities Inactive

If some securities are no longer a part of your current holdings, but may be purchased again in the future, you can "hide" them from the browser box by making them inactive.

1. From the Edit menu select Investments/Securities. The Edit Security box appears.

2. Click on Active Security to remove the "X." The security will not appear in the Security Browser box. When you want to make the security active, just click on Active Security again.

You can include inactive securities in any graph or report.

Recording Expiration Dates

If the security is a bond or option, record the expiration date. The Expiration Report and the Financial Advisor use the expiration dates to remind you when to sell the security.

1. From the Edit menu select Investments/Securities. The Edit Security box appears.

2. Click on Exp Date and type the expiration date.

☒ **E_xp Date:**

03/18/92

Modifying an Existing Security

To modify a security's symbol, price, type, or goal:

1. From the Edit menu, select Investments, then Securities. The Edit Security box appears.

2. Use the Name box to select an existing security.

3. Make the necessary changes to the security.

4. Click on Save to record the changes.

Note: You can also add historical pricing for any security. See *Recording Security Price History* later in this chapter.

Changing a Security Name

To change the security name:

1. From the Edit menu, select Investments, then Securities. The Edit Security box appears.

2. Type part of the security name in the Name area. The Security Browser appears. Highlight a security name, then click OK.

3. Click on Change Name. The Security Name Editor box appears.

4. Type the new name for the security.

5. Click on OK. The new name appears in the Name box.

Managing Your Investments

Selling Securities

Selling a security is essentially the same as buying one. The proceeds from the sale are either added to the cash value of the account or transferred to another account.

1. From the Operations box, choose Sell. The Sell Securities box appears.

2. Type the date of the sale.

3. Use the Name box to choose a security.

4. Type the number of shares with up to three decimal places Enter the share price in decimal (3.5) or fractional (3 1/2) notation.

5. Type the amount of the commission.

6. If you are transferring the proceeds from the sale to a different account, click on Funds To/From and specify the account.

7. Click on Sell to complete the transaction.

   CA-Simply Money automatically uses the difference between the purchase and selling prices to calculate the gain or loss. The amount is attributed to the Realized Gains/Losses category and is displayed in reports.

   CA-Simply Money uses a first-in, first-out method of calculating gains/losses. For information, see *First-in, First-out Costing Method* later in this chapter.

Selling Short

When you sell short, CA-Simply Money still calculates the gain/loss, just as with a standard transaction. Selling short means you sell shares of a security you do not own. You "sell" shares your broker owns and buy them back in the future, hopefully at a lower price. The transaction is the reverse of a standard one—you sell, then buy. When you sell short, select Sell from the Operations menu. Select Buy when you purchase the shares back.

Maximizing Gains or Losses

CA-Simply Money uses a first-in, first-out method of lot matching to track the gains and losses of securities. If you want to record your *maximum* gain/loss for a transaction, see *Lot Grouping* later in this chapter.

Increasing Number of Shares

When you do not want to change the cash balance of the investment account, use the Increase/Decrease operations. By using these operations you can increase or decrease the value of the portfolio without affecting the cash balance.

These operations are useful if you do not care about recording the historical basis and/or cash value of an account. You can just record increases and decreases in the number of shares you hold.

After you set up an investment account, if you do not want to enter previous stock transactions, you can use the Increase operation to enter the number of shares you have and their current price.

You can also use the Increase/Decrease operations is with mutual funds. Mutual fund companies commonly reinvest dividends and capital gains directly into the investor's account. This usually takes the form of shares on your statement. You can add these shares directly to your portfolio. Certain other securities may use reinvestment also. See *Reinvesting Mutual Funds* later in this chapter.

Increasing the holdings for a security is completed in almost exactly the same way as buying a security. You choose the security, then enter shares, prices, and commissions. Transferring funds is not possible with an Increase, however.

To increase the number of shares:

1. From the Operations box, choose Increase. The Increase Securities box appears.

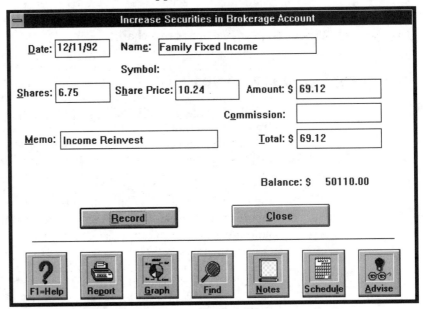

2. Use the Name box to select a security and enter the rest of the transaction information.

   Note: A transfer of funds is not possible with an Increase.

3. Click on Record to complete the transaction. The Operations box appears. The increase in shares appears as an Add in the investment account register.

Decreasing Number of Shares

Decreasing the holdings for a security is almost the same procedure as increasing holdings.

1. From the Operations box, choose Decrease. The Decrease Securities box appears.

2. Choose a security and enter the rest of the transaction information.

3. Click on Record to complete the transaction.

Recording Share Transfers

You may need to transfer shares from one account to another. If you transfer the shares at the current price, investment reports show a gain in the first account. This may be desirable, but most likely you want to transfer shares at cost.

To transfer shares at cost, find the purchase price of the shares by looking at a Transaction Report. Use the Decrease operation to remove the shares at the purchase price. Finally, use Increase to add the shares in the new account at the purchase price.

If you are transferring a group of shares that were acquired in separate lots (at different prices), complete a series of Decrease operations at the original acquisition price. You can determine this price with the Investment Transaction report. To specify the securities you are interested in, choose Filters and Styles from the Options menu on the report window. Then specify a date range in the Report Generator box and click Include.

Recording Stock Splits

When the market price of a company's stock reaches an inconvenient trading range, the company may decide to split the shares. You need to record the split in order to continue tracking your shares under the new share price.

1. From the Operations box, choose Split. The Record Stock Split box appears.

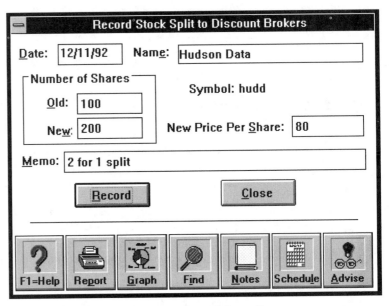

2. In the Date box, type the date of the split.

3. Use the Name box to choose a security.

4. The Number of Shares box has a place for old and new shares. Depending on the type of split, you need to enter the appropriate amounts. A 2:1 split is the most typical, however, other splits are common.

Example: You receive notice of a 2:1 stock split for Hudson Data. You have 100 original shares. The number of new shares would be twice the original or 200.

5. In the New Price for Share box, type the new price of the security. An announcement of a split is usually accompanied by the new price.

6. Click on Record to complete the transaction. The Operations box appears.

The transaction appears in the Investment Register and transaction reports as an Add. The value of your investment account remains the same.

| 03/24/92 | Buy | Hudson Data | 100 | 161 1/2 | 80.00 | 16230.00 | 5290.00 |
| 03/31/92 | Add | Hudson Data
2 for 1 split | 100 | 80 | | 6500.00 | 5290.00 |

Recording Income and Expense

In addition to the buying and selling of securities, your investment account balance changes due to various income and expense. The main sources of income are Interest, Capital Gains, and Dividends. A common expense is Margin Interest. If you receive notice of dividends or interest that are reinvested (usually in a CD or mutual fund), see *Reinvesting Mutual Funds* later in this chapter.

Note: The Dividend calculator calculates the interest rate equivalent to a given dividend return. You can use this calculator to compare the advantage of different investment strategies. See *Using the Dividend Yield Calculator* in Chapter 9.

To record the various types of income and expense:

1. From the Operations box, click on one of the Income or Expense buttons. The related box appears.

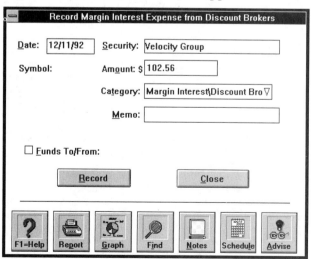

2. Type the date of the transaction.

3. Use the Security box to choose a security.

4. Type the amount of the income or expense.

5. In the Category box, select the appropriate category.

6. Type an optional memo.

7. If the income/expense was transferred to/from another account, click on the Funds To/From box.

8. Click on Record to complete the transaction.

Recording Mutual Fund Transactions

In general, you use the same procedures for recording mutual fund transactions as for recording stock transactions. You buy and sell shares, and CA-Simply Money keeps track of the cost-basis of the shares. However, recording your mutual funds may require these additional transactions:

- Capital gains distributions
- Custodial fees
- Loads
- Reinvestments

Capital Gains Distributions

Capital gains distributions are usually itemized on your statement as reinvestments in shares of the mutual fund. The distributions may be either short-or long-term capital gains.

If your capital gains are reinvested, see *Reinvesting Mutual Funds* later in this chapter. If you receive a cash distribution, you can transfer it to the appropriate account. See *Recording Income and Expense* earlier in this chapter.

IRA Custodial Fees

If you invest your IRA or other retirement funds in a mutual fund, the custodian of the fund might redeem shares to pay your custodial fee.

1. Choose Sell from the Operation window and select the appropriate fund.

2. Type the number of shares and the price of the shares when the shares were redeemed.

3. Type the same dollar amount in the Commission box. This makes the net amount of the transaction equal to zero.

Shares: 1.46	Share Price: 10.28	Amount: $ 15.00
		Commission: 15.00
Memo: Custodian fee		Total: $

Purchasing Load Funds

Most mutual funds are "no-load" funds. However, certain mutual funds add commissions to the purchase price of their shares. This commission is called a "load." The purchase price of a load fund is called the "Offer" or "Buy" price. The "NAV" or "Sell" price is the selling price.

To track the correct market value, use the "Offer" price when you record the purchase of a load fund. Use the "NAV" price when you update the value of your investment.

Reinvesting Mutual Funds

Some securities, particularly mutual funds, pay you dividends, interest income, and capital gains with additional shares. To record the reinvestment, use two transactions:

1. From the Operations box, click on the appropriate income button. Record the information about the transaction (see *Recording Income and Expense* earlier in this chapter).

Managing Your Investments

2. From the Operations box, click on Increase Shares. Record the reinvestment information, including the number of shares and share price. This information is typically included on your statement.

Tax-Free Investment Accounts

Accounts such as an IRA, Keogh, and other retirement plans are tax free. Income is not taxable, even if it comes from a normally taxable source such as bank interest or capital gains. All or part of the money you put into the account may be tax-deductible. All or part of the money you take out may be taxable income. In some states, the rules for state taxation may be different from the federal rules. Consult your tax advisor to determine the tax treatment of a contribution or disbursement.

Example: You create two investment accounts, one called Broker and a second, tax-free account called IRA. In each account, some stock is bought and then sold at a profit. On a Tax Summary report, the profit for the Broker account appears in the category Short-Term Cap. Gains\Broker. The profit for the second account appears in Short-Term Cap. Gains\IRA.

Both of these amounts appear in reports such as Cash Flow. However, in the Tax Summary report, only taxable profit in the Broker category appears. The tax-free profit in IRA does not appear in the Tax Summary report.

For a tax-free investment account, the Operation window still includes buttons for Taxable and Non-Taxable interest. Be sure to select the correct button.

Note: Set up a 401(k) as an asset account (see Chapter 5).

Note: To see which categories are tax-free, select Categories from the Edit menu. Select a category, click on Modify, and see if the Tax-Related box is selected. You can always modify the tax-free status of any account.

Contributing to Tax-Free Accounts

To make a tax-deductible contribution to an IRA or other tax-free account, either:

- record two separate transactions, as shown here

- contribute through payroll deduction, as shown in *Contributing to a 401(k)* in Chapter 6.

Note: If the contribution is partially deductible, use the following procedure for recording the deductible portion, and an account-to-account transfer for the non-deductible portion.

1. Select the account the contribution is coming from. Categorize the transaction as an expense and record it. For example, if you are using funds from your Checking account, write a check and select the appropriate expense category.

    Specify a new category for each tax-free investment, like "IRA Contribution." In the New Category box, select the Tax-Related box.

2. For the tax-free account, choose the type of transaction. Then, type the amount of the contribution and record it. Leave the Category blank.

Choose	For
Deposit	Bank accounts
Misc. Income	Investment accounts
Record Increases	Asset accounts

Withdrawing from Tax-Free Accounts

Funds withdrawn from a tax-free account are generally considered taxable income. To withdraw from a tax-free account:

1. For the tax-free account, select the type of transaction. Then, type the amount of the withdrawal and record it. Leave the Category blank.

Choose	For
Withdrawal	Bank accounts
Misc. Income	Investment accounts
Record Decreases	Asset accounts

2. Select the account to which you are transferring the funds. Record the transfer as an income transaction. Use the income category you created when you made the contribution.

   Another way to withdraw is to disburse the funds directly from the tax-free account. First use the procedure above, transferring the funds from the tax-free account to itself. Then record the expenditure.

   Part of a withdrawal from a tax-free account may be taxable income. Transfer the taxable portion using the previous procedure, and transfer the non-taxable portion with an account-to-account transfer.

Recording Security Price History

The balance of your investment account always reflects the latest prices that you have entered for your securities. CA-Simply Money tracks unrealized paper gains or losses and performance using the last known security price as of your report date.

CA-Simply Money make it easy to add and modify historical prices for any or all of your securities.

Adding a Price

To add a price:

1. From the Edit menu, choose Investments, then Securities. The Edit Security box appears.

2. Use the Name box to select an existing security.

You must add a new security before recording prices for it. See *Adding New Securities* earlier in this chapter.

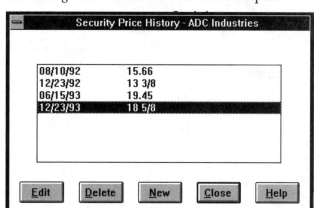

3. Click on Price History. The Security Price History box appears and displays the prices which have already been recorded. The list includes any prices which were recorded from other investment transactions, like Buy and Sell.

4. Click on New. The Price History box appears.

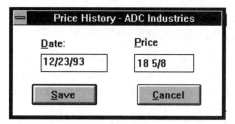

5. In the Date box, type the date of the historical price.

6. In the Price box, type the historical price.

7. Click on Save to save the price. The Security Price History box displays the new price.

Modifying a Price

To modify a price:

1. From the Security Price History box, click on the price you want to change.

Managing Your
Investments

2. Click on Edit. The Price History box appears.

3. Type the changes to the date or price.

4. Click on Save.

Deleting a Price

To delete a price:

1. From the Security Price History box, click on the price you want to delete.

2. Click on Delete. The price disappears from the list.

    Note: You can only restore deleted prices by adding them again.

Viewing Security Price History

CA-Simply Money stores current and historical stock prices so you can assess the performance of your portfolio. By opening certain windows or generating specific reports and graphs, you can see how well your investments are doing.

Reports and graphs base portfolio performance or value on the current security price, which is the last price recorded either automatically or manually. CA-Simply Money assumes that all unsold shares were sold on the last day shown on the report. For complete information on CA-Simply Money calculations, see *Calculating Security Performance* later in this chapter.

To view security prices and assess the performance of your investments, display one of the following windows:

■ **Edit Security box.** This box shows the current stock price. You can scroll through each security, and click Price History to get a price history for each security. To display the Edit Security box, pull down the Edit menu, choose Investments, then Securities.

- **Investment account register.** The register lists the date and price at the time of each transaction in the investment portfolio. To display the register, drag the button for the investment account to the Register button.

- **Security List Report.** This report shows the current price of each security. To display the Security List Report, click on the Reports button and select Investment Reports.

- **Security Price History Report.** This report shows the price history of each security. To display the Security Price History Report, click on the Reports button and select Investment Reports.

Updating Stock Prices by Modem

CA-Simply Money makes it easy to update the prices of your securities. All you need is a modem and software.

The prices are transmitted from the CompuServe® information service. You do not need a CompuServe account, because you can use the Kiplinger's CA-Simply Money Stock Quote Service, which provides 900-number access to a special CompuServe area. The charge of $1.00 per minute (subject to change) is added to your telephone bill. The updating is very fast, usually only a minute or two. The exact length of time depends on the number of quotes you request.

Of course, if you have your own CompuServe account, you can use it instead of the 900 service. If you would like details about joining CompuServe, see the CompuServe information included in your CA-Simply Money package.

CA-Simply Money uses "Basic Quotes" stock prices, which are included in CompuServe's basic monthly subscription. You can retrieve prices for any security or mutual fund listed by CompuServe.

Note: Stock quotes are delayed by at least fifteen minutes from current prices on the stock exchange.

Here is the procedure for updating prices. You need to perform the first two steps only once:

1. Prepare the securities you want to update.

2. Set up your modem.

3. Update the prices.

Note: Use of the Kiplinger's CA-Simply Money Stock Quote Service is subject to the CompuServe Service Agreement Terms found at the end of this chapter.

Setting Up Securities for Price Updating

Before you can update security prices by modem, you must have the securities set up in your investment accounts. The securities must be active and flagged for updating. Once you have flagged a security for updating, you can update the price at any time.

For your convenience, the ticker symbols for the Dow Jones Industrial Average and the S&P 500 are set up in CA-Simply Money. You can update these averages by modem at the same time you update stock prices. Use the following procedure to prepare them for updating by modem.

You need to perform this setup procedure only once.

1. From the Edit menu, choose Investments, then Securities.

2. Type the name of the security in the Name box. The Browser appears.

   Select an existing security or add a new one. If you are adding a new security, be sure to enter all appropriate information. You must include the ticker symbol.

   Note: If you need to look up the ticker symbol, refer to the Wall Street Journal or Investor's Business Daily. You can also find the ticker symbol on CompuServe by typing GO LOOKUP. For mutual fund ticker symbols, you can call the mutual fund.

3. Select Update Price by Modem.

☒ Update Price by Modem

4. Make sure Active is selected.

5. Click Save to save changes for this security.

6. Click Close to leave the Edit Security box.

Setting Up Your Modem

You need to perform this setup procedure only once.

1. From the System menu, select Settings, then Modem. The Modem Settings box appears.

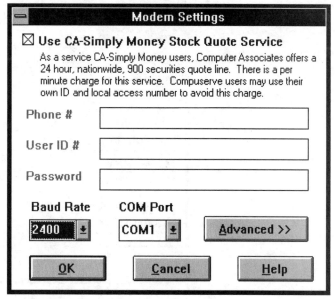

2. If you are using the 900 service, make sure the check box next to Use CA-Simply Money Stock Quote Service is selected.

Managing Your Investments

If you are using your own CompuServe account, type your access information: the local CompuServe phone number, your User ID, and your password. Note that the password shows as asterisks, so make sure you type it correctly.

3. From the Baud Rate list, select the speed of your modem. The default is 2400 baud. Other options are 1200 and 9600.

   Note: If you are using the Kiplinger's CA-Simply Money Stock Quote Service, 9600 baud is not available.

4. From the COM Port box, select the communications port to which your modem is connected. The default is COM1. Other options are COM2, COM3, and COM4.

5. If you need to access an outside line, or temporarily disable call waiting, click on Advanced. Another dialog box appears.

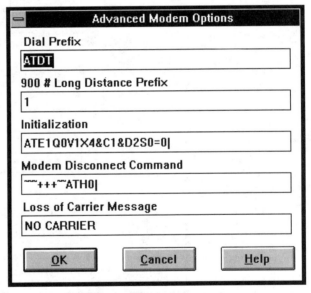

6. In the Dial Prefix area, type the following at the end of the dial prefix "ATDT":

   ■ "9," if you need to dial 9 to get an outside line. For example, the default dial prefix ATDT would become ATDT9.

- "*70" for tone phones or "1170" for pulse phones to disable call waiting for the current call (for example, ATDT9,*70). If you have call waiting, an incoming call would disrupt the transmission of information. The prefixes *70 and 1170 work in most areas. If they do not work for you, consult your local telephone company for more information.

    For information about the other modem commands you can change from this dialog box, see your modem user's guide.

7. If you are using the 900 service, and your telephone system does not require you to dial "1" before a long-distance number, clear the 1 from the 900 # Long Distance Prefix area.

8. Click on OK to save the settings. Your modem setup is now complete.

Updating Prices

Before updating stock prices, make sure your modem and securities are set up properly (see the previous procedures). You need to set them up only once; from then on you can update security prices as often as you like.

CA-Simply Money can store up to one price a day for each security in its price history database. The current price is used to calculate the current value of shares you own or sold short.

To update stock prices:

1. From the Operations menu, select Stock Price Update.

    CA-Simply Money logs on to CompuServe, gets the current price(s), and logs off. A message tells you when the price updating is complete. Updated prices are stored offline in a box that you can scroll.

    Note: If you are using the Kiplinger's CA-Simply Money Stock Quote Service, and you get a disconnect tone or a recording, make sure 900 numbers have not been suppressed from your phone service.

Managing Your Investments

2. Click OK. CA-Simply Money displays a dialog box asking whether you want to update the prices in your price history database.

3. Choose Yes to update the prices, No to leave the price update program without updating the database, and Cancel to look at the prices again.

Assigning Types and Goals

CA-Simply Money provides a simple system for tracking the performance of your portfolio: grouping investments by type or goal. Examples of investment types are Stock, Mutual Fund, and IRA. Typical goals are High Return, Growth, and Income. You can create as many types and goals as you need.

Types are valuable because what you consider successful for your stock portfolio may not be successful for your mutual fund investments. Assigning Types to your investments lets you look at the performance of each type. For example, you may have a stock brokerage account and also own another security outright. You could assign each of these to the Stock type. Reports and graphs could then display the performance of your stock investments as a whole.

Goals let you monitor investments according to the benefits you expect from them. Suppose one of your stock holdings is be for High Return while another is for Growth. You probably have different expectations for the two investments. As with Types, you can display reports and graphs that show you how your goals are being met.

Adding or Changing a Type or Goal

You can add your own types and goals to the ones CA-Simply Money provides, delete unused ones, or modifying existing ones. For example, you may want to add T-Bill, NYSE, AMEX, NASDAQ, and Option as types. As goals, you might add Low Risk, Retirement, or High Return.

1. From the Edit menu, choose either Investments/Types or Investments/Goals. The Security Type Editor or Security Goal Editor box appears.

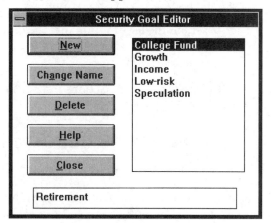

2. To add to the existing list, type a new name into the text box at the bottom of the dialog box and click New.

3. To change the name of a type or goal, select the current name in the list, type a new name in the text box, and click Change Name.

4. To remove a type or goal from the list, select it and click Delete.

Entering Share Prices

You can type share prices as decimal numbers or as fractions. Decimal values that are multiples of 1/16 are automatically converted into fractions. If the price is not a multiple of 1/16, it remains a decimal. For example, the price 12.5 is displayed as 12 1/2, while 12.4 is displayed as 12.4.

Enter fractions as the whole dollar amount, a space, then the fraction. Use a slash (/) between the numerator and denominator, for example, 12 1/8.

First-in, First-out Costing Method

CA-Simply Money uses a first-in, first-out method for tracking the capital gains/losses of your investments. The method is based on the assumption that the oldest shares are sold first. The method is systematic, easy to apply, and conforms to accepted accounting principles.

Example: The transactions in your portfolio for January are:

Jan. 8	Buy	500 shares @ $ 8	$ 4,000
Jan. 25	Buy	1000 shares @ $ 9	$ 9,000
Jan. 30	Sell	1000 shares @ $ 10	$10,000

The costing method assumes that the shares sold on Jan. 30 were those acquired first: the 500 shares bought Jan. 8 and 500 of the shares bought Jan. 25. The cost basis of the sold shares is:

Jan. 8	500 shares @ $ 8	$ 4,000
Jan. 25	500 shares @ $ 9	$ 4,500

	Total cost	$ 9,500

The resulting capital gain for the period is $500 — the proceeds of the sale ($10,000) less the cost ($9,500).

Lot Grouping

You may decide to track individual lots of stocks so you can balance gains and losses during the year. For example, one lot of stocks might show a gain, and the other a loss, depending on the current price. You might decide to sell the winner if you have losses or sell the loser if you have off-setting gains.

Lot Grouping Example

You set up a portfolio to track purchases of SysCom stock. In January you purchase two lots:

Jan. 6   Buy   1000 shares @ $ 6 $ 6,000

Jan. 23   Buy   1000 shares @ $ 8 $ 8,000

To keep track of the lots, you name the first lot "SysCom-1" and the second "SysCom-2." After the second purchase, the Portfolio Value report shows a total SysCom value of $14,000. The two lot groups use the same stock code, so the lots are grouped together on the report under SysCom.

```
                            Portfolio Value
                     Grouped by Investment Account

~~~~~~~~~~~~~~~~~~~~~~~~~~~~~~~~~~~~~~~~~~~~~~~~~~~~~~~~~~~~~~~~~~~~~~

Portfolio Value as of :   04/29/92

Acct Name   Security         # of Shares   Curr. Price   Cost Basis   Gain/Loss   Balance
SysCom

            · Cash ·             N/A          N/A        14,000.00       0.00     14,000.00
                                                        ------------   ---------  ------------
                Total Portfolio                         14,000.00       0.00     14,000.00
```

Two months later the price is $7. You decide to take a gain by selling the first lot. The Realized Gain report shows a profit of $1,000. The value of the SysCom portfolio is now reduced to $7,000.

```
                          Capital Gains Report

       ~~~~~~~~~~~~~~~~~~~~~~~~~~~~~~~~~~~~~~~~~~~~~~~~~~~~~~~~~~~~~~~~~~~~~~~~~
01/01/92    Through   04/29/92

Security          # of Shares    Buy Date    Sell Date   Sales Price   Cost Basis   Gain/Loss
SysCom-1

                      1000       01/06/92    03/23/92     7,000.00      6,000.00     1,000.00
                                                         ----------    ----------   ----------
              Total                                       7,000.00      6,000.00     1,000.00


SysCom-2

                                                         ----------    ----------   ----------
              Total                                           0.00          0.00         0.00
```

The transactions recorded in the Investment Register for this example are as follows:

01/06/92	Cash in	Checking				6000.00	6000.00
01/06/92	Buy	SysCom-1	1000	6		6000.00	0.00
01/23/92	Cash in	Checking				8000.00	8000.00
01/23/92	Buy	SysCom-2	1000	8		8000.00	0.00
03/23/92	Sell	SysCom-1	1000	7		7000.00	7000.00
03/23/92	Cash out	Checking				7000.00	0.00

Tracking and Grouping Lots

To track and group individual lots:

1. From the Edit menu, choose Investments, then Securities. The Edit Security box appears.

2. Add a duplicate of the security for which you want to maximize your loss.

    ■   In the Name box, use a slightly different name.

    ■   In the Symbol box, type the exact symbol used with the original security.

Each lot now appears as a separate item in the Security Browser box. However, the values for lots with the same symbol are grouped in reports and graphs.

Calculating Security Performance

The performance of a security approximates the yearly total rate-of-return. It is similar to an internal rate of return (IRR) calculation, but is not the same calculation.

CA-Simply Money treats shares of stock as single items. The following information is needed for each share of stock: (1) how long it was held, and (2) its buying and selling price. CA-Simply Money assumes that the oldest shares (those owned the longest) are sold before newer shares, unless there is information indicating otherwise.

This section describes the complete calculations used to separate stock performance values.

Terms Used   **Cost Basis**. The total money spent on a stock. It includes the price paid for the stock, commissions, and other expenses.

Buy Price. The price of a share of stock when it is purchased.

Sell Price. The price of a share of stock when it is sold.

Time Held. The length of time a share of stock is owned, in years or fractions of years.

Profit. The percent increase (decrease) in the value of a share.

Performance. The yearly percentage profit or loss per share.

Short sell. The selling of shares a person does not own, but plans to buy later in hopes of a lower price.

Managing Your Investments

The Calculation For each share of a particular stock, CA-Simply Money calculates:

- Cost basis:
  Cost Basis = Buy Price + commissions + expenses.

- Absolute percentage of profit or loss:
  Profit = (Sell Price - Cost Basis) / Cost Basis.

- Yearly percentage of profit or loss:
  Performance = Profit / Time Held.

CA-Simply Money calculates the performance of the entire security by averaging the performance of all the shares.

Special Situations Affecting Performance Calculations

- For shares you still hold, no sell price exists because the sale has not yet happened. In the performance calculations, CA-Simply Money uses the last known price as the sell price. The sell date is the last day of the time period shown in a report or graph. The last day is controlled by the Ending date (System/Settings/Reports & Graphs, or on the graph or report window, Options/Filters and Styles).

  For shares you sold short and have not bought yet, the buy price for performance calculations is also the last known price as of the ending date.

- Income such as interest or dividends is divided evenly among the shares owned when the income is received. When one of these shares is sold, the sell price used in performance calculations is the actual sell price plus the income.

  Example: You buy 1000 shares of stock at $10 per share. A dividend of $.05 per share is recorded two days later. A month after the buy, you sell 500 shares at $10 per share. $10.05 is the selling price (the selling price plus the dividend amount), giving an annual performance of 61%, even though the price never changed.

- For short sales, in which you "sell" shares you do not actually own, the procedure is similar to the one for long (normal) sales, though reversed. The next buy determines how long the shares were held.

Note: Do not record investment income on shares sold short. You cannot get a dividend from shares you do not actually own. If you record such a transaction the performance results may not be a true representation.

Managing Your
Investments

CompuServe Service Agreement Terms

Please do not proceed with using Kiplinger's CA-Simply Money Stock Quote Service unless you have read and agreed to the following CompuServe Service Agreement Terms.

1. The CompuServe Information Service (the "Service") consists of the computing services, software, information services, and information provided by CompuServe Incorporated ("CompuServe"). In addition to the Service, the Service offers access to information and software provided by third parties. These terms and any Operating Rules published over the Service constitute the entire agreement (collectively "Agreement") between CompuServe and Customer with respect to the Service and supersede all other communications.

2. CompuServe may modify this agreement, the Operating Rules or prices. CompuServe may discontinue or revise any or all other aspects of the Service at its sole discretion and without prior notice.

3. Customer agrees to indemnify CompuServe against liability for any and all use of Customer's account.

4. Customer is responsible for and must provide all telephone and other equipment and services necessary to access the Service.

5. CUSTOMER EXPRESSLY AGREES THAT USE OF THE SERVICE, WHICH INCLUDES THE CONTENTS THEREOF AND ANY STORAGE OR USE OF INFORMATION, IS AT CUSTOMER'S SOLE RISK. NEITHER COMPUSERVE NOR ANY OF ITS INFORMATION PROVIDERS, LICENSERS, EMPLOYEES, OR AGENTS WARRANT THAT THE SERVICE WILL BE UNINTERRUPTED OR ERROR FREE; NOR DOES COMPUSERVE OR ANY OF ITS INFORMATION PROVIDERS, LICENSERS, EMPLOYEES, OR AGENTS MAKE ANY WARRANTY AS TO THE RESULTS TO BE OBTAINED FROM USE OF THE SERVICE, OTHER THAN THOSE WARRANTIES WHICH ARE IMPLIED BY AND INCAPABLE OF EXCLUSION, RESTRICTION, OR MODIFICATION UNDER THE LAWS APPLICABLE TO THIS AGREEMENT, THE SERVICE IS DISTRIBUTED ON AN "AS IS" BASIS WITHOUT WARRANTIES OF ANY KIND, EITHER EXPRESS OR IMPLIED, INCLUDING BUT NOT LIMITED TO WARRANTIES OF TITLE OR IMPLIED WARRANTIES OF MERCHANTABILITY OR FITNESS FOR A PARTICULAR PURPOSE OR USE WITH RESPECT TO THE SERVICE OR INFORMATION. NEITHER COMPUSERVE NOR ANYONE ELSE INVOLVED IN CREATING, PRODUCING OR DELIVERING THE SERVICE SHALL BE LIABLE FOR ANY DIRECT, INDIRECT, INCIDENTAL, SPECIAL OR CONSEQUENTIAL DAMAGES ARISING OUT OF USE OF THE SERVICE OR INABILITY TO USE THE SERVICE OR OUT OF ANY BREACH OF ANY WARRANTY. THE PROVISIONS OF THIS SECTION 5 WILL SURVIVE ANY TERMINATION OF THIS AGREEMENT.

6. Except as expressly permitted in the Operating Rules, neither Customer nor its designated Users may reproduce, redistribute, retransmit, publish or otherwise transfer, or commercially exploit, any Information which they receive through the Service.

7. The provisions of paragraphs 5 and 6 are for the benefit of CompuServe and its Information Providers, Licensers, Employees, and Agents; and each shall have the right to assert and enforce such provisions directly on its own behalf.

8. This agreement is, and shall be governed by and construed in accordance with the law of the State of Ohio applicable to agreements, made and performed in Ohio. Any cause of action of Customer or its designated Users with respect to the Service must be instituted within one year after the claim or cause of action has arisen or be barred.

9. This Agreement contains the full understanding of the parties with respect to the subject matter hereof, and no waiver, alteration, or modification of any of the provisions hereof shall be binding on either party unless in writing and signed by duly authorized representatives of the parties. Neither the course of conduct between parties nor trade practice shall act to modify the provisions of this Agreement.

Chapter 8
Business Applications

Chapter 8
Business Applications

CA-Simply Money offers a number of special accounts that help you track your business finances. The ease of use of CA-Simply Money doesn't limit its ability to deal with more complicated financial situations. CA-Simply Money is flexible enough to handle payroll, receivables and payables, petty cash, and more. And the information is easily exported to full-fledged accounting software when necessary.

Accrual vs. Cash Basis Accounting

Certain service businesses (like law, architecture, or hairdressing) often use a cash basis mode of accounting. Cash basis accounting is used primarily because it can provide certain income tax benefits and because it is simple. However, cash basis accounting affects the financial position and operating results of a business. Consequently, most business firms use the accrual basis of accounting. Your accountant can advise you on the best method for your particular business.

Under the accrual basis of accounting, revenue is recognized when it is realized and expenses are recognized when incurred, without regard to the time of receipt or payment. Under the cash basis of accounting, revenue is recognized only when cash is received; expenses are recorded when they are paid in cash.

Payables

The procedures for cash and accrual basis payables are very different. If you are using accrual basis payables, see *Accrual Basis Payables* later in this chapter.

Cash Basis Payables

Cash basis payables are the most common type for small businesses. You record your bills as you receive them, but you don't "recognize" them until you pay them.

Adding Cash Basis Payables

To add cash basis payables:

1. When you receive a bill or invoice, write a check for it. See *Writing Checks* in Chapter 6.

2. Use the due date of the bill for the check date. The pop-up calendar can help you set your dates. See *The Calendar* in Chapter 9.

3. Click on the Print box to remove the "X." You will probably not want to print the check until you are ready to pay it. Unprinted checks are not subtracted from your checking account or detected by the Advisor.

   You can also specify the range of dates for which you want to print checks in the Print Checks box (when you print your checks).

4. Click on Record to complete the transaction.

5. Continue to repeat this procedure for all of your bills and invoices.

Tracking Cash Basis Payables

CA-Simply Money provides reports which help you to keep track of what bills need to be paid. The Accounts Payable report displays all unprinted checks for each payee. See *Business Reports* later in this chapter.

Making Cash Basis Payables

To make cash basis payments:

1. Print the Accounts Payable report and determine which payments need to be made.

2. Use the same check printing procedures you would use with any other check. See *Printing Checks* in Chapter 6.

Accrual Basis Payables

Keeping track of your payables on an accrual basis requires you to set up a separate payables account. A payables account is just a liability account used for a special purpose.

Setting Up a Payables Account

Create a liability account to represent your payables. Add a new account as described in Chapter 5. Use "Liability Acct." as the Account Type. Give the account an appropriate name, like "Payables," or "AP." Use zero as the opening balance.

You will add bills and invoices to this account as you receive them. When you write a check to make the actual payment, the amount is deducted from the payables and checking accounts. The appropriate expense category is also increased.

Adding Accrual Basis Payables

Your payables account uses the same information as the Checkbook. The only difference is that a "check" does not appear. To add accrual basis payables:

1. When you receive a bill from a vendor, drag that vendor's payee button to your Payables button. The Liabilities Increases box appears. The last transaction you entered for that vendor appears.

2. In the Date box, type the due date of the invoice. The pop-up calendar can help you set your dates. See *The Calendar* in Chapter 9.

3. In the Amount box, type the amount of the invoice.

   Note: You don't need to make a selection in the Via box.

4. You can use the ID box to record the reference number of the bill, if it has one. You can also type an optional memo in the Memo box.

5. In the Category box, select the expense category to which the bill applies. The category may already be displayed if you have made a payment to the vendor before.

   You can also use classifications to record project or client numbers. See *Classifications* in Chapter 6.

6. Click on Record to complete the transaction.

7. Continue to repeat this procedure for all of your bills and invoices. Every transaction you add to the Payables account increases your liabilities.

Tracking Accrual Basis Payables

You can create a customized report to help you keep track of what bills need to be paid. To track your payables due:

1. Drag the Reports button to your Payables button. A list of payables due on and before the date of the report appears.

2. From the Options menu, select Filters and Styles. Then, click on Settings. The Report Options box appears.

3. In the Cleared Status box, make sure Blank is selected and Cleared and Newly-Cleared are not.

4. Click OK twice to generate the report.

5. Pull down the File menu on the report window, select Memorize, and type a name for the report such as Accrual AP Report.

6. Click Save to memorize the report.

Making Accrual Basis Payments

When making accrual basis payments you determine which checks to write and then either use the Checkbook or hand write the checks.

1. Click on the Reports button, select Memorized Reports, then choose the report you just memorized in *Tracking Accrual Basis Payables*. Pull down the File menu on the report window and select Print. Look at the report to determine which payments need to be made.

2. Drag your checking account button to the payee button you want to pay. The Checkbook appears, displaying the information from the previous check to that payee.

3. Make any necessary changes to the information. Use the Memo and Classification boxes to help track your payments.

   Note: You can choose to pay all or part of one or more bills with a single check. Keep track of which bills are paid with the ID numbers you used in the Liabilities Increases dialog box.

4. In the Category box, select Liability, then choose your Payables account.

    You do not need to specify an expense category here because you recorded that information when you added the transaction to your Payables account.

5. Click on Record to complete the transaction. Your payables account is decreased by the amount of the check on the date of the check.

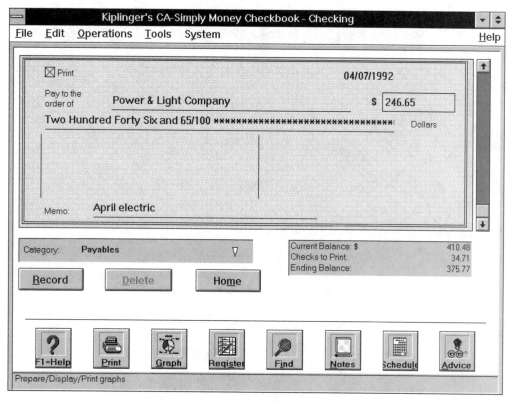

6. If you want to print the check immediately, select Print. Check printing procedures are the same as for any other check.

7. You also need to indicate in the Payables register which transactions have been paid. Double click on your Payables button to display the register.

Date	Via	C	Pay To / Deposit From	Increase	Decrease	Balance
04/01/92	3214	☑	West Telephone April phone Utilities\Telephone ▽	256.98		-256.98
04/03/92	4323	☑	All Ports Travel Travel ▽	576.50		-833.48
04/07/92	659	☑	Power & Light Co. April electric Utilities\Electricity ▽	246.65		-1080.13
04/07/92		☐	▽			

8. If the bill has been paid in full, click the box in the C column. A check mark appears, indicating the invoice has been paid. This keeps the transaction from appearing on the report of current payables due.

9. Click on Record to save the transaction.

10. You can continue to record other payments, or click on Exit to return to the main window.

Credits and Discounts (Payables)

Occasionally you will receive credit from a vendor, if there has been a billing error or you have returned a product. Some vendors also offer discounts if payments are made within a certain discount period. These types of transactions can easily be handled in CA-Simply Money.

There are two ways to handle this:

■ You can modify the original transaction by adding the credit or discount as a split distribution.
-or-
■ You can add the credit or discount as a new, separate transaction.

The split distribution method keeps the entire transaction together and is much faster to complete. The separate transaction method means you don't have to search for the original transaction.

**As a Split
Distribution**

To handle credits or discounts as a split distribution:

1. Double click on your Payables button. The Payables
    Register appears.

2. Select the original transaction to which you want to add the
    credit or discount. See *The Find Feature* in Chapter 9.

3. Click on the Category box. In the Distribution Register, add
    an additional line for the credit or discount. Type a
    negative amount for the value. Use the same category that
    you used for the original transaction.

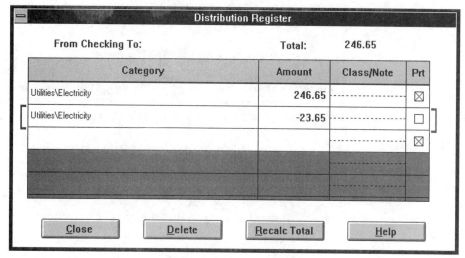

4. Click on Recalc Total, then click on Record.

**As a Separate
Transaction**

To handle credits and discounts as a separate transaction:

1. Click on your Payables button.

2. From the Account Activity box, choose Record Decreases.

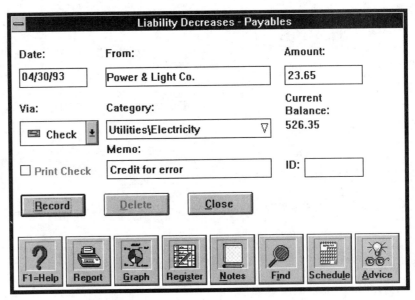

3. Enter the complete transaction information for the discount or credit.

   Type a *positive* number for the amount. The amount will be subtracted from the Payables balance and reduce liabilities.

   Make sure you use the category that was used on the original invoice so that the credit or discount is applied properly.

4. Click on Record.

Setting Up Receivables

A receivables account is an asset account used for a special purpose. Your receivables account in CA-Simply Money can be either cash or accrual basis. The procedure for setting up a receivables account is the same for both accounting methods. However, the procedures for recording the transactions are different. See either *Cash Basis Receivables*, below; or *Accrual Basis Receivables*, later in the chapter.

You can create an Asset Account to represent your receivables, as described in Chapter 5. Give the account an appropriate name such as "Receivables," or "AR." Make the opening balance zero.

When you use a receivables account, the people or companies that owe you money are actually income sources, not payees. So you must set up income buttons for them. In most cases you will use the income source type of "Business Income." For more information, see *Adding Income Sources* in Chapter 5.

Cash Basis Receivables

The cash-basis system described here assumes you recognize income when you receive payment.

Adding Cash Basis Receivables

To add cash basis receivables:

1. First make sure you have followed the procedures described above and have gathered your invoices.

2. Click on your Receivables button.

3. From the Account Activity box, choose Record Increases. The Asset Increases box appears.

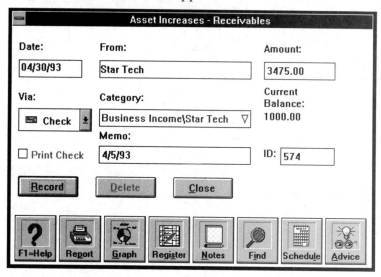

4. In the Date box, type the expected date of payment.

5. In the From box, type the name of the person or company who owes you money. You may need to click Income on the browser to see the name.

6. In the Amount box, type the amount of the invoice.

7. In the Memo box, type the date you issued the invoice.

8. In the ID box, type the invoice number. Use the Memo box also if the invoice number is more than 5 characters.

   If an invoice is paid in installments, record each payment as a separate transaction. Use the ID to identify the installments. For example, invoice #574 might become 5741 and 5742.

9. Click on Record to record the transaction.

10. Repeat this procedure for all your bills and invoices.

   Note: You do not have to use the Via box.

Here are some sample cash basis receivable transactions as they would appear in your Receivables register:

Date	Via	C	To / From	Decrease	Increase	Balance
04/30/93	574	☐	**Star Tech** 04/05/93 Business Income\Star Tech ▽		3475.00	3475.00
05/02/93	575	☐	**DataCom, Inc.** 04/10/93 Business Income\DataCom, Inc. ▽		4236.00	7711.00
05/05/93	576	☐	**AB Systems** 04/02/93 Consulting\AB Systems ▽		2645.50	10356.50
05/05/93		☐	▽			

Tracking Cash Basis Receivables   To track your receivables due:

■ From the Reports List, select the Accounts Receivable report for your receivables account.

A list of receivables due on and before today's date appears. The list is organized by income source and excludes receivables which have been paid (as indicated by being cleared in the register).

Recording Cash Basis Payments

As you receive payments for invoices, you modify the transactions in the Receivables account register. This decreases the value of your Receivables account and increases the value of the account in which you deposit the payment. Use the Distributions Register to update the existing cash basis transactions. To record a cash basis payment:

1. Double click on your Receivables button.

2. Scroll through the register to find the original transaction for the payment you received.

Tip: The Find tool can help you locate a transaction quickly. See *The Find Feature* in Chapter 9. Also, changing the register display can make it easier to find items. Click the Display button in the Register and select the Mid or List display format.

3. In the Date column, enter the date you received the payment. The existing date is the due date you entered.

4. In the Category box, click on the arrow. The Distribution Register appears displaying the income source.

5. In the Category column of the first blank line, type the name of the account to which you want to transfer the payment, such as "Checking" or "Savings." If necessary, click Asset on the Category browser to see the accounts.

6. In the Amount column, type the amount of the payment as a negative number.

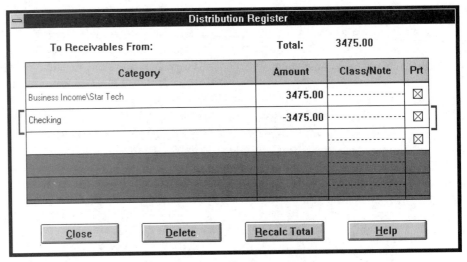

7. Click on Recalc Total to add the new amount to the old amount. The total displayed in the top right of the register becomes "0.00."

8. Click on Close to return to the Receivables Register.

   The Increase and Decrease columns for the transaction should be blank and display "0.00" for the Balance. If the balance is not zero, the customer may owe you money, you may owe the customer money, or you may have made an error in the Distribution register.

9. If the invoice has been paid in full, click the box in the C column. A check mark appears which indicates the invoice has been paid. This keeps the transaction from appearing on the report of current receivables due.

10. Click on Record to save the transaction.

11. You can continue to record other payments, or click on Exit to return to the main window.

Note: In the register of the account to which you distributed the payment, the transfer transaction is displayed against a yellow background. You can only make modifications to this transaction through the Receivables register.

Accrual Basis Receivables

The accrual basis system described here assumes you recognize income when you bill for your services.

Adding Accrual Basis Receivables

To add accrual basis receivables:

1. First make sure you have followed the procedures in *Setting Up Receivables* earlier in this chapter; then gather your invoices.

2. Click on your Receivables button.

3. From the Account Activity box, choose Record Increases. The Asset Increases box appears.

4. In the Date box, type the date of the invoice.

5. In the From box, type the name of the person or company that owes you money. The Browser box comes up. Click on Income. Select an existing income source or type a new one.

6. In the Amount box, type the amount of the invoice.

7. In the ID box, type the invoice number. You can also use the Memo box if the invoice number is longer than 5 characters.

   If an invoice will be paid in installments, record each of the payments as a separate transaction. You can use the ID to identify the installments. For example, invoice #574 might become 5741 and 5742.

8. Click on Record to record the transaction.

   Every transaction you add to the Receivables account increases your assets.

9. Continue to repeat this procedure for all of your invoices.

   Note: You do not have to use the Via box.

Here is a sample accrual basis receivable register:

Date	Via	C	To / From	Decrease	Increase	Balance
04/30/93	574	☐	**Star Tech** 04/05/93 Business Income\Star Tech ▽		3475.00	3475.00
05/02/93	575	☐	**DataCom, Inc.** 04/10/93 Business Income\DataCom, Inc. ▽		4236.00	7711.00
05/05/93	576	☐	**AB Systems** 04/02/93 Consulting\AB Systems ▽		2645.50	10356.50
05/05/93		☐				

Tracking Accrual Basis Receivables

To track your receivables due:

- From the Reports list, select the Accounts Receivable report. A list of receivables due on and before today's date appears. The list is organized by income source and excludes paid receivables (cleared in the register).

Accrual Basis Payments

Several methods exist for recording the receipt of accrued receivables. Your accountant can advise you on the best method for your business. You will probably use one method consistently. The most common method is keeping track of them as separate invoiced transactions.

This procedure has two parts. First, you record a transaction for the payment, then you clear the original billing transaction.

Recording the Payment

1. Double click on your Receivables button to display the register.

2. On the first blank line, change the date to the date you received the payment.

3. Type the name of the person or company that owes you money. In the Decrease column enter the amount of the payment.

4. In the Category line, specify the account to which you deposit the funds (usually the checking account). You can use Memo line for the check number.

5. Click on the C box to indicate the payment was received.

6. Click Record to record the transaction.

Here is a payment transaction:

06/06/92	1396	☐	Star Tech		3450.00	14645.00
			Other Income\Star Tech ▽			
07/07/92		☑	ChipTool, Inc.	4875.00		9770.00
			63112			
			Checking ▽			

Clearing the Original Transaction

7. Scroll through the register to find the original transaction for the payment you received.

Tip: The Find tool can help you locate a transaction quickly. See *The Find Feature* in Chapter 9. Also, changing the register display can make it easier to find items. Click the Display button in the Register and select the Mid or List display format.

8. Click on the C box to indicate the payment was received.

9. Click on Record to save the transaction.

10. You can continue to record other payments, or click on Home to return to the main window.

Here is an original billing transaction:

06/01/92	1374	☑	ChipTool, Inc.		4875.00	4875.00
			Other Income\ChipTool, Inc. ▽			
06/04/92	1375	☐	AB Data		6320.00	11195.00
			Other Income\AB Data ▽			

Recording Payments for Multiple Invoices

Keeping track of the running balance of a customer's account is useful if you receive payments covering several invoices.

To record a payment for multiple invoices:

1. Follow the basic procedure described in *Accrual Basis Payments* earlier in this chapter. However, in the Amount box, type the full amount you received.

2. Clear each of the original billing transactions.

Applying Credits and Discounts (Receivables)

The procedures for applying credits and discounts to your customers are essentially the same as recording credits and discounts you receive from your vendors. See *Credits and Discounts (Payables)* earlier in this chapter. The only difference is that you enter the credits in the receivables register.

As a Split Distribution

Credits and discounts as a split distribution:

1. Drag the Find button to your Receivables account. The Find box appears.

2. Select the original transaction to which you want to add the credit or discount.

3. Click on the Category box and add an additional line for the credit or discount. Type a negative amount for the value. Use the same category that you used for the original transaction.

4. Click on Recalc Total, then click on Record.

As a Separate Transaction

Credits and discounts as a separate transaction:

1. Click on your Receivables button.

2. From the Receivables box, choose Record Decrease.

3. Enter the complete transaction information for the discount or credit.

   Use a positive number for the amount. The amount will be subtracted from the Receivables balance and reduces assets.

Make sure you use the category that was used on the original invoice so that the credit or discount is applied properly.

4. Click on Record.

Business Reports

CA-Simply Money provides several reports which help you track your receivables, payables, and other business accounts. The predefined reports include:

- Cash Flow

- Net Worth

- Category Summary

- Itemized Categories

- Tax Summary

- Balance Sheet

- Accounts Receivable

- Accounts Payable

You can modify any of these reports or add your own. These reports are described in detail in *Reports* in Chapter 9.

Payroll Accounting

Wages and salaries represent a major element in the cost structure of most businesses. The procedures and requirements associated with accounting for salaries and wages include several different current liabilities related to a company's payroll expense.

Although setting up a payroll is more involved than other types of accounts, you will find it easy compared to some other software. The CA-Simply Money Payroll can automate many of your repetitive tasks, including:

- Writing and printing payroll checks.

- Recording employee payroll taxes and deductions.

- Writing and printing checks for payroll liabilities.

- Creating payroll transaction and summary reports.

Liabilities Relating to Payrolls

An employer is by law a tax collector for the federal government with respect to taxes withheld from employees' salaries. An employer may also withhold from salaries and wages amounts for such items as union dues, state disability insurance, group life insurance, pension plans, and for purchase of savings bonds.

When you create a payroll account, CA-Simply Money creates the following liability categories (payroll liability) and expense categories (payroll expense) for tax reporting:

Employer Taxes	FICA	Employer's portion of social security and Medicare.
	FUTA	Federal unemployment tax.
	SUI	State unemployment insurance.
	Disability	Employer liability for disability insurance.
	Misc.	Two miscellaneous categories for other employer-paid taxes or deductions such as union dues, insurance premiums, and retirement plans.
Employee Taxes	FIT	Federal Income Tax.
	SIT	State Income Tax.
	FICA	Employee's portion of social security and Medicare.
	SDI	State disability insurance.

Payroll Setup

Before you start writing payroll checks, you need to perform a few setup procedures. You need to create a payroll account,

employee payee buttons, and possibly a payroll funding
account.

Setting Up a Payroll Account CA-Simply Money makes setting up a payroll much easier than
do many other financial software packages. The main payroll
expense category, and subcategories for employer payroll taxes
and other payroll-related expenses, are automatically created
for you.

To set up a payroll account:

1. In the Account Setup-Add box, name your payroll account.

2. From the Account Type list, choose Payroll, then click OK.

    Note: It may take slightly longer for CA-Simply Money to
    create Payroll than other accounts.

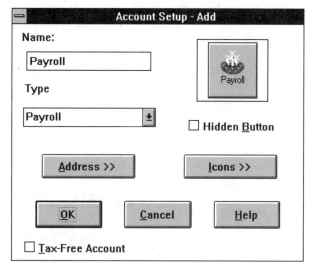

When you create a payroll account, CA-Simply Money creates
the liability categories (payroll liability) and expense categories
(payroll expense).

In addition, there are two miscellaneous categories each for
liability and expense. These can be used for non-standard
deductions, such as charitable contributions or extra
withholding taxes. The payroll expense categories are
automatically flagged for tax reporting in the Tax Summary
report.

Setting Up Employee Payees

Set up Employee accounts as Payees. See *Adding Payees* in Chapter 5. It is also helpful to group the payees. You can then write checks and get payroll reports with a single drag and drop. See *Grouping Buttons* in Chapter 6.

Payroll payees   Payroll group

Setting Up a Payroll Funding Account

If you have just a few employees you can pay them with checks from the firm's regular bank account. However, for many employees, consider setting up a separate bank account for payroll. You set up a separate funding account the same way as any other checking or asset account.

Writing Payroll Checks

Before you writing payroll checks you must set up a payroll account. See *Payroll Setup* earlier in this chapter. To write a check:

1. Click on your Payroll button. The Select an Account box appears.

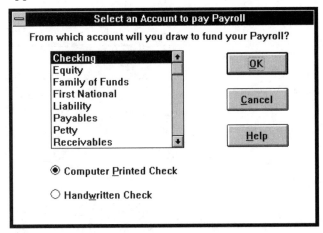

2. Select the account you want to use to fund the payroll; usually the checking account.

3. Choose Computer Printed Check or Handwritten Check.

   Note: If you choose Handwritten Check, a Start No. box appears in the lower right corner. Type the appropriate check number in the box.

4. Choose OK. The Write a Payroll Check box appears.

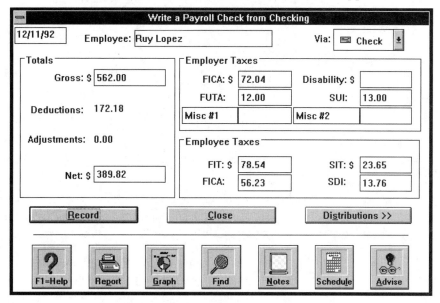

5. Type the date of the check.

6. In the Employee box, type the employee name. Values from the last check written for this payee (if any) appear.

   Tip: If you drag and drop your Payroll button on a payee button, the employee name and previous values automatically appear.

   You may find that the values for many employees may be exactly the same for each pay period. You can then just verify the information and click on Record.

7. In the Gross box, type the amount earned by this employee for this pay period.

8. Type the amounts of the applicable Employer and Employee taxes. These are described in detail in *Liabilities Relating to Payrolls* earlier in this chapter.

Employee deductions are totaled in Deductions and subtracted from Gross to get the amount shown in the Net box.

Note: Your calculation of earnings and deductions needs to be computed elsewhere. Use the Windows calculator to quickly insert values into the appropriate boxes.

Adding Other Deductions

To add other deductions:

1. From the Write a Payroll Check box, click on the Distributions button.

2. The Distribution Register appears. Add extra categories and their deductions. CA-Simply Money adds these to the total deductions in the Write a Payroll Check box. You will see a sum of the extra distributions in the Adjustment box below Deductions.

Note: Employee deductions are entered as negative amounts in the Distribution Register. Employer liabilities are distributed as a negative amount to a liability category and a positive amount to an expense category. Thus they do not affect the employee's net pay. If you enter an employer liability through the Distribution Register, be sure to distribute it as described in this note. To check your work, run a Category Summary report and include the Payroll Expense and Payroll Liabilities categories. For more information, see *Including and Excluding Report Items* in Chapter 9.

Printing Payroll Checks

Printing payroll checks uses the same procedure as printing any other check. If you print on voucher checks, CA-Simply Money prints the first fifteen lines of category information.

Using the Payroll Register

Use the Register to change, delete, or view payroll transactions. You can also use it to record payroll information, but it is better to use the Write a Payroll Check box, since that box lists your common distributions and makes data entry simpler (see *Writing Payroll Checks* earlier in this chapter).

03/06/92	Print ▦	☐	Checking	Ray Lopez	389.82
				Payroll Expns\Gross\Pa) ▼	
03/06/92	Print ▦	☐	Checking	Vera Miller	332.99
				Payroll Expns\Gross\Pa) ▼	
03/06/92	Print ▦	☐	Checking	Donald Bach	297.52
				Payroll Expns\Gross\Pa) ▼	

Changing or Viewing a Payroll Transaction

To change or view a payroll transaction:

1. Drag your payroll button to the Register button.

2. Scroll to the desired transaction.

3. Change the information as needed.

4. Choose Record to update the transaction.

5. When you are finished using the payroll register, choose Home to return to the main window.

Deleting Payroll Transactions

To delete payroll transactions:

1. Drag the your payroll button to the Register button.

2. Scroll to the desired transaction.

3. Choose Delete, then Yes.

4. When you are finished using the payroll register, choose Home to return to the main window.

Paying Withholding Taxes

The methods and schedule you use to pay your payroll liabilities depend on your specific situation. The following is a general procedure.

1. Use a report to find the amount of current liability. Drag your payroll button to the Reports button. The Payroll report appears with a summary of liabilities.

2. Set up a payee for the destination of the withholding funds.

3. Drag the Checking (or other) account button to the payee you set up in step 2.

4. From the Category box, select the payroll liability account you are paying off.

5. Click on Record. CA-Simply Money automatically makes the appropriate changes in the liability, payee, and funding accounts.

   Use the Distribution Register if you make more than one kind of tax deposit per period.

Scheduling Tax Payments

The Scheduler is very helpful in making sure you run your payroll on time and pay your withholding liabilities when they are due.

To schedule a payment:

1. Use the Schedule button, or the Schedule Actions command on the Tools menu, to open the Schedule Actions box. See *The Scheduler* in Chapter 9.

2. In the Schedule Actions box, specify the payee or group name, and the frequency of payment. Use the next scheduled payday as the First Payment Date.

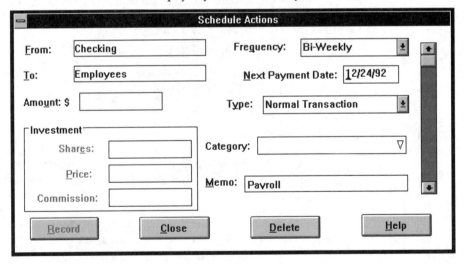

Payroll Reports

CA-Simply Money provides a number of reports to help you. See *Reports* in Chapter 9 if you need to make special reports.

Payroll. Shows employer expenses/liabilities for a period.

Employee Payroll. Shows amounts withheld from employee paychecks.

Payroll Register. Shows payroll transactions with full detail.

Category Summary. Select the payroll expense and liability categories from this report and save it as a memorized report.

Here is a sample Payroll Register report:

```
                                    Payroll Register Report
                                    with Distribution Detail

~~~~~~~~~~~~~~~~~~~~~~~~~~~~~~~~~~~~~~~~~~~~~~~~~~~~~~~~~~~~~~~~~~~~

     02/29/92      Through     03/06/92

Date        Paid From            Paid To                    Amount

03/06/92    Checking             Ray Lopez
            Dist -   Payroll Expns\Gross\Payroll            562.00
            Dist -   Payroll Expns\Employer FICA\Payroll     72.04
            Dist -   Payroll Liab\Employer FUTA\Payroll     -12.00
            Dist -   Payroll Expns\Employer FUTA\Payroll     12.00
            Dist -   Payroll Liab\Employer FICA\Payroll     -72.04
            Dist -   Payroll Liab\Employer SUI\Payroll      -13.00
            Dist -   Payroll Expns\Employer SUI\Payroll      13.00
            Dist -   Payroll Liab\FIT\Payroll               -78.54
            Dist -   Payroll Liab\SIT\Payroll               -23.65
            Dist -   Payroll Liab\FICA\Payroll              -56.23
            Dist -   Payroll Liab\SDI\Payroll               -13.76
                                                        ------------
                                                            389.82
```

Petty Cash

A petty cash fund is a fixed amount used for making small expenditures that are most conveniently paid in cash. The petty cash fund is restored to its original amount at frequent intervals by writing a check to Petty Cash. The replenishment check equals expenditures made from the fund.

The size of the fund should be sufficient to meet normal needs for small cash payments for a period of two or three weeks. As each cash payment is made, you record a transaction in the Petty Cash account.

Typically the person holding the petty cash will keep a list of disbursements showing what was withdrawn, by whom, and for what.

Setting Up a Petty Cash Account

Add a new account as described in Chapter 5. Use "Cash" as the Account Type. Give the account an appropriate name, like "Petty Cash."

You can fund the account in two ways:

An Existing Account

1. Use the current balance in the Starting Account Balance box.

2. Use the other procedures in this section for recording disbursements and replenishing the account.

A New Account

1. Use zero as the amount in the Starting Account Balance box.

2. Drag the button of the funding account (usually the checking account) and drop it on your petty cash button. The Account-to-Account transfer box appears.

3. In the Amount box, type the amount of cash you expect to need in the Petty Cash account.

4. Click on Record to complete the deposit.

5. Use the other procedures in this section for recording disbursements and replenishing the account.

Recording Disbursements

1. Click on your Petty Cash button, then click on Withdrawal. The Cash Out box appears.

   If a payee is already exists, you can drag your petty cash button to the payee button.

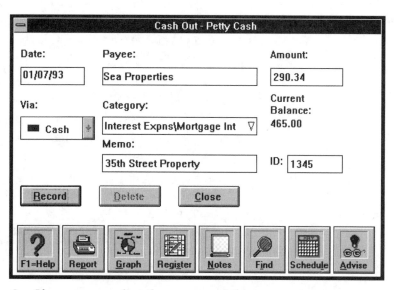

2. If necessary, select the payee and the appropriate category.

3. In the Amount box, type the amount of the disbursement.

4. You can use the ID or Memo fields to describe the disbursement and/or identify the person who withdrew the cash.

5. Click on Record to save the transaction.

Infrequent/One-time Payees   Many petty cash disbursements will be to one-time payees. If the payee is not currently in your list, the Payee Setup-Add box appears. You can click on the one-time only Payee box to prevent the payee from being added to the Payee Browser list. If a payee will be used more than once, but infrequently, you can click on Hidden Button. This adds the payee to the Payee list but prevents a button from displaying in the main window.

Replenishing Petty Cash

The petty cash account is typically replenished every two weeks. Funds are generally transferred from the checking account to the petty cash account.

1. Double click on your petty cash button to view the petty cash register. Use the Windows Calculator to calculate the

amount required to replenish the account. Subtract the current balance from the regular balance of the account to get the replenishing amount.

2. Click on your petty cash button, then click on Deposits. The Cash In box appears.

3. Use the From box to select the account from which you are transferring the replenishing funds. This is usually the checking account.

   You can also drag the button of the funding account and drop it on your petty cash button. The Account-to-Account Transfer box appears.

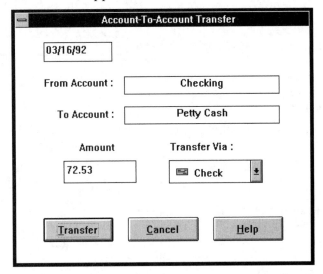

4. In the Amount box, type the amount you calculated in step 1. Click on Transfer.

5. Click on Record to complete the deposit. The balance of the fund is now restored to the original amount.

Using a Petty Cash Fund

Example: On March 2, a petty cash fund of $200 was established for the purpose of paying certain bills. Here is the itemized list of disbursements for the subsequent two weeks:

Mar. 5: Misc. Expense $ 29.00

Mar. 10: Office Expense   <u>$ 43.53</u>

Total $ 72.53

The account was replenished by making a deposit from the Checking account on March 16. The total disbursement was $72.53; the regular balance ($200.00) less the current balance ($127.47).

Here is a sample petty cash register:

Date			Payee / Memo		Amount	Deposit	Balance
03/02/92		☐	**Checking** Bank ▽			200.00	200.00
03/05/92	▪	☐	**Sandy's Deli** Working lunch Misc. Expns\Meals ▽		29.00		171.00
03/10/92	▪	☐	**L&J Office Supplies** Meeting supplies Office Expense ▽		43.53		127.47
03/16/92	▣	☐	**Checking** Bank ▽		72.53		200.00

Chapter 9
Support Tools

Chapter 9
Support Tools

In addition to the main functions and features, CA-Simply Money provides a number of helpful tools.

The Financial Calculators. The Financial Calculators can project or amortize loan costs, calculate investment requirements from investment goals, and more. Information from the calculators can be pasted into any window in CA-Simply Money. The Windows calculator is summoned by choosing Calculator from the System menu.

Reports. Five types of reports cover dozens of topics. You can save ("memorize") any report.

Graphs. Fifteen subjects can be graphed in six charting styles, including bar and pie graphs.

The Scheduler. You can plan ahead to make sure you don't miss payments by scheduling them in advance, and arrange for reminders so you don't forget.

Kiplinger's Financial Advisor. You'll be reminded of scheduled payments and counseled when payments seem out of line, or when your use of finance buttons is inappropriate.

The Find Feature. When you need to locate a transaction, CA-Simply Money offers several ways to search for it.

The Calendar. A calendar is available to you whenever you position your cursor in a date field.

The Notes feature. All transaction windows contain a Notes feature for jotting down the information you want to remember relative to a transaction. The note stays with the transaction until you change or delete it.

Import/Export. You can use data from other programs in your finance groups (Import), or use your CA-Simply Money data files in other programs (Export).

The Financial Calculators

In addition to the standard Windows calculator, CA-Simply Money has five financial calculators. They are the tools you need to make decisions about your loans and investments. With them you can calculate:

- amortization tables

- refinancing costs and benefits

- current interest rates

- annual yield from stock dividends

- amounts to invest to reach your financial goals

Displaying the Calculators

To display any of the financial calculators either:

- Click on one of the calculator icons in the Kiplinger's CA-Simply Money program group in the Program Manager.

- From the System menu, choose Financial Calculator, then the name of the calculator.

Pasting a Calculation into CA-Simply Money

To paste a calculation into CA-Simply Money:

1. Make your calculation.

2. Highlight in any number box the number you want to copy.

3. Press CTRL+C to copy to the Windows clipboard.

4. Select the box where you want to paste the information.

5. Press CTRL+V. The number is pasted into the transaction.

Using the Loan Calculator

The Loan calculator helps you to determine how large a loan you can afford or, given a particular loan amount, what your payments will be. The loan calculator also allows you to build an amortization table that shows the contribution of each payment to principal and interest and the amount of principal remaining after each payment.

Calculating a Loan   To calculate a loan:

1. From the System menu, choose Financial Calculators, then Loan. The loan calculator appears.

2. Choose Principal, Payment, or Annual Interest Rate. CA-Simply Money calculates any one of these values for you.

3. Type the appropriate amounts in the other two boxes.

4. In the Number of Years box, type the length of the loan.

5. In the Payments per Year box, choose the payment frequency.

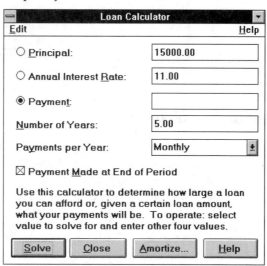

6. If payments will be made at the end of the period, click the Payment Made at End of Period box.

7. Click Solve. CA-Simply Money fills in the missing value.

8. To recalculate with different starting values, type the new value or values into their boxes and click Solve again.

Example: You are looking for a loan of $100,000 to buy a house. Your bank offers you a rate of 10% over thirty years. If you enter these numbers into the loan calculator, it will tell you that your monthly payment will be $870.32.

Displaying an Amortization Table

To display an amortization table:

1. Follow the procedure in *Calculating a Loan*, shown on the previous page.

2. Click Amortize to view an approximate amortization table.

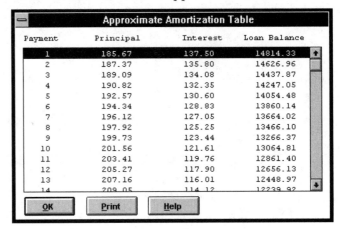

Payment	Principal	Interest	Loan Balance
1	185.67	137.50	14814.33
2	187.37	135.80	14626.96
3	189.09	134.08	14437.87
4	190.82	132.35	14247.05
5	192.57	130.60	14054.48
6	194.34	128.83	13860.14
7	196.12	127.05	13664.02
8	197.92	125.25	13466.10
9	199.73	123.44	13266.37
10	201.56	121.61	13064.81
11	203.41	119.76	12861.40
12	205.27	117.90	12656.13
13	207.16	116.01	12448.97
14	209.05	114.12	12239.92

OK   Print   Help

Using the Refinance Calculator

The refinance calculator helps you to decide if you should refinance a loan. You can enter the amount you are paying now and the new loan parameters, and the refinance calculator figures out how long it will take you to break even on the refinance.

Example: Your bank offers to refinance your $100,000 mortgage at 8% over thirty years for a charge of $2000. Your current monthly payment is $870.32. The refinance calculator tells you that your new payment is $733.76 and that it will take you 14.65 months to break even on the deal.

Calculating a Refinance
To calculate a refinance:

1. From the System menu, choose Financial Calculators, then Refinance. The refinance calculator appears.

2. In the labeled boxes, type your current payment and the parameters of the proposed refinance.

3. Click Solve. The new payment, saving, and break-even time will be shown at the bottom of the calculator.

Using the Interest Conversion Calculator

Interest rates are often quoted as *nominal* rates, which do not take interest compounding into account. The interest conversion calculator allows you to convert between the nominal rate and the *effective* rate (which does include compound interest.)

Converting Interest Rates
To convert nominal and effective interest rates:

1. From the System menu, choose Financial Calculators, then Interest. The Interest Calculator appears.

2. Type the known rate into the appropriately labeled box.

3. Click Solve. The financial calculator displays the other rate.

Example: You have been offered a loan at a nominal rate of 8% interest. With compounding interest, the effective rate is 8.3%.

Using the Dividend Yield Calculator

The dividend yield calculator translates cash dividends for stocks into an annual yield. You can compare the annual yield to other investments that make periodic payments. To calculate the annual yield:

1. From the System menu, choose Financial Calculators, then Dividend. The dividend yield calculator appears.

2. Type the share price and the dividend into the appropriately labeled boxes.

Use the share price at the time the dividend was paid.

3. Click Solve. The dividend yield calculator displays the annual yield.

Example: You have a security that has a price of $28 ¼ and just paid a dividend of $1.43 cents. The annual yield is 5.06%.

Using the Windows Calculator, CA-Simply Money can display the standard Windows calculator. The calculator is useful when you need to adjust figures before recording a transaction.

Example: You paid for four nights at a hotel with a credit card. You want to record the first three nights of a hotel stay as a business expense and the last night as a personal (travel) expense. Instead of calculating the two entries by hand, or looking for a calculator, use the Windows Calculator.

Using the Investment Calculator

The Investment Goal Calculator helps you achieve your financial goals by letting you calculate:

- how much money you will have if you invest a set amount regularly

- how much money to invest regularly in order to accumulate a set amount

- how much money you need to start with in order for a set amount invested regularly to accumulate to a set amount

You specify the number of years your money can accumulate, and how often you invest (monthly, quarterly, and so on). You can enter an inflation rate if you want to see the value of your future money in today's dollars. CA-Simply Money can either subtract taxes, or calculate a tax-free investment.

CA-Simply Money can increase the amount you regularly invest to compensate for inflation. To see the steadily increasing amounts, click on the Payments button. CA-Simply Money displays an amortized investments payment schedule. It is similar to the payment schedule you can calculate for a mortgage or other loan.

Boxes on the Investment Calculator

The Investment Calculator is organized into these areas: Initial Investment, Ongoing Investment, Time and Yield, Inflation, and Taxes. Here is an explanation of contents of each area:

Initial Investment

Starting Amount. How much money you have or need to have at the start of your investment.

Target Amount. The goal amount of your investment.

Future Value (inflation adjusted). The value of the Future Amount in today's dollars. CA-Simply Money calculates this if you enter a percentage in the Expected Inflation Rate (%) box.

Ongoing Investment

Periodic Investment Amount. The amount you invest regularly. This can be a set amount, or it can increase to counteract inflation (click on Increase Periodic Investments for Inflation).

Investments Made. How often you invest. This drop-down list has these choices: weekly, bi-weekly, monthly, bi-monthly, quarterly, semi-annually, annually.

Time and Yield   **Number of Years.** How long you will invest, in years.

Expected Pre-tax Annual Total Return on Investment (%). The percent return you expect to earn on your investment.

Inflation   **Expected Inflation Rate (%).** The annual percent of inflation you expect during the time you invest. If you enter an inflation rate, CA-Simply Money calculates the Future Value (inflation adjusted).

Increase Investments for Inflation. Indicates that you want CA-Simply Money to increase the amount you invest (Periodic Investment Amount) to counteract inflation.

Taxes   **Tax Rate (%).** The percent of taxes you pay (your tax bracket). Enter a tax rate if you want CA-Simply Money to deduct taxes from your investment.

Investment is Tax-deferred or Tax-free. Indicates that you do not want taxes deducted from your investment. CA-Simply Money does not deduct taxes unless you enter a tax rate, so you do not need to click on this if the Tax rate (%) box is empty.

Investing a Set Amount Regularly

This example of the Investment Calculator shows how to calculate the money you will have if you invest a set amount regularly.

Suppose you invest $200 a month for 10 years, earning 9% on your investment. You expect the rate of inflation to be 4%. You already have $10,000. How much will your investment grow to become?

Support Tools

1. Click the option button next to Target Amount. This is the amount you will calculate.

2. Type $10,000 in the Starting Amount box.

3. Type $200 in the Periodic Investment Amount box.

4. Make sure Investments Made is set to Monthly.

5. Type 10 in the Number of Years box.

6. Type 9 in the Expected Pre-tax Annual Total Return on Investment (%) box.

7. Type 4 in the Expected Inflation Rate (%) box. This causes CA-Simply Money to display the Future Value (inflation adjusted).

8. Click Solve. The Target Amount box shows 63,216.43, and the Future Value (inflation adjusted) is 42,403.43.

Calculating How Much to Invest

This example of the Investment Calculator shows how to calculate what you need to invest in order to accumulate a set amount.

Suppose you want to have $100,000 in 10 years. You already have $20,000. If you earn 9% on your investment, how much do you need to invest each month? You want the monthly investments to increase to counteract the effect of inflation.

1. Select the option button next to Periodic Investment Amount. This is the amount you will calculate.

2. Type $20,000 in the Starting Amount box.

3. Type $100,000 in the Target Amount box.

4. Make sure Investments Made is set to Monthly.

5. Type 10 in the Number of Years box.

6. Type 9 in the Expected Pre-tax Annual Total Return on Investment (%) box.

7. Type 4 in the Expected Inflation Rate (%) box. This causes CA-Simply Money to display the Future Value (inflation adjusted).

8. Select the box next to Increase Investments for Inflation.

9. Click Solve. The Periodic Investment Amount box shows 221.12. This is only the amount to invest in the first month, however.

10. Click the Payments button to display the adjusted monthly investments, which steadily increase to account for the 4% yearly inflation rate. The Investment Payments Schedule appears:

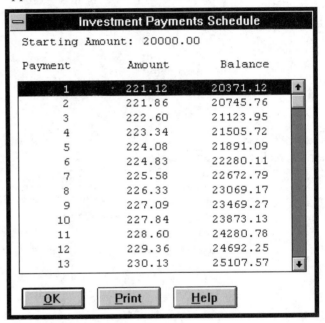

Payment	Amount	Balance
1	221.12	20371.12
2	221.86	20745.76
3	222.60	21123.95
4	223.34	21505.72
5	224.08	21891.09
6	224.83	22280.11
7	225.58	22672.79
8	226.33	23069.17
9	227.09	23469.27
10	227.84	23873.13
11	228.60	24280.78
12	229.36	24692.25
13	230.13	25107.57

11. If you wish, print the payment schedule by clicking on the Print button.

Calculating a Starting Amount This example of the Investment Calculator shows how to calculate the amount you need to start with in order for a regularly invested amount to accumulate to a set amount.

Suppose you want to have $100,000 in 10 years, after taxes. You can invest $300 a month. If you earn 9% on your investment, how much do you need to start with?

1. Click the option button next to Starting Amount. This is the amount you will calculate.

2. Type $100,000 in the Target Amount box.

3. Type $300 in the Periodic Investment Amount box.

4. Make sure Investments Made is set to Monthly.

5. Type 10 in the Number of Years box.

6. Type 9 in the Expected Pre-tax Annual Total Return on Investment (%) box.

7. Type 31 in the Tax Rate (%) box.

8. Click Solve. The Starting Amount box shows 27,059.73.

Displaying the Windows Calculator

To display the Windows Calculator:

1. From the System menu, choose Calculator. The calculator appears on top of the CA-Simply Money window.

2. Click on the onscreen buttons as you would press the buttons of a real calculator. To copy the number in the display to the Clipboard, choose Copy from the Edit menu or press Ctrl+C.

See your *Windows User's Guide* for other details on using the calculator.

Reports

CA-Simply Money can generate a variety of reports to help you manage your finances. Displaying or printing a report is as easy as choosing the type of report you want. You can choose date ranges, page numbers, and fonts. You can also choose from numerous formatting options to customize your reports.

Generating a Report

You can generate either a quick transaction report, or one of the special reports that comes with CA-Simply Money.

Quick Transaction Report   Drag the Report button to one of your income, account, or payee buttons. Or, if another report is displayed, choose Report List from the Options menu on the report window.

Other Reports   CA-Simply Money offers six groups of reports: Transaction, Financial, Button, Investment, Miscellaneous, and Memorized. The reports in each group are explained in *Choosing the Right Report* later in this chapter. To generate a report:

1. Click on Reports.
    -or-
    From the Tools menu, choose Produce Reports. The Report Selections box appears.

2. From the Report Selections box, choose one of the six types of reports. The list of available reports for the chosen report type appears in the box to the right.

3. Click on the report you want to generate, then click on OK.

    The report appears in the Report display window. If the report is larger than the window, use the scroll bar to browse through the report.

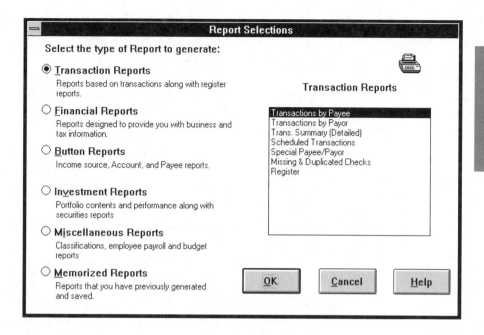

Printing a Report

To print a report:

1. Display the desired report. From the File menu on the Report window, choose Printer Setup to verify that you have selected the correct printer.

2. From the File menu on the Report window, choose Print Report. The report prints on the selected printer.

3. From the File menu on the Report window, choose Home.

Choosing the Right Report

CA-Simply Money offers six groups of reports: Transaction, Financial, Button, Investment, Miscellaneous, and Memorized. Besides these, you can also generate a quick transaction report by dragging and dropping a button onto the Reports button.

Transaction Reports   **Transactions by Payee.** Groups transactions alphabetically by payee, and includes the transaction amount, date, and the account from which the amount was paid. For each payee, transactions are sorted by date and totaled. Use the report to verify payments for a payee, to determine how many installments you have already paid on an item, or to see how much business you are giving to a payee.

Transactions by Payor. Groups transactions alphabetically by payor, and tracks transactions from payor to account and from account to payee. Transactions are sorted by date and totaled for each payor.

Transaction Summary (Detailed). Provides a detailed summary by date of all transactions. Includes Paid From (including memos and categories), Paid To, and Amount columns.

Scheduled Transactions. Shows all scheduled transactions that have been completed within the date range. Includes transaction date, Pay To and Pay From, amount, and frequency of payment.

Special Payee/Payor. Lists all payments transacted as Special activities, such as deposit, withdrawal, and transfer. See *Adding Specials* in Chapter 5.

Missing & Duplicated Checks. Lists all handwritten checks in sequence, noting when a check number is skipped or duplicated. If you print checks with CA-Simply Money, a check that is written but not marked for printing shows as a duplicate check.

Register. Presents Pay To/Deposit From information chronologically. Includes memos and categories. You can generate a Register report by clicking the Report button in an account Register.

The Register Report with Distribution Detail is a printout of the Register for an account. It shows everything in the Register, including whether the transaction has cleared. It provides a running balance of an account. You can use the Register Report as printed backup or support for an account's activity.

Financial Reports   **Cash Flow.** Shows inflow and outflow of funds. Lists all categories and totals without itemizing transactions. Gives total cash outflow at the end, and the overall total, positive or negative.

Net Worth. Lists assets and liabilities by account name. Accounts are sorted by decreasing amounts. Gives total assets, total liabilities, and net worth. Assets include all asset accounts. Liabilities include all liability accounts and categories (for example, payroll liabilities such as FICA or federal income tax).

Category Summary. Groups account balances by income, assets, liabilities, and expenses, and gives totals for each category and subcategory.

Itemized Categories. Lists all transactions by category within Income and Expense. Gives date, check number, Payee/Payor, memo, cleared status, and amount. Has an Income Total, an Expense Total, and Total Income Less Expense.

Tax Summary. Itemizes and totals taxable income and expense categories.

Tax Schedule. Lists expenses for each tax schedule (Schedule A, B, and so on). Use this report at tax time to help prepare your return.

Balance Sheet. Groups account activities into assets, liabilities, and equity. Totals assets, liabilities, equity, and liabilities and equity combined (which equals Assets). The Balance Sheet Report shows the health of your company.

Accounts Receivable. Lists transactions for a single account by payor (you must select an account from the Select Account window). Gives the transaction date and amount, subtotals for each payor, and the total for all receivables.

Accounts Payable. Lists transactions for a single account by payee. Gives the transaction date and amount, subtotals for each payee, and total for all payables.

Support Tools

Button Reports   **Income Report.** Lists transactions by date (regardless of income source). It shows the income amount, account it was transferred to, and categories. Gives an income total at the bottom. To see all transactions for an income source grouped together, run this report for only one income source or run the Transactions by Payor report.

Account Report. Lists transactions by inflow and outflow, sorted by date (regardless of account). Shows Paid From/To names and amounts, total inflow and outflow, and account balance. To see all transactions for an account grouped together, select this report for just one account.

Payee Report. Lists transactions by date (regardless of payee). It shows amount, account paid from, and total paid. To see all transactions for a payee grouped together, run this report for only one payee or run the Transactions by Payee report.

Investment Reports   **Portfolio Value.** Lists current value of each investment account. Tracks each security (cash, stock, etc.) within that account by number of shares and current price (if applicable), cost basis, gain/loss, and account balance. Totals securities by account.

Portfolio Market Value. Lists market value of the stocks within each investment account. Tracks each stock by number of shares and current price. Totals the market value of each stock, each account, and all accounts.

Portfolio by Type. Lists current value of each security, grouped by type of security (stocks, mutual funds, etc.). Tracks each security within that type by number of shares and current price, cost basis, gain/loss, and account balance. Within each type the balances are totaled, then all investments are totaled.

Portfolio by Goal. Lists current value of each security, grouped by the financial goal for that security (college education, income, etc.). Tracks each security for that goal by number of shares and current price, cost basis, gain/loss, and account balance. Within each goal the balances are totaled, then all investments are totaled.

Investment Performance. Lists a performance value for each security. The performance value approximates the percentage yearly rate of return yielded by an investment. The calculation used to generate the performance ratings is described in *Calculating Security Performance* in Chapter 7.

Investment Income/Expense. Lists Income (categorized by dividends, short term capital gains, etc.) for each investment account. Totals each category within Income and Expenses. Totals Income and Expense categories. Calculates difference between Income and Expenses.

Capital Gains. Lists each security (stocks, mutual funds, etc.) and its Short- and Long-Term Capital Gains. Tracks each security's "sell" transaction by number of shares sold, buy date, sell date, sales price, cost basis, and gain/loss. Within each security the gains/losses are totaled, then all gains/losses are subtotaled for short- and long-term. Finally, all gains/losses are totaled.

Investment Transaction Detail. For a selected investment account, lists each transaction made during a specified time period. The report shows the starting balance. For each transaction, the report lists transaction date, action taken with which security (buy stocks, sell mutual funds, etc.), number of shares, price (either buying or selling), commission, cash value, investment value, and total value (cash value + investment value). The last three values are each totaled. The unrealized gain/loss is calculated at the end of the time period and added to the investment value to equal the account's ending balance.

Securities List. Lists each security by name, symbol, type (stock, mutual fund, etc.), financial goal (income, college education, etc.), expiration date, number of shares held, current share price, and market value of the security.

Securities Expiration Date. Lists securities in chronological order by expiration date. It shows security name, symbol, type (stock, mutual fund, etc.), financial goal (income, college education, etc.), number of shares held, current share price, and market value.

Security Price History Report. Lists each security, dates when share price was recorded, share price, and variance (positive or negative) from the previous date. Negative changes are

highlighted in red. If there is no change, the column contains
"N/C."

Miscellaneous Reports

Classification Report. Groups transactions by classification, giving date, account name, and amount.

Class/Dist. Report. For each classification and category, transactions are shown with date, account name, and amount. Amounts are subtotaled by category and classification.

Employee Payroll Report. Shows total payroll expenses and liabilities. This report is useful for analyzing the salary paid and deductions made for each employee. It is particularly useful for determining amounts owed to state and federal tax authorities.

Category List. Groups categories by income, assets, liabilities, and expenses. Shows whether a category is tax-related, and lists any category description.

Button List. Groups buttons by Income, Account, and Payee, and sorts in the order they were created. This report lists phone, account number, and contact. Indicates whether buttons are hidden, a one-time payee, or have been deleted.

Budget (Actual vs. Budgeted). Lists expense categories alphabetically, gives an actual and budgeted amount for each, and calculates the difference. The amounts under budget are negative.

Over/Under Budget. Shows the same information as Budget (Actual vs. Budgeted), but presents the Difference as a percentage over or under budget. The percentages under budget are negative.

Memorized Reports

By clicking the Memorized Reports button in the Report Generator box, you can see a list of the report formats you have saved (see *Memorizing a Report Format* later in this chapter).

Customizing Your Report

Each report represents a special view of your finances. That view changes based on the information you choose to include and the format in which you display it. You can specify the dates you want the report to cover, include or exclude items such as accounts or payees, indicate how often you want the amounts subtotaled, and more.

Setting Default Dates and Colors

You can specify a default range of dates for your reports to cover, and decide on color or monochrome reports.

Note: You can also set date ranges for individual reports, rather than for all of them. See *Setting Title and Date Options* immediately following.

1. From the System menu, choose Settings, then Reports & Graphs. The Reports & Graphs Settings box appears.

Note: You can access the System menu on the main window from within the Report display, but the default changes do not take effect until the next report is generated.

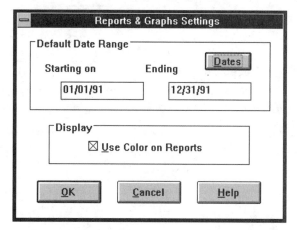

2. In the Default Date Range area, either type dates in the Starting and/or Ending boxes, or click Dates to see a list of date ranges. If you select a date range from the list, the starting and ending dates change accordingly.

3. If you are using a monochrome laptop, you may want to turn off the red and blue colors that reports normally have. In the Display area, clear the X from the Use Color on Reports box.

4. Choose OK to set the defaults and return to the main window.

Note: You can save a date range if you memorize the report (see *Memorizing a Report Format* later in this chapter).

Setting Title and Date Options

1. Generate a report.

2. From the Options menu on the report window, choose Filters and Styles. The Report Generator box appears.

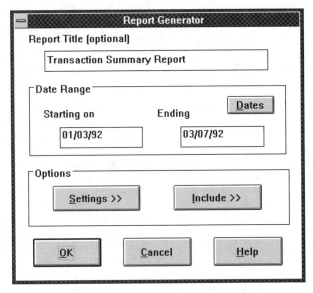

3. If you want to change the title, enter a new title in the Title box.

4. If you want to change the time period of the information shown on the report, either type dates in the Starting on and Ending boxes, or click on Dates to see a list of date ranges. If you select a date range from the list, the starting and ending dates change accordingly. You can also set a default date range, as described in the previous procedure, *Setting Default Dates and Colors*.

Including and Excluding Report Items

5. If you want to include or exclude income sources, accounts, payees, categories, or classifications, or securities, click on Include. The Include in Report box appears.

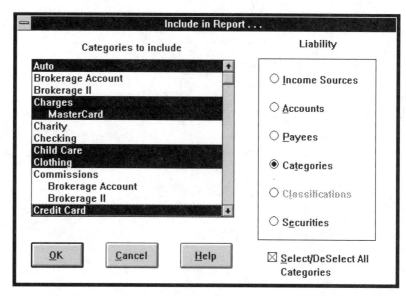

By default, CA-Simply Money includes all items that apply. Therefore, when the box opens, all items under Categories to include are highlighted, and the Select/DeSelect option is turned on. Highlighted items are included in the report, and items not highlighted are excluded.

The items in the Include in Report box depend on the type of report you are generating. You can get a different list of items by choosing a button in the Liability area. Buttons that do not apply to your report are dimmed.

6. To deselect a highlighted item, click on it. To deselect all items, turn the Select/DeSelect All box off. You can then select items by clicking on them.

   Example: You want a report showing all transactions for Barton's Pharmacy and Albert's Food. In the Include box choose Payees, then DeSelect All. Click on Barton's and Albert's in the Payee list.

7. Click OK to get back to the Report Generator box.

Setting General Options

8. Click the Settings button on the Report Generator box. The Report Options box appears. Choose one or more of the options, which are described below.

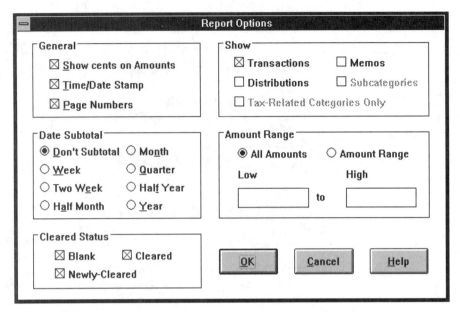

The Report Options box is divided into five option boxes: General, Date Subtotal, Cleared Status, Show, and Amount Range. The General options are described first.

Show cents on Amounts. Include two decimal places for cents (on) or whole-dollar amounts only (off).

Time/Date Stamp. Show the time and date the report was generated (on) or not (off).

Page Numbers. Print page numbers (on) or not (off). This option applies only when the report is printed.

Setting Date Subtotal Options You can subtotal weekly, every two weeks, twice a month, monthly, quarterly, twice a year, and annually. You can use only one option at a time.

Setting Cleared Status Options

For reports with checking transactions, you can choose which checks to include. Select one or more of these options:

Blank. Shows checks that have not cleared.

Cleared. Shows checks that have cleared and have been reconciled.

Newly Cleared. Shows checks that have cleared but have not been reconciled.

Setting Show Options

For reports containing transactions, you can choose which parts of transactions to include or exclude.

Transactions. Shows Date and Paid From information (on) or not (off).

Distributions. Shows categories (on), or not (off).

Tax-Related Categories Only. Shows only information in tax-related categories (on), or not (off).

Memos. Shows memos for transactions (on), or not (off).

Subcategories. Shows amounts in subcategories (on), or only amounts in top-level categories (off).

Setting Amount Range Options

If you are reporting on transactions, you can select a range of amounts to show in the report, or you can show all amounts.

All Amounts. Shows every transaction.

Amount Range. Shows all transactions within the range you set:

Low. An amount for the bottom of the range.

High. An amount for the top of the range.

Choosing Report Fonts

To choose fonts for a report:

1.   From the Options menu on the Report window, choose Title Font or Body Font. The Report Font box appears.

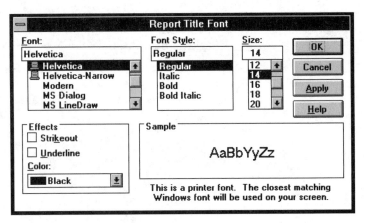

2. From the Font box, choose a typeface.

3. From the Font Style box, choose a style.

4. From the Size box, choose a font size.

5. In the Effects box, choose any or all of the options.

    Text appears in the Sample box with the selected typeface, font style, and size. The Font, Font Style, and Size boxes list all of the options you installed in Windows for your printer. A message appears under the Sample box indicating whether you have selected a printer or screen font. See your *Windows User's Guide* for more information about using fonts. Printer fonts are accompanied by the 🖳 icon.

6. Choose OK to return to the Report display. Your report appears with the font selection you made.

Exporting a Report to Another Program

The Export Report command converts the report to a standard ASCII or database (comma-delimited) format. If you want to export to a tax program, do not use this procedure; see *Exporting to Tax Programs* later in this chapter.

1. From the File menu in the Report display window, choose Export. The Print Report to Disk box appears.

2. In the Report type box, choose ASCII (PRN) file or Comma delimited. ASCII creates standard text files for use with word-processing software. Comma delimited converts reports into data records for use with database or spreadsheet software.

3. In the Filename (with path) box, type the full path destination for the report file, or use the Browse button.

4. Click on the Include header box to include the date, title, and column labels in the exported report.

5. If you export in ASCII format, you can specify the maximum number of Lines/page.

6. Choose OK to export the report and return to the Report window.

Memorizing a Report Format

If you regularly use the same customizing options with the same report types, you can "memorize" the format instead of selecting the options every time you generate a report. In the future, you simply choose the memorized format.

1. Generate a report and choose the options you want from the Report display window's Options menu.

2. From the File menu on the report window, choose Memorize Report. The Save Memorized Report box appears.

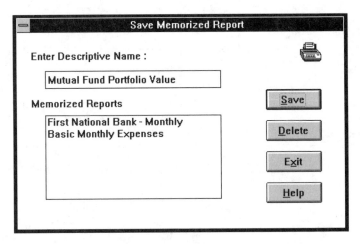

3. In the Enter Descriptive Name box, type a name that describes your report. Reports you have already memorized are displayed.

4. Choose Save.

Using a Memorized Report

To use a memorized report:

1. Click on the Reports button in the main window.
    -or-
    From the Tools menu, choose Produce Reports.
    -or-
    On the report display, pull down the Options menu and choose Report list.

    The Report Generator box appears.

2. Choose Memorize Reports on the left side of the Reports Selection box. The list of memorized reports appears.

3. Choose a report name from the list, then click OK.

4. If necessary, choose items to be displayed and click OK to draw the report.

Deleting a Memorized Report

To delete a memorized report, highlight the report name in the Save Memorized Report box and choose Delete.

Graphs

CA-Simply Money can present your financial picture in a variety of area, bar, line, and pie graphs. You can customize them by choosing a range of dates, including or excluding information, and more.

Drawing a Graph

You can generate a quick transaction graph, or one of the pre-set graphs that come with CA-Simply Money.

Quick Transaction Graph
Drag the Graph button to one of your income, account, or payee buttons. Or, if another graph is displayed, choose Graph List from the Options menu in the graph window.

Other Graphs
CA-Simply Money provides groups of graph types for you to choose from: Income and Expense, Asset and Liability, Investment, Budget, and Memorized. The graphs in each group are explained in *Choosing the Right Graph* later in this chapter.

1. Click on Graphs.
    -or-
    From the Tools menu, choose Draw Graphs. The Graph Selections box appears.

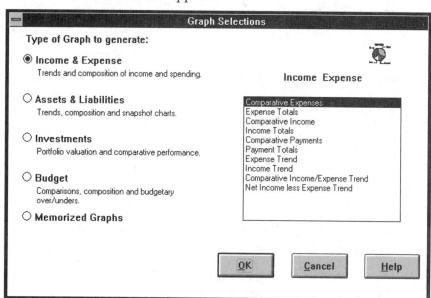

2. Choose a graph type: Income & Expense, Assets & Liabilities, Investments, Budget, or Memorized Graphs.

3. Choose the graph you want from the list box on the right.

4. Click OK to display the graph.

Tip: You can display the detail for the components of any graph. Click on a bar or pie slice to view the data that is represented.

Printing a Graph

To print a graph:

1. Display the desired graph. From the File menu on the Graph window, choose Printer Setup to verify that you have selected the correct printer.

2. From the File menu on the Graph window, choose Print.

3. From the File menu on the Graph window, choose Home.

Choosing the Right Graph

The CA-Simply Money offers several groups of graphs: Income and Expense, Asset and Liability, Investment, Budget, and Memorized. Besides these, you can also generate a quick transaction graph by dragging & dropping a button onto the Graphs button.

Income and Expense

Comparative Expenses. Shows expenses by category over time.

Expense Totals. Draws a pie chart showing expenses in each category as a percentage of total expense. The slice Other represents categories whose combined amounts are less than 10% of the total.

Comparative Income. Shows income by category over time.

Income Totals. Shows total income from each source as a percentage of total income.

Support Tools

Comparative Payments. Shows payments to various payees over time.

Payment Totals. Shows total payments to each payee as a percentage of total payments.

Expense Trend. Draws a bar chart of expenses over time.

Income Trend. Draws a bar chart of income grouped by time.

Comparative Income/Expense Trend. Compares income and expenses over time.

Net Income Less Expense Trend. Subtracts expenses from income to show, in general, how you did over time.

Assets & Liabilities

Asset/Liability Snapshot. Shows the balance of each category.

Net Balance Trend. Subtracts liabilities from assets and shows how the balance changes over time.

Asset Composition. Shows assets by category as a percentage of total assets.

Liability Composition. Shows liabilities by category as a percentage of total liabilities.

Asset Trend. Shows how your assets change over time.

Liability Trend. Shows how your liabilities change over time.

Investment

Comparative Investment Performance. Displays a bar graph representing the performance of each security. See *Calculating Security Performance* in Chapter 7 for the calculation.

Portfolio Value by Account and Security. Displays the value of your portfolios (investment accounts), broken down by securities.

Portfolio Value by Goal. Displays the value of your portfolios, broken down by goals.

Portfolio Value by Type. Displays the value of your portfolios, broken down by types.

Security Price History. Displays the price history of each security.

Budget **Comparative Budget/Actual Expense Trend**. Displays a bar graph comparing budgeted amounts to actual expenses.

Comparative Budget/Actual Income Trend. Displays a bar graph comparing budgeted amounts to actual income.

Over Budget Expenses. Displays a bar graph of expenses that exceeded budgeted amounts.

Over Budget Income. Displays a bar graph of income that exceeded budgeted amounts.

Under Budget Expenses. Shows expenses that are below budgeted amounts.

Under Budget Income. Shows income that is below budgeted amounts.

Actuals Less Budgeted Expenses. Shows the difference between your budget for each category and your actual expenses.

Actuals Less Budgeted Income. Shows the difference between your budget for each category and your actual income.

Composition of Expense Budget. Shows expense categories as a percentage of the total expense budget.

Composition of Income Budget. Shows income categories as a percentage of the total income budget.

Customizing a Graph

You can change the period of time represented on a graph, the title, the information included, and the graph type and style.

Setting Default Dates You can specify a default range of dates for your graphs to cover.

Note: You can also set date ranges for individual graphs, rather than for all of them. See *Setting Title and Date Options* immediately following.

1. From the System menu, choose Settings, then Reports & Graphs. The Reports & Graphs Settings box appears.

Note: You can access the System menu on the main window from within the graph display, but the default changes do not take effect until the next graph is generated.

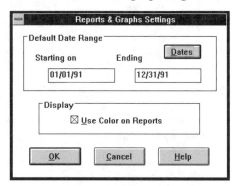

2. In the Default Date Range area, either type dates in the Starting on and/or Ending boxes, or click Dates to see a list of date ranges. If you select a date range from the list, the starting and ending dates change accordingly.

3. Choose OK.

Note: You can save a date range if you memorize the graph (see *Memorizing a Graph Format* later in this chapter).

Setting Title and Date Options

1. Draw a graph.

2. From the Options menu on the graph window, choose Filters and Styles. The Graph Generator box appears.

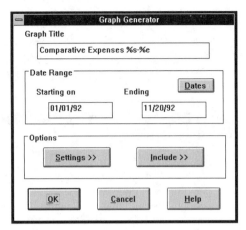

3. If you want to change the title, enter a new title in the Title box. You can use the following codes to add information automatically:

%s	Start date
%e	End date
%b	Button name

4. If you want to change the time period of the information shown, either type dates in the Starting on and Ending boxes, or click on Dates to see a list of date ranges. If you select a date range from the list, the starting and ending dates change accordingly. You can also set a default date range (see *Setting Default Dates* earlier in this chapter).

Including and Excluding Graph Items

1. If you want to include or exclude income sources, accounts, payees, categories, classifications, or securities, click on Include. The Graph Includes box appears.

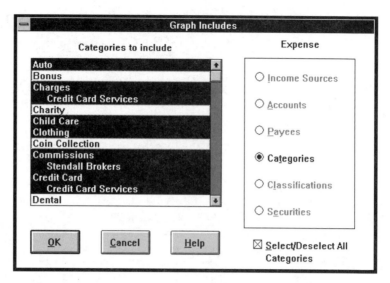

By default, CA-Simply Money includes all items that apply. Therefore, when the box opens, all items under Categories to include are highlighted, and the Select/DeSelect option is turned on. Highlighted items are included on the graph, and items not highlighted are excluded.

The items in the Graph Includes box depend on the type of graph you are generating. You can get a different list of items by choosing a different button in the right side of the dialog box. Buttons that do not apply to your graph are dimmed.

2. To deselect a highlighted item, click on it. To deselect all items, turn the Select/DeSelect All box off. You can then select items by clicking on them.

3. Click OK to get back to the Graph Generator box.

Choosing Graph Types and Styles

1. If you want to change the type of graph (bar, 3D bar, pie, 3D pie, line, area), or change the style of formatting, click Settings in the Graph Generator box. The Settings box appears.

   Note: You can also go directly to the Settings box by pulling down the Options menu on the graph window and selecting Settings.

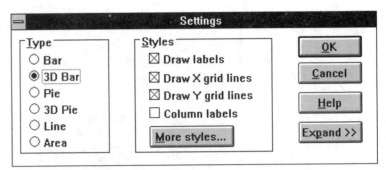

2. To choose a different graph type, click the type of your choice. The following table illustrates and briefly explains the types of graphs.

Graph Types	Uses
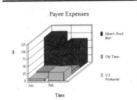	**Bar Graph.** Shows individual figures or draws comparisons between items (but not to a whole).
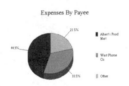	**Pie Graph.** Shows the relationship of parts to a whole (always contains just one data series); good for highlighting a significant element.
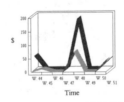	**Line Graph.** Shows trends or changes over time; similar to an area graph, but emphasizes the rate of change rather than the amount of change.
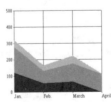	**Area Graph.** Shows the relative importance of values over time; similar to a line graph, but emphasizes the amount of change (magnitude of value) rather than the rate of change.

Support Tools

Setting Basic Graph Styles

To specify labels or draw grid lines on your graph, select one of these options:

Draw labels. Labels the segment on pie graphs; labels the axis on bar, line, and area graphs.

Draw X / Y Grid lines. Includes grid lines on bar, line, and area graphs. Usually, a graph without grid lines has a cleaner look.

Column labels. Puts labels in a column on the right side of the graph. For certain graph types, you cannot deselect this option.

Setting Bar Graph Styles

To customize a bar graph further, click on More styles. Choose one or more of the following options:

Draw clustered bar. Displays a bar for each item value.

Draw stacked bar. Combines values for all items in a stacked bar.

Draw percentile bar. Depicts percentages of total rather than dollar amounts. Use for graphs with more than one set of bars.

Draw bars horizontally. Draws horizontal instead of vertical bars. Horizontal bars put more emphasis on time than vertical bars do.

Cluster bars in Z-axis. Shows items in different rows along the Z-axis.

Setting Pie Graph Styles

To customize a pie graph further, click on More styles. Choose one or more of the following options:

Omit label lines. Leaves out the lines connecting the label to the segment in a pie graph.

Label colors = segments. Draws the label in the same color as the segment. The default color for labels is black.

Give percentages. Labels segments with a percentage.

Use % symbol. Displays percent signs (%) next to percents.

Setting Other Graph Options

To limit values on the graph, request subtotals, or type your own labels, click on Expand. The Settings box now looks like this:

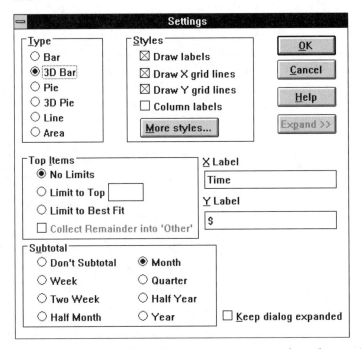

Top Items. You can limit the items in your graph to those within a certain percentage of the largest value.

- **No Limits.** Shows all values.

- **Limit to Top.** Shows only values within, say, the top 10%. You enter the percent.

- **Limit to Best Fit.** Sizes the graphical elements to display the best looking distribution.

- **Collect Remainder into 'Other.'** Displays the remaining items as one graphical element.

Subtotals. For graphs representing a period of time, you can select when to subtotal the amounts. The subtotals are represented by the data points of the graph.

X Label, Y Label. You can specify your own labels for the X and Y axes by typing in these text boxes.

Keep Dialog Expanded. You can keep the Setting box expanded by clicking on the Keep Dialog Expanded box.

Copying a Graph

You can copy a graph to the Windows clipboard so you can use it in Windows documents. From the File menu on the Graphs window, choose Copy.

Memorizing a Graph Format

If you regularly use the same customizing options with the same graph types, you can "memorize" the format instead of selecting the options every time you draw a graph. In the future, you simply choose the memorized format.

1. Generate a graph and customize it by using the Options menu on the graph window.

2. From the File menu on the graph window, choose Memorize. The Save Memorized Graph box appears.

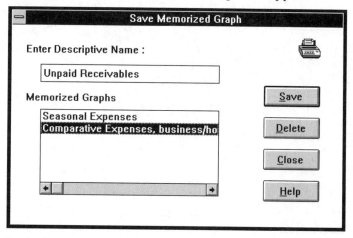

3. In the Enter Descriptive Name box, type a descriptive name for your graph. The Memorized Graphs box displays the graphs you have already memorized.

4. Choose Save. The graph format is memorized and you return to the graph window.

Using a Memorized Graph

To use a memorized graph:

1. Click on the Graphs button in the main window.
   -or-
   From the Tools menu, choose Draw Graphs. The Graph Generator box appears.

2. Choose Memorized Graphs. The Memorized Graphs list appears.

3. Choose a graph name from the list, then choose OK. The memorized graph is displayed.

Deleting a Memorized Graph

To delete a memorized graph, highlight the graph name in the Save Memorized Graph box and choose Delete.

The Scheduler

If you have recurring bills, you can have CA-Simply Money automatically prepare them and remind you to pay them at the same time each month. Transactions are prepared using the information you supply in the Schedule Actions box. You receive reminders from the Financial Advisor, explained later in this chapter. When you "act" on scheduled transactions, you can edit them.

Here are a few ways to use the Scheduler:

- Get reminders when scheduled transactions are due.

- Set up payment of standard monthly bills (rent, for example).

- Set up an insurance payment that is due every six months.

- Set up a payment in advance, so you won't forget to pay it.

- Set up routine deposits or account-to-account transfers.

- Write memos to yourself and have displayed at the time you want to see them. For example, if you are expecting a refund by a certain date, you can schedule it and then take appropriate action if you do not receive it.

Scheduling a Transaction

You can easily schedule transactions when you enter them by clicking the Schedule button in a transaction entry box such as the Checkbook.

1. Click on the Schedule button.

   -or-

   From the Tools menu, choose Schedule Actions. The Schedule Actions box appears.

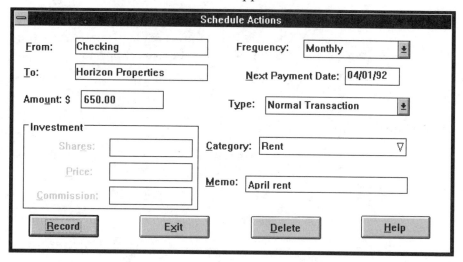

2. In the From box, enter the account to fund the payment.

3. In the To box, enter the payee to receive the payment.

4. In the Amount box, type the amount of the transaction.

5. Select from the Frequency box if the action occurs other than monthly.

6. In the Next Payment Date, specify the next date of a recurring payment or the date of a one-time payment.

   Note: The Calendar feature, explained later in this chapter, may help you select a date.

7. If you are scheduling an investment transaction , choose the transaction type from the Type box (buy shares, for example). The Schedule Actions box changes to "Account" instead of "From" and "Security" instead of "To."

If you are going to buy, sell, or change the number of shares, fill in the Investment box:

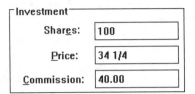

8. In the Category box, type the category for the transaction.

9. Type an optional memo.

10. Click on Record to schedule the transaction or memo. A blank Schedule Actions box appears.

11. Choose Home to return to the main window.

Scheduling a Memo

You can have the Scheduler remind you to do something, without processing a transaction.

1. Click on the Schedule button.

2. In the Memo box, type the message you want to schedule.

3. From the Type list, select Memo Only.

Performing a Scheduled Action

1. Choose Action Items from the Operations menu. The Action Items box appears, showing all the scheduled actions.

2. Click on any action item to see a short description. Double-click on the item, or click on the Act button, to open the dialog box for that action.

3. Complete the action.

Note: Skipping a recurring action removes it from both the Action Items list and the Scheduled Actions list in the Scheduler. Skipping a one-time scheduled item removes it from the Action Items list but leaves it in the Scheduled Action list to be reset or deleted.

Editing a Scheduled Action

To edit a scheduled transaction:

1. In the Schedule Actions box, use the scroll bar to find the scheduled transaction or memo you want to change.

2. Make the desired changes.

3. Click on Record.

Note: A scheduled action is either a deposit or a withdrawal, depending on the information you enter in the From and To boxes of the Schedule Actions box. Deposits occur when From is an income source and To is an account. Everything else is a withdrawal. The only way to change a withdrawal to a deposit, or a deposit to a withdrawal, is to delete the scheduled transaction and enter a new one.

Deleting a Scheduled Action

To delete a scheduled action:

1. Use the Schedule Actions box scroll bar to locate the transaction or memo you want to delete.

2. Click on Delete. The transaction is removed from the schedule.

Kiplinger's Financial Advisor

Kiplinger's Financial Advisor helps you manage your finances by monitoring your transactions and displaying helpful messages. The messages are of two types: Action Items and Advice Messages.

Action Items. The Financial Advisor keeps track of scheduled and post-dated transactions, and reminds you when you need to complete the transactions. It also warns you if a recurring transaction seems unusually large or small. For example, if your electric bill never exceeded $80 last year, but this month you recorded a payment for $923, you would see a message saying the amount seems excessive. This warning goes into an Action Items list that displays the check number and date.

Advice Messages. Kiplinger's Financial Advisor has dozens of useful tips relevant to your specific financial situation. For example, suppose you are paying large amounts of interest on your credit cards, yet you have a large amount of home equity. The Advisor suggests that you take out a home equity loan to pay off the credit card interest to realize significant savings.

After you review a piece of advice, the Advisor does not act again on that advice until the next session. Some Advisor warnings pop up infrequently; for instance, some reminders about your taxes appear only once a year.

The Advice button appears in the main window, the Register, the Checkbook, and in transaction windows. The Advisor performs different functions depending on where it is selected. For instance, clicking on the Advice button while in the Checkbook displays a list of advice specific to the current checking account, such as "Balance is in the red." The Advice button in the main window displays all current advice. The Action Items notice ("Scheduled, recurring, or due transactions") always appears if actions are pending, regardless of the current window.

Note: You can disable the Financial Advisor by selecting General Settings from the System menu. See *Optional System Settings* in Chapter 10.

Viewing and Deleting Advisor Messages

The Advisor signals you to read your messages by displaying a message on the window message line, and visibly animating the eyes on the Advice button. If you have Audio option turned on (see *Optional System Settings* in Chapter 10), a short tune plays. The Advice button eyes move until you look at the messages.

1. Click on the Advice button
   -or-
   From the Tools menu, choose Get Advice. The General
   Advice box appears.

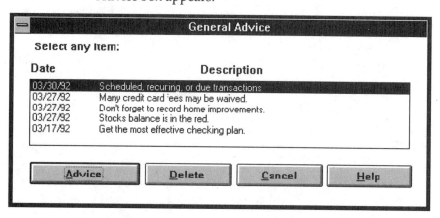

2. Highlight the message by clicking on it.

3. To get more information, click Advice. You can also
   double-click on the message for the same result.

   To delete the message, click Delete. This simply removes
   the message from the display. For example, if you have
   overdrawn an account, the problem does not go away until
   you deposit more funds. You cannot delete the Action
   Items warning "Scheduled, recurring, or due transactions."
   This item always appears at the top of the advice list.

4. To leave the Advice box, click Close.

Completing Transactions Using the Advisor

If the Advisor detects a situation that may require a transaction,
the Advice History box contains a line called "Scheduled,
recurring, or due transactions."

1. Follow the previous procedure to open the General Advice
   box.

2. Double-click on the "Scheduled, recurring, or due
   transactions" item. The Action Items box appears.

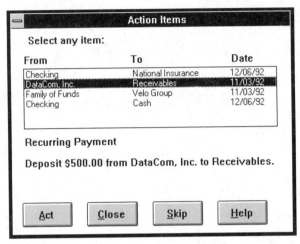

3. Highlight an item in the list. CA-Simply Money displays information about it underneath the list. You can choose to act on the item (Act button), skip it (Skip button), or ignore it.

Note: Skipping a recurring action removes it from both the Action Items list and the Scheduled Actions list in the Scheduler. Skipping a one-time scheduled item removes it from the Action Items list but leaves it in the Scheduled Action list to be reset or deleted.

4. To pay a scheduled or recurring bill, click on Act. The Record Transaction box appears. It contains the information you supplied when you scheduled the action in the Scheduler, or the information from the last payment made to a recurring payee.

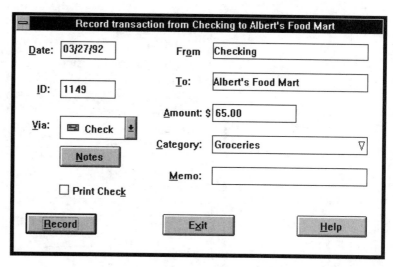

5. Make any changes required to the transaction information in the Record Transaction box, and choose Record.

6. When you have completed all your transactions, choose Close to return to the General Advice box.

Getting Advice

To receive advice from Kiplinger's Financial Advisor:

1. Click on the Advice button.

2. In the General Advice box, choose a description other than the Scheduled, recurring, or due transactions item, and click on Advice (or double-click on the message). A message box appears explaining the problem and offering one or more solutions.

Use the Advice message box the same way you use the online Help. For information on using Help, select Using Help from the Help menu.

Using Reminders

CA-Simply Money provides several reminder settings that let you control the Financial Advisor to some extent, and make sure your financial data is backed up when you exit. To set reminders:

1. From the System menu, choose Settings, then Reminders. The Reminder Settings box appears.

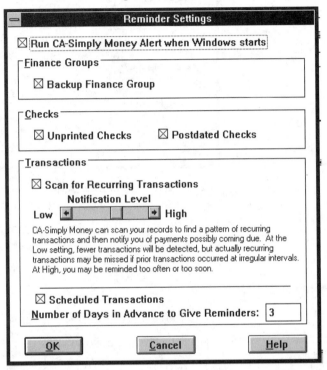

2. All reminders are on by default. Click to clear a reminder and turn it off. When you are finished, click OK. The reminders are:

Run CA-Simply Money Alert when Windows Starts. Alerts you to Action Items when you first open Windows, before you start CA-Simply Money. You can jump directly to CA-Simply Money to view the action items and act on them.

Backup Finance Group. Reminds you to back up your finance group to disk (in a location separate from the CA-Simply Money data files) each time you exit CA-Simply Money.

Support Tools

Unprinted Checks. Tells the Advisor to remind you that you have written but not printed checks. The message is removed from the Action Items list when you print checks.

Postdated Checks. Tells the Advisor to notify you that pending checks are postdated. The message is removed from the Action Items list when you print checks.

Scan for Recurring Transactions. Tells the Advisor to look for recurring transactions and notify you when they may be due. Each recurring transaction is removed from the Action Items list as you act on it or skip it.

Notification Level. Raises or lowers the number of transactions needed before the Advisor displays a recurring transaction message. Move the slider toward High if you want a high degree of sensitivity to catch any recurring transactions. Move the slider toward Low if you want only transactions that have occurred many times.

Scheduled Transactions. Tells the Advisor to list all scheduled transactions in the Action List and notify you when they are due. See *The Scheduler* earlier in this chapter.

Number of Days in Advance to Give Reminders. Lets you specify how much in advance you want the Advisor to alert you about scheduled transactions.

The Find Feature

The Find feature lets you search for transactions by using one or more of these selection criteria:

- Date ranges
- Specific accounts
- Specific Payees/Payors
- Memo text
- Dollar amounts
- Transfer methods
- Cleared transactions

The more explicit the selection, the fewer transactions you will have to wade through to find the desired transaction. CA-Simply Money selects only the transactions that meet all of the criteria.

Finding a Transaction

To find a transaction:

1. Click on the Find button
    -or-
    From the Tools menu, choose Find.
    -or-
    Drag the Find button to the button of the account you want to find a transaction in.

    The Find Transactions box appears.

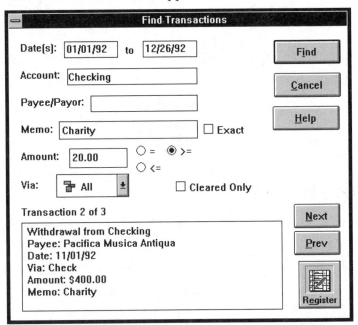

2. In the Find Transactions box, type or select the criteria you want to use to narrow your search:

    Date(s). Specify a range of dates or use the default range.

    Account. Specify an account.

Payee/Payor. Specify a payee, account, or income source.

Memo. Specify all or part of a memo in one or more transactions. To search for an entire memo exactly as you typed it, click on Exact.

Amount. Specify dollar amounts. Type an amount, then choose one of these operators:

= finds the exact amount.

<= finds any amount less than or equal to the amount.

>= finds any amount greater than or equal to the amount.

Via. Click the down arrow and select a transfer method.

Cleared Only. Specify only transactions that have cleared.

3. Choose Find to search for all transactions matching your criteria. Information for the first found transaction appears in the text box, and a message above it lists the number of transactions found.

4. To see other transactions, click on the Next and Prev buttons.

5. If you want to modify or delete the transaction, click on Register to go to the register entry of the currently displayed transaction.

The Calendar

CA-Simply Money makes it easy for you to consult a calendar and enter dates automatically into your transaction.

Inserting Today's Date

To insert today's date, click on any date in CA-Simply Money and press F3. Today's date is automatically entered in the field.

Inserting a Different Date

You can insert a calendar date into any CA-Simply Money date field.

1. Click on a date box and press F4. A calendar appears.

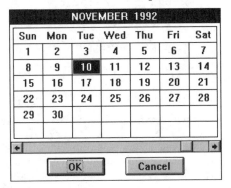

2. If you need to change the month or year, click on the scroll bar arrows.

3. Click on a date, then OK. The date is automatically inserted into the date field.

The Notes Feature

Use the Notes feature to record notes about a transaction. You can add, edit, or view notes in the Register, the Checkbook, and in many transaction dialog boxes. Notes are like memos, but they can be longer and are private. Notes do not appear on checks or reports. You can use notes to:

■ Document circumstances or conditions at the time of purchase, such as a salesclerk's name or other information.

■ Remind yourself what a payment was for.

■ Give reasons for unusually high or low payments (as in monthly utilities during unusual weather).

You can make a note any time during or after completion of a transaction. A note is "attached" to the transaction, just like other transaction information.

To view a note, select the transaction line and click on the Notes button.

Example: If you dispute a charge on a credit card bill, you can make a note that the payment does not include the amount of the disputed item and to look for credit on the next bill. You could also schedule a memo to remind you to check the bill when it arrives (see *Scheduling a Memo* earlier in this chapter).

Creating and Editing a Note

To create or edit a note:

1. In a Register or the Checkbook, click on a transaction line to begin a transaction or select a completed transaction.

2. At the bottom of the window, click on the Notes button. The Notes box appears. If a note has already been recorded with this transaction, it appears in the Note box. You can drag the edges of the box to a more readable width and height.

3. Type your note regarding the transaction, or make changes to the existing note.

4. Close the Notes window to make any further entries for this transaction.

5. Click Record to save the note with the transaction and return to the Register.

Note: If the Confirm Cancel option is turned on (see *Optional System Settings* in Chapter 10) when you close the note and leave the transaction without recording the note, CA-Simply Money asks if you want to save this entry and reiterates the transaction information. Choose OK to save the note.

Exporting and Importing Data

CA-Simply Money makes it easy to export transactions to these file types: QIF (**Q**uicken Interchange Format), MXF (CA-Simply **M**oney Exchange Format), and TXF (**T**ax Exchange Format). You can import from QIF, MXF, and BMF (BillPay USA Format).

QIF Files

Many financial software applications, including CA-Simply Money, support QIF for transferring data to other applications. QIF uses special characters to identify transactions in a text file.

Note: Some of the data you may have in CA-Simply Money cannot be transferred with QIF. Some mortgage information, program customization information, and stock price histories will be lost. Therefore, use QIF only for sending data to and from programs that accept only QIF. Use MXF whenever possible.

Exporting and importing with QIF files is useful for:

- Moving data to other financial programs.

- Adding transactions from Quicken or other programs.

MXF Files

MXF produces a text file containing all transaction information in CA-Simply Money. MXF exports everything except General Advice comments. Exporting and importing MXF text is useful for:

- Exporting finance groups between CA-Simply Money programs.

- Merging income from two or more finance groups.

- Merging portions of finance groups.

- Archiving data in a format you can read as text.

- Transferring transactions from one account to another. If you entered transactions in the wrong account, you could export them from the account and import them to the proper account.

TXF Files

The TXF file format is used by many tax programs. After you assign Tax Codes to your categories, and categorize your financial transactions, CA-Simply Money has most of the information needed for your tax returns. The TXF format exports this information to your tax software. See *Exporting to Tax Programs* later in this chapter.

BMF Files

BMF is the BillPay USA format. If you pay your bills electronically through Prodigy and BillPay USA, you can export a record of your payment transactions to a BMF file, then import the file to CA-Simply Money to update your accounts. See *Importing BillPay USA Records* later in this chapter.

Exporting Data in MXF or QIF Format

CA-Simply Money provides several options for exporting data. When exporting to QIF, you can include or exclude transactions, thus making it easy to work with specific data. This feature is not available in many financial programs. You can also filter transactions in either QIF or MXF by selecting a date range.

Another way to export data is to print a report to disk. See *Exporting a Report to Another Program* earlier in this chapter.

For exporting in TXF format, see *Exporting to Tax Programs* later in this chapter.

To export items:

1. From the File menu, choose Export. The Export Data box appears.

2. In the File Name box, type a name and (optional) extension for the exported data file, or use the Browse button. The Export CA-Simply Money Data box appears.

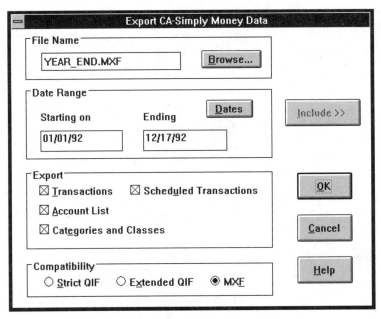

3. Type starting and ending dates for the transactions you want to export, or click the Dates button.

Note: You can also set a default date range for exporting by choosing the System menu, then Settings, then Reports and Graphs. For more information, see *Setting Default Dates* earlier in this chapter.

4. If you are exporting to a QIF file, click the Include button if you want to include or exclude incomes sources, accounts, payees, categories, or classifications.

5. Choose the appropriate options in the Export and Compatibility areas:

Setting Export Options

Transactions. Transactions are exported by default. Deselect this item only if you want to limit the export exclusively to one or more of the other export options.

Account List. Exports the account list. If you are exporting to QIF, you can export multiple accounts into one file.

Categories and Classes. Exports a list of categories and classes.

Scheduled Transactions. Exports all scheduled transactions.

Setting Compatibility Options

Strict QIF. Quicken-compatible format. This is most useful if you are importing data into a Quicken version earlier than 5.0. The export file contains no investment accounts and only one account from the include list.

To export to:	Select:
Quicken 4.0 or Windows	Strict QIF; transactions only.
Quicken 5.0	Strict QIF; any combinations.

Extended QIF. Useful for recent versions of Quicken. You can export an account list with multiple accounts using this format.

MXF. CA-Simply Money Exchange Format. Includes groups and icons; the most complete export/import option.

Completing the Export

6. Click on OK to export the file.

7. If any problems occur during the export, you can review messages about them after the export is complete. In MXF exports, these messages are duplicated as comments in the export to help you find and fix the problems. The Appendix in this guide lists the messages you may see and offers solutions.

Exporting to Tax Programs

Before you can export tax information, you need to use Tax Related categories. You also need to assign a Tax Code for each tax-related category (see *Using the Category Editor* in Chapter 6). The Tax Codes are grouped by tax form and listed alphabetically within each tax form.

To export information in TXF format:

1. From the File menu, choose Tax Export.

   The Tax Export box appears.

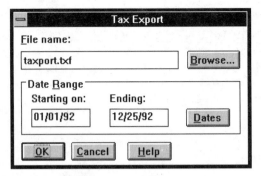

2. Type a file name or click the Browse button. Use the extension .TXF.

3. Type starting and ending dates, or click Dates.

4. Click OK.

Importing an MXF File

To import a MXF file:

1. Select Import from the File menu. The Import Browse dialog box appears.

2. Type or select a file name with an .MXF extension. The MXF Import dialog box appears.

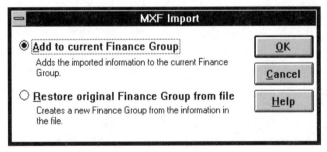

4. Choose Add to current Finance Group (the default) or Restore original Finance Group from file.

5. Click on OK to begin importing the file.

Handling MXF Import Problems   If a problem occurs when you import an MXF file, you can choose to view the error or warning message.

1. In the error and warning box, click Yes.

2. Click on a problem to see the code in the file that caused the message to appear.

3. Fix the problem by following the instructions for the specific message. The messages and suggested solutions are contained in the Appendix of this guide.

Importing a QIF File

To import a QIF file:

1. From the File menu, choose Import. The Import Browse box appears.

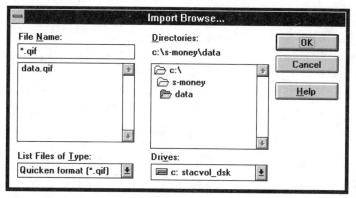

2. In the Import Browse box, type or select a filename with the .QIF extension.

3. Click OK. The Import from File box appears.

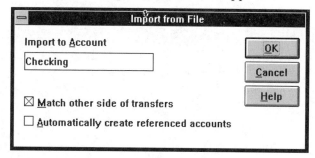

The options on the QIF Import box are:

Import to Account. Type the name of the CA-Simply Money account the imported transactions should go into, if the QIF file does not specify an account. (Quicken for Windows and Quicken version 4 do not specify accounts.) Normally you export Quicken transactions one account at a time. CA-Simply Money prompts you every time it encounters a possible account and/or new category. This allows you to control how accounts and categories are added to the finance group. See the following procedure, *Handling QIF Import Problems.*

Match other side of transfers. Select this option to eliminate duplicate transfer transactions between accounts. Duplicates may occur when you import multiple accounts with transfers to CA-Simply Money. If the file contains transfers, make sure you use the name of the account whose transactions you are importing in the Import to Account box. This ensures that transfers are imported correctly.

Automatically create referenced accounts. Select this option to create automatically any accounts referenced in the imported transactions. Use this option only to import checking account information. Do not use it for other account types.

4. Specify an account if necessary, and/or click to select the other options.

5. Click on OK to begin importing the file.

Handling QIF Import Problems

Imported data may include a category or account that is not used in the current finance group. When this happens, the Import box appears. It lets you to indicate whether an account or category should be created. You can also specify the category type, which may not exist in the QIF file.

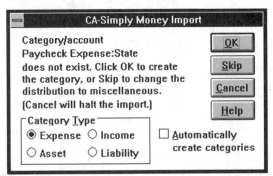

1. If you want to stop the import, click on the Cancel button.

   If you want CA-Simply Money to use the Miscellaneous category instead of creating a new one, click on the Skip button. Otherwise, if you want CA-Simply Money to create the account or category, go on to steps 2 through 4.

2. Select the category type: Expense, Income, Asset, or Liability.

3. If you do not want CA-Simply Money to prompt you if it encounters another unknown account or category, select Automatically create categories. The imported category name is used.

4. Click on OK to proceed with the import.

Merging Payees Imports from Quicken may produce several buttons for the same payee. You can merge them by using the Payee Merge feature; see *Grouping Buttons* in Chapter 6.

Importing BillPay USA Records

BillPay USA allows you to pay your bills electronically, without writing or printing checks at all. This service is available through Prodigy; see the Prodigy leaflet in your CA-Simply Money package for information about obtaining an account. BillPay USA keeps a record of all your payments, and this record can be imported to CA-Simply Money.

Note: If you use BillPay USA, be sure your credit card and mortgage are set up as payees rather than accounts.

To import from BillPay USA:

1. In BillPay USA, export your records. Your payment records go into a file called PAYMENT.BMF.

2. In CA-Simply Money, from the File menu, choose Import. The Import Browse box appears.

3. In the List Files of Type box, choose the BillPay USA format, .BMF. Select PAYMENT.BMF, then click OK. You get the Import from File box for BMF files.

4. In the Import to text box, type the name of the account the payments were made from.

Note: Specify Match other side of transfers to prevent recording payments twice. By default, BillPay USA exports your entire transaction history, so after the first import you import the older transactions again. You can specify a date range for the export, but checking for duplicated transactions is a useful caution.

5. Click OK. CA-Simply Money records the payments made through BillPay USA and adjusts your account balance.

Note: Your imported records include only transactions that have actually been completed, not necessarily all the payments you have just told BillPay USA to make. Completion is not immediate, but should take no more than a few days.

Importing Other Files

If you import a file that does not have an .MXF, .QIF or .BMF extension, CA-Simply Money chooses the most likely type of file by looking at the contents.

Merging Finance Groups

You may find it necessary to move transactions from one finance group to another. For example, you might decide that transactions involving auto maintenance should be in your business group instead of your personal group because you use the car for business. To move transactions between Finance Groups, use the Import and Export options.

1. Export the appropriate data to an MXF file.

2. Open the finance group to receive the transactions.

3. From the File menu, select Import. The Import Browse box appears.

4. Select the file you exported in step 1.

5. In the MXF Import box, choose whether to add the imported information to the open finance group or to restore the imported information as another finance group.

6. Click on OK to import the file.

Chapter 10
Other Options

Other Options

Chapter 10
Other Options

Several CA-Simply Money options help you protect your data and customize the screen.

Password. Protection for finance groups.

Backup. Daily backup, restore, and archiving functions.

Settings. Numerous settings to customize the operation of CA-Simply Money.

Button Arrangement. Selection of automatic or manual arrangement of finance buttons.

Color Schemes. Customization of the patterns and colors of the various CA-Simply Money displays.

Passwords

CA-Simply Money provides you with the ability to prevent casual snooping into your financial affairs. You can create a password that protects any or all of your finance groups. If you use CA-Simply Money at your job, you can assign security to your personal finances.

Please note that although the CA-Simply Money password is encrypted, it may not deter an experienced and determined snoop. Also, the password protects only the currently displayed financial group. If you want to protect more than one group, you must assign a password to each. You can use the same password for each group if you like.

Creating a Password

Caution! It is imperative that you make a written note of your password, and keep it in a safe place. If you forget your password, you will not be able to access your data.

To create a password:

1. From the System/Settings menu, choose Password. The Password box appears.

2. In the New Password box, type the password. An asterisk appears for each letter you type.

3. Choose OK. CA-Simply Money prompts you to type the password again, to make sure you typed it correctly.

4. Type the password and choose OK to record it.

    You will now be required to type the password each time you open the current finance group.

Correcting Password Errors

1. Try typing the password again. If you get the error message again, choose Cancel to return to the Password box.

2. Delete the asterisks in the New Password box and repeat steps 2 through 4 of the previous procedure.

Changing Your Password

To change your password, you type the current (original) password first, then the new password.

1. From the System/Settings menu, choose Password. The Password box appears.

2. In the Original Password box, type the current password. You will see only asterisks.

3. In the New Password box, type the new password, then choose OK.

4. Type the password again and choose OK.

Note: You can remove password protection by leaving the New Password box empty and choosing OK. When prompted to type the password again, leave the box empty and choose OK. This removes any password associated with the finance group.

Using Your Password

The next time you load the current finance group, a password box appears.

■ Type your password, then click on OK.

Backup

We strongly recommend that you back up your data on a regular basis. This will protect you in the event of a hard drive failure or other calamity. A good plan is to back up after each CA-Simply Money session to a set of diskettes that you rotate systematically. The built-in CA-Simply Money backup function makes it easy to back up, restore, and archive your data.

The Reminders feature has a default setting that reminds you to back up your finance groups each time you exit CA-Simply Money. You can turn this reminder message off at any time (see *Using Reminders* in Chapter 9).

Backing Up Data

When you back up your data , all information from a finance group is copied to a separate directory or disk. Backups can be made as often as you wish. Each new backup replaces the previous backup file. If something should happen to your original data, you can recover each finance group by using the Restore feature described in *Restoring Data*, later in this chapter.

Note: If you want to keep a copy of a finance group as of a certain date, use the Archive feature described in *Archiving Data*, later in this chapter.

To back up finance group data:

1. The first time you back up data, format a floppy disk and create a backup directory from the Windows File Manager. We recommend backing up to a floppy disk so that your data is protected if something happens to your hard disk.

2. Return to CA-Simply Money and choose Backup from the File menu. The Backup Finance Group box appears.

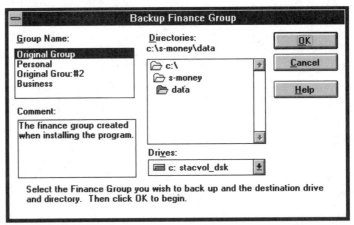

3. In the Group Name box, click on the group you want to back up.

4. In the Directories and Drivers areas, choose a path for the backup.

5. Choose OK. The Continue Backup box appears to ask if it's okay to back up the named finance group to the named directory. Choose OK.

6. If the data files already exist, CA-Simply Money asks if you want to overwrite the files or create a new finance group. Choose Overwrite Finance Group to overwrite.

7. When the backup is complete, the Backup box appears to tell you the backup is successful. Choose OK to return to the main window.

Restoring Data

The Restore feature lets you copy backup finance groups to the main CA-Simply Money data directory. You may need to restore your data if something happens to the disk containing the original data. You may also find Restore useful for transferring data into a new finance group.

Note: The Restore feature can only restore data that was backed up using the Backup feature. Make frequent backups. The data that you restore is only as recent as the date of the last backup.

Restoring to an Existing Finance Group

To restore data to an existing finance group:

1. From the File menu, choose Restore. The Restore Finance Group box appears.

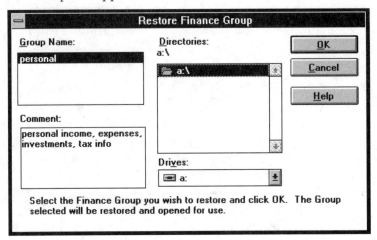

2. In the Group Name box, click on the name of the group you want to restore from backed up files.

3. In the Directories and Drivers Area, choose a path to restore from.

4. Click on OK. If the backup file you want to restore already exists, the Continue Restore box appears.

5. Make sure you have selected the right file to restore, then click on OK to continue. The Restore box appears.

6. Click on Overwrite Finance Group. The backup copy of your data will be copied over the current data in the specified finance group.

7. The Restore box appears when the operation is complete. Choose OK to return to the main window.

Restoring to a New Finance Group

You may find the Restore feature useful for creating a copy of an existing finance group. You could then use the new finance group for a different purpose. The Archiving feature can be used for the same purpose.

To restore data to a new finance group:

1. Follow steps 1 through 5 in the previous procedure.

2. In the Finance Group Options box, click on Create New Finance Group. The New Finance Group box appears.

3. Type a name for the new finance group. You can also type a comment to describe the new group.

4. Click on OK to continue. A new finance group will be created using the data from the backup copy you have chosen.

Archiving Data

Use the Archive feature to create an exact copy of your data as of a certain date. This is useful if you want to keep copies of your finances at different points in time. Archiving is different from a backup because you can have many different archived copies of the same finance group. With a backup, you only have the latest copy of your data. You can use Archive to:

- Close out your accounting for a year. Make the end date of the archive the last day of the year in question, then select Remove Transactions.

- Archive your current data at the end of each month. This gives you a "snapshot" of your finances at the time of the archive.

- Fix mistakes. If you find that you made a major error in the past, you could open an archived copy of the finance group from before the time of the error. Then you would only have to add the transactions which were added since that archive.

- Remove transactions from a finance group for a certain period of time.

Once you archive a file, it becomes just another finance group. You can open it, modify it, add transactions, and perform any other CA-Simply Money operations.

To archive a finance group:

1. From the File menu, choose Archive. The Archive of box appears.

Other Options

2. You can choose to archive a range of data by typing a date in the End Date box. The default is today's date. All transactions on or before the end date are archived.

3. Choose OK. CA-Simply Money creates a copy of the specified finance group in the \S-MONEY\DATA directory.

   The Archive box appears to tell you the Archive was successful.

4. Choose OK to return to the main window.

Renaming an Archived Group

An archived finance group retains the same name as the original group. You may want to rename either the original group or the archived group by using the File/Change Name command. See *Modifying a Finance Group* in Chapter 5. You can also use the Comment to distinguish archived groups. The comment for all archived files shows the date the archive was created.

Deleting an Archived Group

You can delete archived finance groups the same way you delete other finance groups, using the File/Delete command. See *Deleting a Finance Group* in Chapter 5.

Removing Transactions During an Archive

You can remove transactions from a finance group during an Archive procedure. This is useful at the end of the year for storing past transactions and continuing with only transactions from the beginning of the new year. By choosing Remove Transactions, you delete all transactions occurring on or before the End Date. Your archived copy contains all transactions; your current finance group contains transactions beginning at the End Date.

To delete transactions using Archive:

1. Follow steps 1 and 2 described in the previous procedure.

2. In the Archive of Finance Group box, click on the Remove Transactions box.

3. Choose OK to make an archive copy of the finance group and to delete the data from the original group.

Optional System Settings

The System menu option Settings provides many choices for making CA-Simply Money look and act as you wish.

Changing System Settings

To change system settings:

1. From the System/Settings menu, choose General. The General Settings box appears.

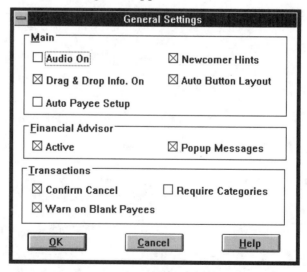

The CA-Simply Money settings are grouped into three categories: Main, Financial Advisor, and Transactions.

2. Choose any or all of the settings, then click on OK.

Main Settings	**Audio On**. Default ON. A beep sounds upon completion of every transaction, including setting up and modifying accounts, income sources, and payees. A brief tune plays when the Advisor has a message and when you delete transactions, buttons, and Financial Advisor messages.

Drag & Drop Info On. Default ON. Displays descriptive text in the Help line that is relative to the position of the mouse cursor over buttons or menu items.

Auto Payee Setup. Default OFF. When writing a check to a new payee, the Payee Setup-Add box appears. When you turn the option ON, a new payee is added without using the Add box. The payee button will be hidden.

Newcomer Hints. Default ON. Help text appears when you encounter significant program features. The help text provides information to aid in the proper use of the features.

Auto Button Layout. Default ON. Changes the order of main window buttons on the basis of most often used accounts. For more information, see *Button Arrangement*, later in this chapter.

Financial Advisor Settings	**Active**. Default ON. Advisor messages are accessible at any time by clicking on the Advisor button. When information is available, the Advisor icon animates to give you a visual indication that you have a message. When you turn this option OFF, the Advisor does not analyze your data and the icon does not animate.

Popup Messages. Default ON. Advisor messages will appear in popup boxes on your screen. Clicking on the popup box will close it.

Transaction Settings	**Confirm Cancel**. Default ON. If you attempt to exit from a modified transaction without choosing Record, you are prompted to save the changes. If Confirm Cancel is turned OFF, the transaction is canceled automatically.

Warn on Blank Payees. Default ON. Pops up a warning box if a payment transaction is entered with no payee.

Require Categories. Default OFF. This option can remind you to select a category when making a transactions. If you turn this option ON, the warning message appears when you record a transaction without providing a category.

Button Arrangement

When you create a new finance group, your first task is to create your income sources, accounts, and payees. By default, CA-Simply Money automatically arranges your finance buttons according to how often you use them for transactions, putting the most frequently used buttons at the top. You may not even notice the buttons have moved. The system setting for this feature is Auto Button Layout. When you turn off the Auto Button Layout option, you can rearrange your finance buttons in any order that you choose.

Rearranging Buttons

To manually rearrange buttons:

1. From the System menu, choose Settings/General. The General Settings box appears.

2. From the Main box, turn the Auto Button Layout option to OFF. Choose OK to return to the main window.

3. While holding down the Shift key, drag and drop a button into the desired position (you must place the button in an area currently occupied by another button). It is automatically repositioned.

   When buttons are not visible on the window, use the scroll bar to see the button you want to move. Hold down the Shift key and drag the button to the up or down arrow on the scroll bar. The buttons will begin to scroll. Drop the button in the desired position.

Background Patterns

CA-Simply Money gives you choices for the background colors and patterns of your main window, the Register, the

Other Options

Checkbook, and the check itself. You can even edit the patterns or design your own.

Selecting a Background Pattern

To select a background pattern:

1. From the System menu, choose Background Pattern. The Background Patterns box appears.

2. In the Apply to box, choose the area of CA-Simply Money you want to change—the Main Screen, Check Book, Check, or Register.

3. From the Select/Change box, click on a pattern. Use the scroll bar to view over 30 backgrounds.

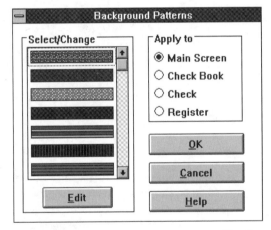

4. Choose OK. The pattern automatically changes in the area you selected.

Editing a Background Pattern

You can modify any of the patterns included in CA-Simply Money, or add your own.

To edit a pattern:

1. From the Select/Change box, click on a pattern to edit.

2. Choose Edit. The Edit Pattern box appears.

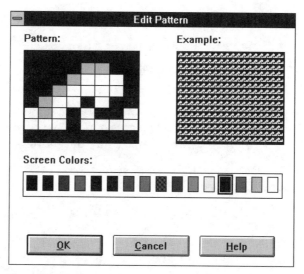

3. From the Screen Colors box, choose a color with which you want to work. Any of the 16 colors in this palette can be added to the pattern.

4. In the Pattern box, click on a square. The color of the square changes to the screen color you have selected. Each square you click on changes to the color selected in the Example box.

   The Pattern box represents a very small portion of the Example box. Notice that as you work on your design pattern, the Example box gradually changes to reflect your developing pattern.

5. Continue to select colors and add them to the pattern. Choose OK when you have completed your pattern design.

6. From the Background Patterns box, choose OK.

   The new pattern appears in the appropriate CA-Simply Money window area. This pattern remains in your gallery of patterns, whether you currently use it or not.

Changing Squares of Color

If you want to change all squares of one color to a different color, you can use the Pattern Select method:

To color multiple squares:

1. From the Screen Colors palette, choose a color.

2. Use the right mouse button to click on one square in the pattern.

   All of the squares of the same color as the square you clicked on are changed to the new color. If all the squares are the same color, the entire box changes color.

Adding a Background Pattern

A number of blank pattern boxes are available so you can create your own designs.

To add a new pattern:

■ Scroll through the Select/Change list and choose a blank box. Create your pattern as described in the previous procedures.

Appendix.

Appendix

Appendix

Table of Categories

This table shows the default expense categories provided in the Personal and Business finance groups. The "Both" type of finance group includes all categories.

Expense	Personal	Business
Advertising		•
Auto	•	•
Charity	•	•
Child Care	•	
Clothing	•	
Commissions		•
Dental	•	
Dining	•	
Entertainment	•	
Gifts	•	•
Groceries	•	
Home Repair	•	
Insurance	•	•
Auto	•	•
Interest	•	•
Invest Expns	•	
Leasing		•
Legal Fees		•
Medical	•	

continued...

...continued

Expense	Personal	Business
Misc. Expns	•	•
Office Expense		•
Property Tax	•	
Recreation	•	
Rent	•	•
Repairs		•
Service Chrg	•	•
Subscriptions	•	•
Travel	•	•
Utilities	•	•
Electricity	•	•
Gas	•	•
Sanitation	•	•
Telephone	•	•
Water	•	•

Online Help

CA-Simply Money Help is a convenient, quick way to look up information about features, functions, procedures, and commands. You will find Help buttons in nearly every dialog box and window in the CA-Simply Money program.

To display online Help:

1. Click Help on the menu bar.

```
                          Help
    Contents
    Keyboard
    Commands
    Procedures
    Using Help

    Windows Tutorial

    About CA-Simply Money...
```

2. Click the Help category you want. You will see either
    information about the category or a list of topics for the
    category.

    For further information on using Help, see the Windows
    User's Guide.

Ordering Supplies

You can save time by printing checks directly from
CA-Simply Money. Choose from a wide variety of custom
checks designed to work with CA-Simply Money. Ordering
your own personalized checks is as simple as making a phone
call to the CA-Simply Money toll-free number. You can also
print the order form and fax or mail it to the CA-Simply Money
store.

Using the Supplies Order Form

To use the supplies order form:

1. From the System menu, choose Order Supplies. The
    Supplies box appears.

2. Use the scroll bar to browse through the supply list.

3. When you have finished browsing the supply list, choose
    Exit from the Supplies File menu.

    If you order over the telephone, you will probably want to
    print the form and fill it in for your records. Use the
    supplies order form File menu to print the form, or print the
    form to a disk for export to a word processing program.

Printing the Supplies Order Form

To print the supplies order form:

■   From the Supplies box File menu, choose Print.

Exporting the Supplies Order Form

To export the supplies order form:

1. From the Supplies box File menu, choose Export. The Print Report to Disk box appears.

2. Follow the procedure *Exporting a Report to Another Program,* in Chapter 9.

Copying and Pasting

Copying and pasting is a technique for moving contents from one place to another in the Windows environment. You can move contents between CA-Simply Money and other Windows applications. The information moves through the Clipboard, a temporary storage space that understands information from all Windows programs. See your *Windows User's Guide* for further information.

Cut Command

Removes the selected text and places it on the clipboard.

Copy Command

Places a copy of the text on the Clipboard, leaving the original information unchanged.

Paste Command

Copies text from the Clipboard to the active window, inserting it at the Windows cursor.

Setting Up Your Printer

You must select a printer driver and a printer connection so that CA-Simply Money can send the correct printing instructions to the printer. The printer connection is the port on your computer where the printer cable is plugged into the computer.

Windows handles many details of setting up your software to print correctly. For more information on printers and printer setup, see your *Windows User's Guide*.

Choosing a Printer

To choose a Printer:

1. From the File menu, choose Printer Setup. The Printer Options box appears.

2. From the Printer list, choose the printer you want to use.

3. Click on the OK button to continue.

Note: The printer you choose must be the active Windows printer. If you want to change the active printer, you need to make the change in the Windows Control Panel. See your *Windows User's Guide* for further information.

Reconfiguring a Printer

The CA-Simply Money printer configuration is a convenient shortcut to the Windows printer configuration utility. You can change or add printers, change paper sizes, and more. See your *Windows User's Guide* for more information.

To reconfigure the printer:

1. From the File menu, choose Printer Setup. The Printer Options box appears.

2. Click on Setup. A Windows printer configuration box appears for the active printer.

3. Make the desired changes in printer configuration.

4. Click on OK to return to the Printer Options box.

Customizing Some Operations at Startup

By taking advantage of some features of the Windows Program Manager, you can do the following when you activate CA-Simply Money:

- open a specific finance group
- control some operations of the registers and the checkbook

RunTime Codes

To affect only the CA-Simply Money session you are about to start, use the Windows Run command. To affect every session, change the Program Manager command line. Either way, you enter the following codes:

-k This "keep position" switch affects the behavior of the Register button in the checkbook and in account transaction dialogs (paying a mortgage, adding to savings, and so on). When an existing transaction is active and you click on the Register button, CA-Simply Money opens the account register and goes directly to that transaction. Without this switch, the cursor goes to the end of the register.

-r This switch causes the Return key to record the current check in the checkbook. Otherwise, by default, the Return key moves the cursor to the next field.

-c This switch causes check printing on dot matrix printers to always be done in character mode. Otherwise, by default, printing is done in the best available mode.

"finance group" Opens the finance group whose name you specify. If the name is more than one word, surround it with double quotation marks.

If you have several finance groups, you can make each one appear with a separate CA-Simply Money icon in the Program Manager. This enables you to start CA-Simply Money with the finance group of your choice. See *Copying Icons* later in this section.

Using the Run Command

To affect only the CA-Simply Money session you are about to start, use the Run command.

1. Select Run from the File menu on the Windows Program Manager window. A dialog box appears.

2. Click on the Browse button. Another dialog box appears.

3. Select the directory containing the CA-Simply Money files (usually S-MONEY), then double click on CASMMAIN.EXE. The first dialog box reappears, with CASMMAIN.EXE and its path in the Command Line text box.

4. Type one or more of the codes (-k, -r, -c, "finance group"), leaving a space before and after them.

    Here are examples. The lowercase letters are the ones you type:

    C:\S-MONEY\CASMMAIN.EXE -k "my finances"
    C:\S-MONEY\CASMMAIN.EXE personal -c

5. Click on OK. CA-Simply Money starts.

Changing the Command Line

To affect every session of CA-Simply Money, change the command line in the Program Manager.

Note: If you want to assign icons to finance groups, follow the next procedure, *Copying Icons*, before doing this procedure.

1. In Program Manager, click once on the CA-Simply Money icon.

2. From the File menu, choose Properties. The Program Item Properties box appears.

3. At the end of the command line, add one or more of the codes (-k, -r, -c, "finance group"), leaving a space before and after them. For example, if you add a finance group named "original," the Properties box would look like this:

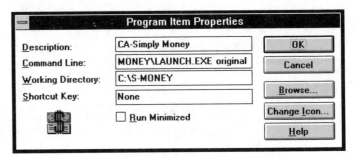

4. Click OK.

5. If you copied icons, repeat steps 1 - 4 for each icon.

Copying Icons

This procedure shows how to copy icons. After copying, follow the previous procedure, *Changing the Command Line*.

1. In Program Manager, click once on the CA-Simply Money icon.

2. From the File menu, choose Copy. The Copy Program Item box appears.

3. From the To group drop-down list box, select the program group you want the icon copied to (usually the group the icon is copied from).

4. Click OK, and follow the previous procedure, *Changing the Command Line*.

MXF Export and Import Messages

If a problem occurs when you export or import an MXF file, you can choose to view the error or warning message. This section explains the messages you may see and offers solutions. For exporting and importing procedures, see *Exporting and Importing Data* in Chapter 9.

MXF Export Messages

Category does not have a valid type. The category is not one of these valid types: income, expense, asset, liability, equity. Edit the MXF file to give the category a valid type.

Invalid date. A date is not correct. Edit the finance group, then export the data again. Or edit the MXF file.

Unknown reference type in field X. A field contains a reference to something that does not exist. Edit the finance group, then export the data again. Or edit the MXF file.

Reference in field X not found. A field contains a reference to something that does not exist. Edit the finance group, then export the data again. Or edit the MXF file.

Reference to nonexistent button. A field contains a reference to something that does not exist. Edit the finance group, then export the data again. Or edit the MXF file.

Database error - invalid ID ref. A field contains a reference to something that does not exist. Edit the finance group, then export the data again. Or edit the MXF file.

WARNING - INVALID <Field Name> <Value>. A field contains an invalid value. Restoring the MXF file will set the field back to a default value and fix the problem.

MXF Import Error Messages

Attempt to put numeric value X into non-numeric field. Non-numeric data is in an amount or number field. Edit the original finance group, then export the data again to create a new MXF file. Or edit the MXF file.

Badly formed category name X. A category name does not have the "grandparent\parent\child" format. Edit the original finance group, then export the data again to create a new MXF file. Or edit the MXF file.

Budget must be a value or list of values. The data for a budget field can only be a single amount or a list of amounts enclosed in parentheses. Edit the original finance group, then export the data again to create a new MXF file. Or edit the MXF file.

Button name must contain text. A button record in the MXF file has no name. Edit the original finance group, then export the data again to create a new MXF file. Or edit the MXF file.

Category creation failed for X. A database, memory, disk, or internal error prevented the creation of the given category. Close other applications, make sure you have enough disk space, and import again.

Database problem - X. A disk or database problem occurred, perhaps because of a full disk, disk problems, or internal errors. Close other applications, make sure you have enough disk space, and import again.

Name required for buttons. A button record in the MXF file has no name. Edit the original finance group, then export the data again to create a new MXF file. Or edit the MXF file.

Name required for securities. A security record in the MXF file has no name. Edit the original finance group, then export the data again to create a new MXF file. Or edit the MXF file.

Need type data for X reference. A reference to a category or button does not specify the type (expense, income, asset, liability, equity). Edit the original finance group, then export the data again to create a new MXF file. Or edit the MXF file.

Price history date information missing. A price history record has no date, which is required. Edit the original finance group, then export the data again to create a new MXF file. Or edit the MXF file.

Reference unknown. The button or category referred to in a transaction does not exist. This error may occur with an MXF file containing only transactions (no buttons or categories). You must import this type of MXF file into an existing finance group that contains all the necessary buttons and categories. Do not use it to restore a finance group from scratch.

Security name must contain text. A security record in the MXF file has no name. Edit the original finance group, then export the data again to create a new MXF file. Or edit the MXF file.

Surprising input (X) - expecting Y. A field has the wrong kind of data (for example, a string in an amount field). Edit the original finance group, then export the data again to create a new MXF file. Or edit the MXF file.

Syntax error. The file may not be in MXF format, or it may be badly damaged. Select another file format to import, or export the data again to create a new MXF file.

Type required for buttons. A button record has no type (expense, income, asset, liability, equity), which is required. Edit the original finance group, then export the data again to create a new MXF file. Or edit the MXF file.

Unresolved forward reference to button X. A category in the MXF file refers to a button that does not exist. This error may occur with an MXF file containing only transactions (no buttons or categories). You must import this type of MXF file into an existing finance group that contains all the necessary buttons and categories. Do not use it to restore a finance group from scratch. This error always occurs after the entire MXF file has been processed.

Record was not correctly imported to DB. Some information in the record was omitted. Check the last imported transaction carefully; it may not contain all the information that was exported.

MXF Import Warnings

Button X already exists - import data ignored. A button of the same name already exists in the Finance Group. Imported information about the button is ignored, and any imported transactions are applied to the button already in the Finance Group. If you want to import the button in the MXF file, either delete the button in the finance group or change its name before importing the MXF file.

Category X conflicts with an existing category of the same name. A category with the same full name ("grandparent\parent\child" format) and type already exists in the Finance Group. The imported category is ignored. If you want to import the category in the MXF file, either delete the category in the finance group or change its name before importing the MXF file.

Extra type information ignored. A reference contains more than one type (expense, income, asset, liability, equity). Only the first is used. The MXF file may be bad, so you might need to export the data again to create a new MXF file.

Memory running low. The importer is having problems allocating needed memory. Close other applications and try to import the file again.

Monthly budgets beyond the twelfth were ignored. Only 12 monthly budget amounts are imported; the extra amounts are ignored. The MXF file may be bad, so you might need to export the data again to create a new MXF file.

Security X already exists - import data ignored. A security of the same name already exists in the Finance Group. Imported information about the security is ignored, and any imported transactions are applied to the security already in the Finance Group. If you want to import the security in the MXF file, either delete the security in the finance group or change its name before importing the MXF file.

Some parent categories of X did not exist and were created. Defaults were used to create some categories. This should not happen with a properly constructed MXF file. The MXF file may be bad, so you might need to export the data again to create a new MXF file.

Excel Applications

CA-Simply Money for Windows supports Dynamic Data Exchange (DDE). CA-Simply Money acts as a server (providing information to) with other Windows applications.

CA-Simply Money needs to be running to service any application in Windows (but the client can always start CA-Simply Money if needed). The Excel sample starts CA-Simply Money from within Excel if it is not already loaded.

The following examples discuss how to request information into Microsoft Excel. However, any Windows application that supports DDE may access CA-Simply Money data. See the sample Excel worksheet and macro or other Windows application documentation for more information.

The sample Excel macros fill or read the sample worksheet starting from the top row on down as far as it needs to run. When viewing the sample worksheet, move horizontally across to view the different buttons provided to execute the macros.

The technical reference sections describe the actual macro DDE calls made from Excel to CA-Simply Money. These same calls may be used in any other Windows application's macro language that supports DDE.

- From Excel, open the file CASMXDDE.XLW. This loads the Excel worksheet CASMXDDE.XLS and the macro CASMXDDE.XLM.

Exporting Securities Information to Excel

There are four sets of information about securities that can be retrieved from CA-Simply Money into Excel (or any other DDE-compatible worksheet or database program).

- A list of individual securities.

- Updating prices for individual securities.

- A securities transaction report.

- A securities price history report.

List of Individual Securities

This provides a list of all individual securities in the current finance group. This is useful for the Update current market prices macro below. This list retrieves the security name, symbol, number of shares held, current market price and the current market value of each holding.

- Click on the Securities Report button in the sample worksheet to obtain a listing.

Technical Reference

Call these in the following order to retrieve information from the same record. You may call these repeatedly in this order for additional securities. If you only want the security name, just call it repeatedly.

```
Application Name=      "Dollars"
    Topic=             "Securities"
    Items=             Name, Symbol, Shares, Price
    channel=           INITIATE("Dollars","Securities")
    name=              REQUEST(channel,"Name")
    symbol=            REQUEST(channel,"Symbol")
    shares=            REQUEST(channel,"Shares")
    price=             REQUEST(channel,"Price")
```

Update Prices for Individual Securities

This automatically updates the current market price of each holding. However, the number of shares and the symbol are not updated.

1. First, use the List of Individual Securities macro or manually add the appropriate data into the worksheet.

2. Click on the Current Price button underneath the Securities Report button in the sample worksheet to obtain price updates.

Technical Reference

```
Application Name=      "Dollars"
    Topic=             "System"
    price=             REQUEST(channel,"GetPrice")
    channel=           INITIATE("Dollars","System")
    return success=    EXECUTE(channel,"GetPrice
                       ("&stockname&")")

                       pass in the stock name OR
                       symbol for the price you are
                       requesting.

                       the call may evaluate to:
                       GetPrice("SPUD").
    price=             REQUEST(channel,"GetPrice")
```

Call this immediately following the call above to retrieve the price from CA-Simply Money.

Repeat these last two calls to retrieve additional prices.

Securities Transaction Report

This report provides a list of all transactions within a specific date range. The list includes any securities transactions recorded in the currently open finance group within the specified date range. CA-Simply Money provides the transaction date, security name, type of securities transaction, symbol, number of shares, total cost (excluding commission,) commission and current price. The date range is optional.

■ Click on the Securities Transactions button on the sample worksheet to obtain this report.

Technical Reference

```
Application Name=      "Dollars"
    Topic=             "System"
    security table=    REQUEST(channel,
                       "GetNextSecurity")
    channel=           INITIATE("Dollars","System")
    return success=    EXECUTE(channel,
                       "GetNextSecurity("&startdate
                       &","&enddate&")")
```

Call this so that a comma-delimited table is prepared in CA-Simply Money.

Appendix

The call may evaluate to:

```
GetNextSecurity("01/01/92","02/01/92")
```

To leave out the date range, pass in blanks.

```
security table=    REQUEST(channel,
                   "GetNextSecurity")
```

Call this immediately following the call above to retrieve the table. The table returned may look like:

```
"01/01/92","Budweiser","Buy","SPUD","100",
"10000","10","100"
```

Call these last two calls repeatedly for additional tables.

Securities Price History Report This provides a price history of all securities within a certain date range in the currently open finance group. The report provides the reference data, security name, symbol, and price per share. The date range is optional.

- Click on the Securities Price History button to access price history within CA-Simply Money.

Technical Reference

```
Application Name=        "Dollars"

  Topic=                 "System"

  history table=         REQUEST(channel,
                         "GetNextSecHistory")

  channel=               INITIATE("Dollars","System")

  return success=        EXECUTE(channel,
                         "GetNextSecHistory
                         ("&startdate&","&enddate&")")
```

Call this so that a comma-delimited table is prepared in CA-Simply Money.

The call may evaluate to:

```
GetNextSecHistory("01/01/92","02/01/92")
```

Pass in blanks if you do not want to specify a date range.

```
history table=         REQUEST(channel,
                       "GetNextSecHistory")
```

Call this immediately following the call above to retrieve the table. The table returned may look like:

```
"01/01/92","Budweiser","Buy","SPUD","100"
```

Call these last two calls repeatedly for additional tables.

Exporting Transaction Information to Excel

You can export three sets of transaction information from CA-Simply Money into Excel:

- A transaction report.

- A transaction summary.

- The amounts of unique transactions.

Transaction Report

This provides a transaction report within a specified date range from the currently open finance group. The date range is optional. The transaction report provides the transaction date, payee name, payor name and transaction amount

- Click on the Transaction Report button on the sample Excel worksheet.

Technical Reference

```
Application Name=        "Dollars"
    Topic=               "System"
    Transaction Table=   REQUEST(channel,
                         "GetNextTran")
    channel=             INITIATE("Dollars","System")
return success=          EXECUTE(channel,"GetNextTran
                         ("&startdate&","&enddate&",
                         "FALSE")")
```

Call this so that a comma-delimited table is prepared in CA-Simply Money.

Start date and end date is the date range specified. You will retrieve all records if these are blank.

FALSE indicates that you are retrieving just unique transactions, but want all transactions in the date range. See Listing of Unique Transactions for an example using TRUE.

```
transaction table=    REQUEST(channel,"GetNextTran")
```

Call this immediately following the call above to retrieve the table. The table returned may look like:

```
"01/01/92","PG&E","Checking","50.00"
```

Call these last two calls repeatedly for additional tables.

Transaction Summary

This provides a list of unique transactions. This macro is for use with the Amounts for Unique Transactions macro. A unique transaction is a transaction with the same payee name and payor name. The list provides a start date, end date, payee name and payor name. The start date is the first transaction date for the unique transaction and the end date is the last recorded transaction.

- Click on the Transaction Summary button on the sample Excel worksheet.

Technical Reference

```
Application Name=         "Dollars"

    Topic=               "System"

    Transaction Table=   REQUEST(channel,
                         "GetNextTran")

    channel=             INITIATE("Dollars",
                         "System")

return success=          EXECUTE(channel,
                         "GetNextTran("&startdate&",
                         "&enddate&","TRUE")")
```

Call this so that a comma-delimited table is prepared in CA-Simply Money.

Start date and end date is the date range specified. You will retrieve all unique records if these are blank.

TRUE indicates that you are retrieving just unique transactions, not all transactions in the date range. See Transaction Report for an example using FALSE.

```
transaction table=      REQUEST(channel,"GetNextTran")
```

Call this immediately following the call above to retrieve the table. The table returned may look like:

```
"01/01/92","PG&E","Checking","50.00"
```

Call these last two calls repeatedly for additional tables.

Amounts for Unique Transactions

This provides transaction amounts for each unique transaction. The amount represents all transaction amounts recorded between the start date and end date for the payee name and payor name.

1. First, use the Transaction Summary macro or manually add the appropriate data into the worksheet. If you type the data manually, you must add the payee name and, optionally, any or all of the following: start date, end date, and payor name.

2. Click on the Amount button underneath the Transaction Summary button on the sample Excel worksheet.

Technical Reference

```
Application Name=        "Dollars"
    Topic=               "System"
    amount=              REQUEST(channel,"GetSum")
    channel=             INITIATE("Dollars","System")
return success=          EXECUTE(channel,"GetSum
                         ("&startdate&","&enddate&",
                         "&payeename&","&payorname&")")
```

Call this to request an amount from CA-Simply Money.

The EXECUTE may evaluate to the following:

```
GetSum("01/01/92","02/01/92","PG&E","Checking")
amount=     REQUEST(channel,"GetSum")
```

Call this immediately following the call above to retrieve the amount.

Call these last two calls repeatedly for additional amounts.

Categories

There are two ways to view categories:

- A category list.

- A category balance.

Looking at a List of Categories

This provides a list of all categories within a specified date range in the currently open finance group. This list includes the category name, whether or not it is a taxable category, and the category balance. The date range is optional. The list defaults to providing all categories within the date range. Use the zero suppression flag to only get those categories with non-zero balances.

- Click on the Category Report button on the sample worksheet. Set the zero-suppression flag to TRUE if you want to suppress reporting on categories with zero balances. The flag is located underneath the Category Report button on the sample worksheet.

Technical Reference

```
Application Name=        "Dollars"

    Topic=               "System"

    category Table=      REQUEST(channel,"GetNextCat")

    channel=             INITIATE("Dollars","System")

return success=          EXECUTE(channel,"GetNextCat
                         ("&startdate&","&enddate&",
                         "TRUE")")
```

Call this so that a comma-delimited table is prepared in CA-Simply Money.

The EXECUTE may evaluate to the following:

```
GetNextCat("01/01/92","02/01/92","TRUE")
```

TRUE indicates that you would only like category tables with non-zero balances. Use FALSE if you would like all categories.

```
category table=  REQUEST(channel,"GetNextCat")
```

Call this immediately following the call above to retrieve the amount. The table returned may look like:

```
"Utilities","Expense","Y","50.00"
```

"Y" indicates that this category is considered taxable.

Call these last two calls repeatedly for additional tables.

Looking at Category Balances

This provides a category balance for the categories for any distribution amounts within the specified date range.

1. First, use the Category List macro or manually add the appropriate data into the worksheet. If you type the data manually, you must add the category name and optionally any or all of the following: start date, end date, and category type.

2. Click on the Balance button underneath the Category Report button on the sample worksheet.

Technical Reference

```
Application Name=      "Dollars"

Topic=                 "System"

amount=                REQUEST(channel,"GetCatSum")

channel=               INITIATE("Dollars","System")
                       EXECUTE(channel,"GetCatSum
                       ("&startdate&","&enddate&",
                       "categorytype","&categoryname&")")
```

Call to request an amount from CA-Simply Money.

The EXECUTE may evaluate to the following:

```
GetCatSum("01/01/92","02/01/92","Expense",
"Utilities")
```

```
amount= REQUEST(channel,"GetCatSum")
```

Call this immediately following the call above to retrieve the amount.

Call these last two calls repeatedly for additional amounts.

Glossary

account A place where you hold your money. In CA-Simply Money, accounts are the records of each way you transfer funds. They can include checking accounts, credit cards, investments, and more.

accrual basis accounting A method of keeping books where revenue is recognized when realized and expenses are recognized when incurred, without regard to the time of receipt or payment.

adjustment *See* balance adjustment.

annual yield The amount of money you make in a year on an investment.

asset A non-monetary item you own (such as a coin collection, a car, or a computer) that has real value.

balance adjustment An amount automatically added during account reconciliation by CA-Simply Money if you choose to make an adjustment to an unbalanced account. Balance adjustment is a special.

balance sheet A listing of total assets, liabilities, and equity designed to give an overall picture of the health of a company.

bank balance The amount of money the bank says you have. It is determined by the amounts of cleared transactions, and is different from the *current balance*, which is your up-to-date record that may contain deposits, checks, and other transactions that have not cleared the bank. Also known as a statement balance.

bond An investment in the form of a loan to a government or corporation. Usually represented by a certificate which details the terms of the loan.

book value The purchase price of securities (net of commissions) plus the cash balance in an investment account.

brokerage account A CA-Simply Money account that represents the account your broker uses for you. As you receive your statements, you can copy the transactions into CA-Simply Money.

Browser box A feature of CA-Simply Money that helps you enter information in a field without having to type it each time. Typing one or more letters in certain boxes produces a pop-up browser box which contains a list of related buttons, categories, or classifications.

budget Simply a plan of how much you intend to spend in various categories throughout the year.

capital gains distribution The part of a payment received from a mutual fund which is the result of realized profits from the sale of securities. For tax-reporting purposes, these are technically not income.

cash basis accounting A method of keeping books where revenue is recognized when cash is received and expenses are recorded when they are paid in cash.

category A method of organizing and tracking income and expenditures. CA-Simply Money provides a list of common categories you can use and modify. You can also create your own categories. *See also* classification.

classification Used to group related distributions. You might use the classification to assign a client code to track expenditures for specific clients across categories. *See also* category.

cleared balance The balance of your account excluding the credits and debits that have not yet cleared (have been transacted between the time your statement was prepared and now).

compounding When the calculation of interest occurs more than once per year. The interest rate is divided by the period (for example, monthly). Then the periodic interest rate is multiplied by the principal at the end of each period and the resulting interest is added to the principal. Subsequent calculations include the previously added interest as well as the principal; the result is the effective interest rate, which is higher than the annual rate.

cost basis The total money spent on a stock including the actual price paid, commissions, and other expenses.

costing methods Refers to tracking capital gains/losses of your investments. CA-Simply Money assumes that the oldest shares of a stock are sold first.

current balance The actual amount of money you have available in an account. This is different from the *bank balance*, which is the bank's total of cleared transactions.

distribution The assignment of transaction amounts to one or more categories.

dividend A sum paid, usually quarterly, to the owner of a security to return some of the company's profit to the investor.

Drag & Drop A feature of CA-Simply Money that makes it easy to accomplish all your financial activities. Drag a button over another then release it, to perform an action.

Dynamic Data Exchange (DDE) A method that Windows applications use to exchange information.

effective rates The interest rates based on compounding interest. *See also* compounding.

equity The money value of a property you own minus the amount you owe on it.

expense Anything you spend money on.

Export Move data from CA-Simply Money to other programs.

finance group A collection of financial income and outflows.

Financial Advisor A special feature of CA-Simply Money that reminds you of regularly-scheduled events, tells you when payments seem unusually high, and offers valuable, money-saving tips. Transactions that you make trigger advice tailored to your particular situation.

first-in, first-out method The method that CA-Simply Money uses to track capital gains/losses of your investments, based on the assumption that the oldest shares are sold first. *See also* costing method.

Import Bring data from other programs into CA-Simply Money.

income source Places where you obtain (earn) money.

investment account One or more securities that you want to track as a group. Also called a portfolio.

IRA *See* tax-free accounts.

Keogh *See* tax-free accounts.

liability Something for which you owe money. The principal on a mortgage is one example of a liability.

load The commission added into the price of some mutual funds.

lot grouping Tracking individual groups (lots) of stocks to balance gains and losses between lots during a year. In CA-Simply Money you do this by assigning slightly different names to each lot of a particular security.

money market accounts A type of mutual fund which invests only in short term loans to companies or governments.

mutual funds A group of stocks, bonds, and other securities purchased by a professional management company and sold as shares to individual investors.

net worth The sum of all your assets minus the sum of your liabilities.

Newcomer Hints A feature of CA-Simply Money that displays helpful instructions on the screen when you use a feature for the first time. You can turn Newcomer Hints on or off from the Settings box.

nominal rates Interest rates that do not take compounding into account.

paid-in equity The amount of your real property (such as your house) that you have paid for. Every payment on your mortgage increases your paid-in equity.

payable An item you owe. A term usually reserved for business accounts. *See also* receivable.

payee A person or company to whom you owe money.

Payee Summary An information box which allows you to see instantly all the pertinent information about a payee. To view, click on the payee's button.

payroll An account used for recording payments to employees and for accruals of income tax and social security deposits.

performance The yearly percentage profit or loss per share of a security.

portfolios *See* Investment account.

principal In a loan, the actual amount you borrowed or the amount you have left to pay off.

profit The percentage increase (or decrease) in the value of a share of stock. *See also* performance.

receivable Money that comes to you. A term usually reserved for business accounts. *See also* payable.

reconcile To compare your records with those of your bank. Usually you do this by checking your monthly bank statement against your check register. CA-Simply Money streamlines this process. With CA-Simply Money, you may also reconcile your credit cards.

reinvestments Some securities, particularly mutual funds, pay you dividends, interest income, and capital gains with additional shares instead of cash.

Reminders A CA-Simply Money feature which lets you schedule your transactions to make sure you don't miss important dates like a mortgage payment or a CD coming to term.

Scheduler A CA-Simply Money feature that helps you track your regular payments and other transactions.

security Any investment which has a value that is expressed in shares.

SEP-IRA *See* tax-free accounts.

short sell When you sell shares of stock you do not actually own, but plan to buy later in hopes that the buying price will be lower.

Special Some transactions require transferring funds but don't warrant setting up a payee button. These situations are listed in the special Browser box, and you can designate a special when you record transactions in the Register. Some examples are balance adjustments, deposits, and service charges.

split Dividing a transaction amount into two or more categories.

statement balance *See* bank balance.

stock Shares of stock represent shared ownership of a corporation by investors.

stock split When the market price of a company's stock reaches an inconvenient trading range, the company may reduce the price of their shares by a percentage and issue compensatory shares to maintain investors' equity.

tax-free accounts Some income from investment accounts such as Keogh, IRA, SEP-IRA, 401(k) plan, and other retirement accounts may be tax-free. Consult your tax advisor for more information.

Tool Rack The row of buttons at the bottom of the main window in CA-Simply Money.

unrealized equity The value of your real property minus the amount you owe on the property. Improvements made on property (such as your house) that are not yet paid for will increase your unrealized equity.

Welcome A step-by-step introduction to CA-Simply Money that illustrates the available features and allows you to start a finance group. The Welcome appears the first time you run CA-Simply Money.

Glossary

Index

Index

Index

M

Make Groups box, 6–58
Margin
    account, 7–5
    interest, 7–8, 7–23
Memo
    line in register, 6–12
    scheduling, 9–42
Memorized
    graphs, 9–39
    reports, 9–27
Memory requirements, 2–3
Merge
    Category box, 6–53
    Payees box, 6–59
Merging
    categories, 6–53
    finance groups, 9–62
    payee buttons, 6–59
Miscellaneous reports, 9–20
Missing & Duplicated Checks report, 9–16
Modem
    setup, 7–33
    stock price updates, 7–31
    updating security prices, 7–16
Modify
    Category box, 6–51
Modifying
    button groups, 6–59
    buttons, 5–19
    categories, 6–51
Money market accounts, 7–4
    definition of, GL–3
Monthly Budget box, 6–61, 6–65
Mortgage accounts, advantages of, 5–12
Mortgage Payment box, 6–37
Mortgages, 6–36
    account setup, 5–14
    accounts, 5–12
    editing transactions, 6–39
    increasing equity, 6–39
    paying, 6–37
    recording home improvements, 6–39
    recording other costs, 6–39
Move Category box, 6–52

Multiple invoices
    recording payments on, 8–18
Mutual funds, 7–24
    definition of, GL–4
    reinvesting, 7–25
    setting up, 7–5
MXF files, 9–54
    errors exporting, APP–10
    errors importing, APP–11, APP–13
    exporting, 9–55, 9–62
    importing, 9–58, 9–62

N

Net Income Less Expense Trend graph, 9–31
Net worth
    and mortgages, 5–12
    definition of, 1–7, GL–4
Net Worth report, 9–17
New
    Finance Group box, 5–4, 10–9
    Security box, 7–15
Newcomer Hints, 3–9, 10–12
    definition of, GL–4
    turning off, 3–10, 10–11
Nominal rates, definition of, GL–4
Notes, 9–52
    box, 9–53
    editing, 9–53

O

One-time payees, 6–12
Online Help, APP–4
Opening Finance Group, 5–5
Operations box, 7–11, 7–12, 7–15, 7–18, 7–20, 7–21
Operations menu
    Action Items, 9–42
    Make Group, 6–58
    Modify Group, 6–59
    Pay Expenses, 6–16
    Sell, 7–25
    Transfer Funds, 6–16
Options

Index

S

Index

Kiplinger's™
CA-Simply Money™

For Microsoft Windows

Quick Reference

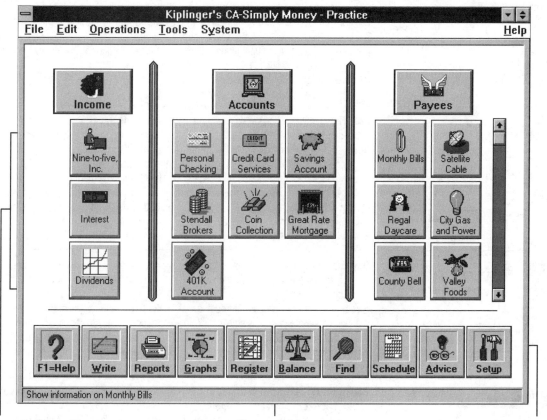

Finance Group Buttons   **Message Line**   **Tool Rack**

Dragging and Dropping

Drag one button over another and release it to perform a transaction. For example, to see transactions in your checking account, drag the Register button to the checking button, then release it. (Or drag the checking button to the Register button.)

If a drag and drop action cannot take place, a circle with a line through it appears:

The Menus

The menus let you perform the following tasks. (The Tool menu, not shown, does the same things as the Tool buttons described on page 8.)

New - Create a new finance group.

Open - Access another finance group.

Delete - Remove a finance group that is not currently active.

Change Name - Change the name of a finance group or the comment about it.

Backup - Make a backup of a finance group.

Restore - Bring a backed up finance group into CA-Simply Money.

Archive - Create a copy of your data as of a certain date.

Import - Bring in MXF, QIF, or BMF data.

Export - Save data in MXF or QIF format to use with another product.

Tax Export - Save data in TXF format to use with tax preparation software.

Printer Setup - Access the Windows printer setup feature.

Exit - End the current CA-Simply Money session.

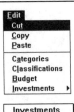

Cut - Remove a selected word or amount and put it in the Windows clipboard.

Copy - Put a copy of the selected word or amount into the Windows clipboard.

Paste - Place the contents of the Windows clipboard at the current cursor location.

Categories - Modify categories.

Classifications - Modify classifications.

Budget - Make a budget.

Investments Securities - Change information about a security (name, symbol, price, etc.).

Investments Types - Add to or change the kinds of investments you have (stock, mutual fund, CD, etc.).

Investments Goals - Add to or change your investment goals (high risk, growth, income, etc.).

Pay Expenses - Make payments on an account (same as single click on an account button).

Record Income - Add income through an income source (same as single click on an income button).

Transfer Funds - Move money from one account to another.

Action Items - See a list of pending tasks.

Modem Stock Update - Update stock prices through Compuserve.

Make Group - Group income sources, accounts, or payees to automate tasks or see summary reports or graphs.

Modify Group - Change the members of a group.

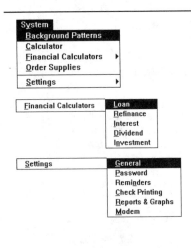

Background Patterns - Select patterns for the background of the main screen, check screen, check, and/or registers.

Calculator - Display a calculator.

Financial Calculators Loan - Determine an affordable loan size or payment amount.

Financial Calculators Refinance - See when you will break even after refinancing your mortgage.

Financial Calculators Interest - Convert nominal interest rate to effective (annual) rate.

Financial Calculators Dividend - Translate dividends into annual yield.

Financial Calculators Investment - Calculate amounts to invest.

Order Supplies - See information about ordering checks.

Settings General - Control settings for audio, button layout, financial advisor, newcomer hints, confirmation messages, and more.

Settings Password - Enter or change a password for the current finance group.

Settings Reminders - Control reminder messages.

Settings Check Printing - Specify date format and other options for checks.

Settings Reports & Graphs - Specify ranges of dates, or turn color on or off for reports and graphs.

Settings Modem - Set up communications information.

Procedures for Basic Tasks

Creating a New Finance Group

1. Select New from the File menu.
2. Type a descriptive name for the finance group. If you wish, add a comment.
3. Click on OK.
4. Select the type of finance group you want by clicking on Personal, Business, or Both.

Opening a Finance Group

1. Select Open from the File menu.
2. Click on a finance group name.
3. Click on OK.

Setting up Income Sources, Accounts, and Payees

1. Gather all paperwork (pay stubs, checkbook, statements).
2. Drag the Income, Accounts, or Payees button down to the Setup button, then release the mouse button.
3. Click on whichever of these buttons is on your screen: Add Income Source, Add an Account, Add a Payee.
4. Type the name of an income source, account, or payee.
5. Select the type of income, account, or payee:
   - click the down arrow near Type
   - click on one of the types listed
6. Add an address, telephone number, contact person, and/or account number:
   - click on the Address button
   - type the information in the spaces provided
   - click OK
7. If desired, change the icon:
   - click on the icons button
   - locate the icon you want
   - click on the icon of your choice
   - click OK
8. If desired, check the box next to Hidden Button.
9. If you are adding a tax free account such as an IRA, 401(k), or annuity, check the box next to Tax-free Account.
10. Click on OK.
11. If you are adding an account, fill in the starting amounts CA-Simply Money asks for.
12. Click on OK.

Preparing Checks For Printing

The checkbook register is updated automatically when you prepare checks for printing.

1. Drag the checking account button down to the Write button, then drop it.
2. Type any letter on the Pay to the Order of line, then choose a payee by either:
   - Clicking on a payee, then on the OK button.
   - Typing a name, then clicking on the New button. (You are then prompted to add the new payee.)
3. Enter an amount. Type a memo if you wish.
4. If desired, enter a category. (See "Assigning One Category" or "Assigning Several Categories (Making a Distribution).")
5. Click on the Record button.
6. Prepare as many checks as needed. Print them now or later by clicking on the Print button and then on OK.
7. Click Home to return to the main screen.

Recording Checks in the Checkbook Register

1. Drag the checking account button down to the Register button, then drop it.
2. Type a letter, then choose a payee by either:
   - Clicking on a payee, then on the OK button.
   - Typing a name, then clicking on the New button. (You are then prompted to add the new payee.)
3. Enter an amount.
4. If desired, enter a category. (See "Assigning One Category" or "Assigning Several Categories (Making a Distribution).")
5. If necessary, change the date (See "Entering Dates").
6. If you are going to print a check with CA-Simply Money, type a "p" in the Via column.

   If you are recording a check you wrote, type the check number in the Via column.
7. Click on the Record button.
8. Click on the Home button.

Procedures for Basic Tasks (continued)

Printing Checks

1. If necessary, change printing options: from the System menu select Settings, then Check Printing.

2. Drag the checking account button down to the Write button, then drop it.

3. If necessary, write some checks.

4. Click on the Print button.

5. Click on OK.

Paying a Mortgage or Credit Line

By updating the mortgage or credit line account, you also automatically enter the information in the check register, and prepare a check for printing.

1. Click once on the button for the account.

2. Click on whichever of these buttons appears: Pay Mortgage or Pay Bill.

3. If you amortized your mortgage, change (if necessary) any amount in the Amortized Payment box, then click on OK.

4. Enter principal and interest.

5. Type a letter in the space labeled From Account or Income Source.

6. If necessary, click the button next to Income, Accounts or Special in the Account browser.

7. Indicate the income source or account by either:

   - Clicking on an income source or account, then clicking on the OK button.

   - Typing a name, then clicking on the New button. (You are then prompted to add the new income source or account.)

8. Click on the Record button.

9. Click on the button next to either of these: Prepare Check for Printing, Just Record Transaction.

10. Click on OK.

Transferring Funds Between Accounts

1. Drag the button for one account to the button for the other account, then drop it.

2. Type an amount.

3. If necessary, click the down arrow near Transfer Via, then click on the method of transfer: Cash, ATM, Wire, or Direct.

4. Click on the Transfer button.

Depositing Money in an Account

1. Drag the account button down to the Register button, then drop it.

2. Type a letter.

3. Click the button next to Special, then either:

   - Click on a type of deposit, then on the OK button.

   - Type a method of deposit that is not on the list, then click on the New button.

4. Type an amount in the Deposit column.

5. If desired, enter a category. (See "Assigning One Category" or "Assigning Several Categories (Making a Distribution).")

6. If necessary, click the down arrow near Transfer Via, then click on the method of transfer: Cash, ATM, Wire, or Direct.

7. Click on Record.

Depositing Your Paycheck

1. Drag your paycheck button to an account button, then drop it.

2. Record gross income and deductions. (To record extra deductions such as health insurance, click on the Distribution button, then enter amounts.)

3. If necessary, click the down arrow near Via, then click on the method of transfer: Cash, ATM, Wire, or Direct.

4. Click on the Record button.

Withdrawing Money from an Account

1. Drag the account button down to the Register button, then drop it.

2. Type a letter.

3. Click the button next to Special, then either:

   - Click on Withdrawal, then on the OK button.

   - Type a method of withdrawal that is not on the list, then click on the New button.

4. Type an amount in the Payment column.

5. If desired, enter a category. (See "Assigning One Category" or "Assigning Several Categories (Making a Distribution).")

6. If necessary, click the down arrow near Transfer Via, then click on the method of transfer: Cash, ATM, Wire, or Direct.

7. Click on Record.

ssigning One Category

tegories let you track your finances by grouping similar nsactions for budgets, reports, and graphs. Sample categories utilities, dental, and clothing. You assign categories while cording income, updating accounts, or writing checks.

Drag an account button down to the Register button, then drop it.

Type a letter on the category line (the line with the small arrowhead).

If necessary, click the button next to Expense, Asset, Income, or Liability on the browser.

Indicate the category by either:

- Clicking on a category in the list, then on OK.

- Typing a new category, then clicking on the New button. Enter a description for the category, and indicate whether it is tax related. Click on OK.

ssigning Several Categories (Making a stribution)

tribute the amount to more than one category if, for example, a is for clothing and food.

Drag the checking account button down to the Write or Register button, then drop it.

Enter a payee, then the amount of a bill.

Click on the small arrowhead on the category line.

Type a letter in the Category column.

If necessary, click the button next to Expense, Asset, Income, or Liability on the browser.

Indicate the category by either:

- Clicking on a category in the list, then on OK.

- Typing a new category, then clicking on the New button. Enter a description for the category, and indicate whether it is tax related. Click on OK.

Type an amount for that category in the Amount column.

Repeat steps 3 - 6 for every category.

If necessary, click on the Recalc Total button.

Click on the Close button.

Click on the Home button.

Grouping Income Sources, Accounts, or Payees

Grouping income sources, accounts, or payees lets you summarize information on reports and graphs, and automate tasks such as check writing. For example, if you group payees before writing checks, CA-Simply Money displays a check for each one automatically, one after the other.

Temporary group:

1. Hold down the Shift key and click on the buttons you want to group. (To deselect a button, press Shift and click on it again. To deselect all buttons, click on the background.)

2. To generate reports or graphs, drag any one of the grouped buttons to the Reports or Graphs button.

   To write checks, drag any of the grouped buttons to the button for your checking account.

Permanent group:

1. Make a temporary group.

2. Drag any one of the grouped buttons to the Setup button.

3. Type a group name.

4. If desired, add a member to the group by clicking on an unselected income source, account, or payee. Omit a current member by clicking on a highlighted item.

5. If desired, select a new icon or hide the button.

6. Click on the OK button.

Reconciling an Account

1. Drag the account button down to the Balance button, then drop it.

2. Enter statement balance, any service charge, interest earned or paid, then click on OK.

3. For transactions included on the statement, click in the column labeled C (cleared). (To clear consecutive checks, click on the Clear Range button and enter the range of check numbers.)

4. If you need to change or record any transactions, click on the Register button.

5. Click on the Home button.

6. If the account does not balance, click on the Add or Don't Add button.

Procedures for Basic Tasks (continued)

Generating a Quick Graph or Report

- Drag an income, account, or payee button down to the Graphs or Reports button.

Generating a Report

1. Click on the Reports button.
2. Click on the button for the type of report you want.
3. Click on the report you want, then on OK.

If you want to print the report, pull down the File menu on the report window and choose Print.

If you want to use the data on the report in another application, pull down the File menu on the report window and choose Export.

Customizing a Report

Before generating the report:

- To specify a range of dates, select the System menu, then Settings, then Reports & Graphs.
- To specify the income sources, accounts, or payees for your report, group their buttons.

After generating the report, while it is on the screen:

- To change the title, pull down the Options menu on the report window, then choose Filters and Styles.
- To specify the income sources, accounts, or payees for your report, pull down the Options menu on the report window. Choose Filters and Styles, then click on Include. Select (highlight) or deselect items by clicking on them.
- To control totals, number format, and more, again choose Filters and Styles from the Options menu on the report window. Click on Settings.
- To specify fonts, choose Title Font or Body Font from the Options menu on the report window.

Saving a Report Format

This procedure lets you keep the format of a customized report for future use.

1. Customize a report. (See the preceding procedure.)
2. Choose Memorize from the File menu of the report window.
3. Use the format in the future by clicking the Reports button to generate a report, then the button next to Memorized Reports.

Making a Graph

1. Click on the Graphs button.
2. Click on the button for the type of graph you want.
3. Click on the graph you want, then on OK.

If you want to print the graph, pull down the File menu on the graph window and choose Print.

If you want to include the graph in another Windows application, copy it to the clipboard. Pull down the File menu on the graph window and choose Copy.

Customizing a Graph

Before generating the graph:

- To specify a range of dates, select the System menu, then Settings, then Reports & Graphs.
- To specify the income sources, accounts, or payees for your graph, group their buttons.

After generating the graph, while it is on the screen:

- To change the title, pull down the Options menu on the graph window, then choose Filters and Styles.
- To specify the income sources, accounts, or payees for your graph, pull down the Options menu on the graph window. Choose Filters and Styles, then click on Include. Select (highlight) or deselect items by clicking on them.
- To switch to another type of graph, choose Settings from the Options menu on the graph window.
- To control whether items such as grid lines and labels appear again choose Settings from the Options menu on the graph window.

Saving a Graph Format

This procedure lets you keep the format of a customized graph for future use.

1. Customize a graph. (See the preceding procedure.)
2. Choose Memorize from the File menu of the graph window.
3. Use the format in the future by clicking the Graphs button to make a graph, then the button next to Memorized Graphs.

udgeting

From the Edit menu choose Budget.

If necessary, click the button next to Expense or Income.

Either:

- Enter amounts in the Amount column (for expenses) or the Income column (for income).

- Click on AutoBudget, make selections, then click on OK.

If you want to make a budget for several months, click on the Variable button.

If you want to sort by value, or show top-level categories only, click on the Options button.

nporting Data

u can import these file formats:

MXF (CA-Simply Money Exchange Format)
QIF (Quicken Interchange® Format)
BMF (BillPay USA Format)

From the File menu choose Import.

Select a file, then click on OK.

If it is a MXF file, choose to add the data to the current finance group or make a new finance group.

If it is a QIF or BMF file, specify the account to receive the data.

Click on OK.

porting Data

u can export these file formats:

MXF (CA-Simply Money Exchange Format)
QIF (Quicken Interchange Format)

From the File menu choose Export.

Type a name for the file, or select a name by clicking on the Browse button.

If necessary, indicate a date range and file compatibility.

Specify the items to be exported.

If you want to specify the income sources, accounts, or payees to be exported, click on the Include button. Select (highlight) or deselect items by clicking on them.

Click on OK.

Exporting Tax Information

1. From the File menu choose Tax Export.

2. Type a name for the file, or select a name by clicking on the Browse button.

3. If necessary, indicate a date range.

4. Click on OK.

Preventing Others from Seeing Your Finances

1. From the System menu choose Settings, then Password.

2. Type a password (asterisks appear for each letter), then click on OK.

3. Type the password again, and click on OK.

4. Write down your password and keep it in a safe place separate from your computer.

Moving Buttons

By default CA-Simply Money positions your most frequently used buttons at the top of the work area. To change the button positions:

1. From the System menu choose Settings, then General.

2. Click on the box next to Auto Button Layout to deselect it, then click on OK.

3. Hold down the Shift key and drag a button. The new location must currently be occupied by another button. If the desired location is off the screen, position the button over the up or down arrow on the scroll bar until the location comes into view.

Entering Dates

To insert today's date:

- Click on a date field and press F3.

To insert another date:

1. Click on a date field and press F4. The calendar appears.

2. If necessary, change the month by clicking on the scroll bar arrows. Change the year by clicking on the scroll bar.

3. Click on a date, then on OK.

The Tools

Click on the tools at the bottom of the screen to do common tasks:

Explains how to use CA-Simply Money.	Lets you write a check.	Generates a report.	Displays a graph.	Lets you make transactions in an account.

Lets you reconcile an account.

Searches for a transaction based on one or more of these factors: date, account, payee, memo, amount, method of payment.

Lets you set up a recurring transaction such as paying rent each month. CA-Simply Money reminds you to make the transaction, and automatically uses the amount and other information you enter in the Scheduler.

Displays a list of financial advice topics tailored to your situation. To see detailed advice, select a topic by clicking on it, then click on the Advice button.

Lets you add income sources, accounts, payees, and special types of fund transfer

Clicking on Buttons

Button	Single click	Double click
Income Accounts	Shows the name, type, number of transactions, and balance of every income source or account.	Lets you add, modify, or delete an income source or account.
Payees	Lets you choose a payee, then see information about it. (Same as single clicking on individual payee button.)	Lets you add, modify, or delete a payee.
Individual income buttons	Lets you record income.	Lets you modify or delete the button.
Individual account buttons	Lets you add to or withdraw from the account.	Shows the register for the account.
Individual payee buttons	Shows information about the payee. (Same as single clicking on Payees button.)	Lets you modify or delete the button.
Tool buttons at bottom of screen	Does the task assigned to the button (display online help, write checks, and so on).	Same as single click.